109

MIRIAM BRATU HANSEN is Ferdinand Schevill Distinguished Service Professor in the Humanities at the University of Chicago, where she teaches in the Department of English and the Committee on Cinema and Media Studies. She is the author of *Babel and Babylon: Spectatorship in American Silent Film* (Harvard, 1991) and has published essays on a wide range of topics in film history, film theory, and debates on mass culture and the public sphere. Currently a fellow at the American Academy Berlin, she is completing a study on "The Other Frankfurt School: Kracauer, Benjamin, and Adorno on Cinema, Mass Culture, and Modernity."

ELIZABETH HUTCHINSON teaches at Barnard College and Columbia University and writes on a variety of visual cultures of the American West. She is currently completing a book titled *The "Indian Craze": Primitivism, Modernism and Transculturation in America, 1890–1914.*

MELISSA RAGONA teaches critical theory and media and sound studies at the School of Art at Carnegie Mellon University. She is completing a book on the uses of sound in experimental film work (1970 to present) as well as a project on the recordings of Andy Warhol.

FEDERICO WINDHAUSEN is a doctoral candidate in cinema studies at New York University. He is completing a dissertation on didactic tendencies in American avant-garde film and video of the 1970s.

MICHAEL WOOD was a longtime colleague of Edward Said's at Columbia University, and currently teaches English and Comparative Literature at Princeton. His most recent book is *The Road to Delphi* (Farrar Straus Giroux, 2003).

MICHAEL ZRYD is Assistant Professor in the Department of Film and Video at York University in Toronto, where he teaches cinema studies with a focus on experimental and documentary film. He was curator of a retrospective of Hollis Frampton's extant *Magellan* films at Anthology Film Archives in 2003. He is currently writing a book on the *Magellan* project, and researching institutional and cultural relationships between late-twentieth-century experimental film and the academy in North America.

Please address all editorial correspondence to *October*, 611 Broadway, #610, New York, NY 10012. We reserve the right to edit letters and responses selected for publication. We review manuscripts of no more than 8,500 words, double-spaced and submitted in duplicate.

Room-for-Play: Benjamin's Gamble with Cinema*

MIRIAM BRATU HANSEN

For Lisa Fittko

> . . . *What is lost in the withering of semblance* [Schein], *or decay of the aura, in works of art is matched by a huge gain in room-for-play* [Spiel-Raum]. *This space for play is widest in film.*

> —Walter Benjamin, "The Work of Art in the Age of Its Technological Reproducibility" (1936)

During the past three decades, Walter Benjamin's essay "The Work of Art in the Age of its Technological Reproducibility" may have been more often quoted than any other single source, in areas ranging from new left media theory to cultural studies, from film and art history to visual culture, from the postmodern art scene to debates on the fate of art, including film, in the age of the digital. In the context of these invocations, the essay has not always acquired new meanings, nor has it become any less problematic than when it was first written. Not quite ready to throw in the towel and follow Peter Wollen's suggestion that the essay should be shelved altogether, I wish to return to it yet once again.[1]

* For critical comments, suggestions, and inspiration, I wish to thank Paula Amad, Susan Buck-Morss, Frances Ferguson, Hal Foster, Michael Fried, Michael Geyer, Ron Gregg, Martin Jay, Rob Kaufman, Roberta Malagoli, James Schamus, Heide Schlüpmann, Susan Stewart, and Yuri Tsivian, as well as audiences who responded to earlier versions of this paper at Princeton University, Indiana University, the 2003 meeting of the Film Studies Association of Canada in Halifax, Nova Scotia, and the University of Chicago Graduate Workshop on Mass Culture. Special thanks to Bill Brown and Dan Morgan for urging me at every stage of this project to take things further and to Michael Geyer for making me let go of it. A shorter version appears in *Canadian Journal of Film Studies/Revue Canadienne d'études cinématographiques* 13, no. 1 (Spring 2004).
1. Peter Wollen, "Detroit: Capital of the Twentieth Century," lecture presented at the centennial symposium on Walter Benjamin, Wayne State University, Detroit, April 1992; earlier versions of this text, "Cinema/Americanism/the Robot," appeared in *New Formations* 2 (1989) and *Modernity and Mass Culture*, ed. James Naremore and Patrick Brantlinger (Bloomington: Indiana University Press, 1991); also reprinted in Wollen, *Raiding the Icebox* (Bloomington: Indiana University Press, 1993).

More precisely, I'd like to turn to the version of the essay which Benjamin considered his "*Ur*-text," that is, the typescript completed in February of 1936 which appeared later the same year, with a few fiercely contested cuts and modifications, in a French translation by Pierre Klossowski.[2] This long-lost second (German) version of the essay—the first was a shorter, handwritten draft—was published in 1989 and is now available in English in volume three of the Harvard edition of Benjamin's *Selected Writings*. Whether in response to criticism by Theodor W. Adorno, the unsympathetic reception of the essay on the part of friends such as Gershom Scholem and Bertolt Brecht and the Paris organization of communist writers, or the increasingly grim political situation, Benjamin kept revising the text between 1936 and 1939, hoping in vain to get it published in the Moscow literary exile journal *Das Wort*.[3] It is this (third) version that first appeared in *Illuminationen* (1955), edited by Adorno and Friedrich Podszus, and which entered the English-speaking world, in a rather unreliable translation, with the 1969 publication of *Illuminations*, edited by Hannah Arendt. It is this multiply compromised and, for Benjamin, still unfinished version that has become known all over the world as *the* Artwork essay.

Benjamin's second version differs significantly from the third, familiar one, although the basic argument is already in place. A rough sketch of that argument might go somewhat like this: the technical reproducibility of traditional works of art and, what is more, the constitutive role of reproduction in the media of photography and film have affected the status of art in its core. Evolving from the large-scale reorganization of human sense perception in capitalist-industrial society, this crisis is defined, on the one hand, by the decline of what Benjamin refers to as "aura," the unique modality of being that has accrued to the traditional work of art, and, on the other, by the emergence of the urban masses whose mode of existence correlates with the new regime of perception advanced by the media of technological reproduction. The structural erosion of the aura through the technological media converges with the assault on the institution of art from

2.   "L'oeuvre d'art à l'époque de sa reproduction mécanisée," *Zeitschrift für Sozialforschung* 5, no. 1 (1936), pp. 40–68; reprinted in Walter Benjamin, *Gesammelte Schriften*, ed. Rudolf Tiedemann and Hermann Schweppenhäuser, vol. 1 (1974), pp. 709–39. Hereafter cited in the text as *GS*. This volume (pp. 431–49) also contains the first (handwritten) version of the essay which Benjamin composed during the autumn of 1935.
3.   See letter to Margarete Steffin, March 4, 1936, in Benjamin, *Gesammelte Briefe*, ed. Christoph Gödde and Henri Lonitz, vol. 5 (Frankfurt a.M.: Suhrkamp, 1999), pp. 254–55; letter to Alfred Cohn, July 4, 1936, ibid., vol. 5, p. 325; and letter to Gretel Adorno, early April 1939, ibid., vol. 6, p. 246f.; Gershom Scholem, *Walter Benjamin: The Story of a Friendship* (1975), trans. Harry Zohn (Philadelphia: Jewish Publication Society of America, 1981), pp. 202, 207; Bertolt Brecht, *Journals*, ed. John Willett, trans. Hugh Rorrison (London: Methuen, 1993), p. 10. For further material on the essay's reception and publication history, see the editors' commentary in Benjamin, *GS* 1, pp. 982–1028, esp. pp. 1024ff., and *GS* 7, pp. 661–65; 681–82; also see Werner Fuld, *Walter Benjamin: Zwischen den Stühlen: Eine Biographie* (Munich: Hanser, 1979), pp. 260–61. Adorno's well-known letter of March 18, 1936, which first appeared in translation in *Aesthetics and Politics* (London: Verso, 1977), clearly responds to the second version of the essay: a number of passages make no sense at all if, as commonly assumed, they were directed at the later version. See Theodor W. Adorno and Walter Benjamin, *The Complete Correspondence 1928–1940*, ed. Henri Lonitz, trans. Nicholas Walker (Cambridge, Mass.: Harvard University Press, 1999), pp. 127–34; the editor's notes refer the reader to the second version of the essay.

within by avant-garde movements such as Dada and Surrealism. In terms of the
political crisis that is the essay's framing condition, two developments have entered
into a fatal constellation: one, the aestheticization of political life as practiced by
fascism, which gives the masses an illusory expression instead of their rights and
which culminates in the glorification of war; two, within the institution of art, the
cult of the decaying aura of belated aestheticism, as in the George circle and
among individual avant-gardists such as F. T. Marinetti who supplies a direct link to
fascism. In this situation of extreme emergency, Benjamin argues, the only remaining strategy for intellectuals on the left is to combat the fascist aestheticization of
politics with the "politicization of art" as advanced by communism.

One of several problems with this by now well-worn argument is that it turns
on a rhetoric of binary oppositions. This strategy arrests the dynamic of Benjamin's
distinctive—and distinctively productive—mode of thinking in which concepts are
hardly ever stable or self-identical; rather, they tend to overlap, blend, and interact
with other concepts, just as their meanings oscillate depending on the particular
constellations in which they are deployed.[4] In the Artwork essay, however, Benjamin
establishes the terms "aura" and "masses" as unequivocally defined opposites that
correspond to related dichotomies throughout the essay: distance versus nearness,
uniqueness versus multiplicity and repeatability, image versus copy, cult versus
exhibition value, individual versus simultaneous collective reception, contemplation
versus distraction (significantly, the only term that eludes this dichotomous structure
is the concept of the optical unconscious). Building up a crisis at the textual level
designed to crystallize the options remaining to intellectuals in the ongoing political
crisis, this binary logic culminates in the closing slogan that pits communist political
art against the phantasmagoria of fascism.

This conclusion raises more questions than it answers. What did communist
art politics mean in 1936 (or, for that matter, in 1939)? What did Benjamin mean
by politics? What was his underlying concept of revolution? Which "masses" did he
have in mind, the movie-going public or the proletariat? How does the conclusion
tally with the argument about the revolutionary role of film in relation to art,
sense perception, and technology?

The "*Ur*-text" of the essay, while not directly addressing the first, engages with
all these questions. Most important, this version complicates the binary opposition
of aura and masses, and it does so from both ends. In a long excursus relegated to a
footnote, Benjamin offers what is probably the most extensive discussion in his
whole work of the problem of "the masses," which, among other things, should clear
him at least partially from the charge of technological determinism.[5] As for the

4.   On Benjamin's modes of theorizing, see Theodor W. Adorno, "Erinnerungen," in *Adorno, Über
Walter Benjamin* (Frankfurt a.M.: Suhrkamp, 1964; 1990), p. 83; Sigrid Weigel, *Entstellte Ähnlichkeit: Walter
Benjamins theoretische Schreibweise* (Frankfurt: Fischer, 1997) and, partly overlapping, Weigel, *Body- and
Image-Space: Re-reading Walter Benjamin*, trans. Georgina Born (London: Routledge, 1996); and Michael
Opitz and Erdmut Wizisla, *Benjamins Begriffe*, 2 vols. (Frankfurt a.M.: Suhrkamp, 2000), editors' preface.
5.   This discussion met with particular approval on the part of Adorno: ". . . I find your few sentences
concerning the disintegration of the proletariat into 'masses' [*sic*] through the revolution, to be

declining aura, he makes the term part of a different conceptual trajectory, defined by the polarity of "semblance and play" [*Schein und Spiel*].

In the following, I will reopen the Artwork essay from the perspective of *Spiel*, understood in its multiple German meanings as "play," "game," "performance," and "gamble." *Spiel*, I will argue, provides Benjamin with a term, and concept, that allows him to imagine an alternative mode of aesthetics on a par with modern, collective experience, an aesthetics that could counteract, at the level of sense perception, the political consequences of the failed—that is, capitalist and imperialist, destructive and self-destructive—reception of technology. Not least, Benjamin's investment in the category of *Spiel* will help us better to understand why and how film came to play such a crucial role in that project. I will trace this connection with the goal of extrapolating from it a Benjaminian theory of cinema as a "play form of second nature" (*Spielform der zweiten Natur*).[6]

*

In Benjamin's writings, the term *Spiel* appears in a variety of contexts, which span the range of meanings attached to the German word. His theoretical interest in *Spiel* in the sense of *play* is most explicit in his book reviews and exhibition reports on children's toys (1928). In these articles he argues for a shift in focus from the toy as object [*Spielzeug*] to playing [*Spielen*] as an activity, a process in which, one might say, the toy functions as a medium.[7] He develops such a notion of playing—whether the child uses toys or improvises games with found objects, materials, and environments—in several vignettes in *One-Way Street* (e.g., "Child Hiding") and *Berlin Childhood* (e.g., "The Sock," "The Mummerehlen," "Hiding Places"), as well as the texts on the "mimetic faculty."[8] Here the emphasis is on the child's penchant for creative mimicry, for pretending to be somebody or something else: "The child plays at being not only a shopkeeper or teacher, but also a windmill and a train" (*SW2*, p. 720).

In the playful osmosis of an other, that is, a world shot through with "traces of an older generation" (*SW2*, p. 118), the child engages with an "alien . . . agenda

amongst the most profound and most powerful statements of political theory I have encountered since I read [Lenin's] State and Revolution" (*Complete Correspondence*, p. 132f.).
6.   Fragment relating to Artwork essay, *GS* 1, p. 1045.
7.   "The Cultural History of Toys," in Benjamin, *Selected Writings*, vol. 2, ed. Michael W. Jennings, Howard Eiland, and Gary Smith, trans. Rodney Livingstone et al. (Cambridge, Mass.: Harvard University Press, 1999), pp. 113–16. "Toys and Play: Marginal Notes on a Monumental Work," *Selected Writings* 2, pp. 117–21. Hereafter cited in the text as *SW*. An additional reference to the German edition indicates that the translation has been modified.
8.   *One-Way Street* (written 1923–26; published 1928), *Selected Writings*, vol. 1, ed. Marcus Bullock and Michael W. Jennings (Cambridge, Mass.: Harvard University Press, 1996), pp. 444–88; esp. p. 465f.; "Berlin Childhood around 1900" (final version, 1938; 1934 version), *Selected Writings*, vol. 3, ed. Jennings et al. (Cambridge, Mass.: Harvard University Press, 2002), pp. 344–413, esp. pp. 374–76, 390–93; "On the Mimetic Faculty" (1933), *SW* 2, pp. 720–22, as well as the earlier, longer version, "Doctrine of the Similar" (1933), *SW* 2, pp. 694–98.

imposed by adults" (as Jeffrey Mehlman paraphrases Benjamin), though not necessarily in ways intended or understood by them.[9] However, since the child's mimetic reception of the world of things centrally includes technology, children's play not only speaks of generational conflict. More significantly, it elucidates the way in which the idea that "each truly new configuration of nature—and, at bottom, technology is just such a configuration—" is incorporated "into the image stock of humanity." The cognitive experience of childhood undercuts the ideological abuse of technological progress by investing the discoveries of modernity with mythic yet potentially utopian meanings: "By the interest it takes in technological phenomena, its curiosity for all sorts of inventions and machinery, every childhood binds the accomplishments of technology to the old worlds of symbols."[10]

Benjamin complicates the mimetic, fictional dimension of play ("doing as if") with an interest, following Freud, in the "dark compulsion to repeat," the insatiable urge to do "the same thing over and over again" (*SW* 2, p. 120; *GS* 3, p. 131). Referring explicitly to an "impulse 'beyond the pleasure principle,'" Benjamin attributes to repetition in play a function at once therapeutic and pedagogic: "the transformation of a shattering experience into habit" (*SW* 2, p. 120). He thus modifies Freud's pessimistic slant to some extent by imputing to repetition in play an existential quest for happiness and, as we shall see with regard to cinema, a liberating and apotropaic function.

The notion of play as creative mimicry shades into a second meaning of the German word: *Spielen* as *Schauspielen*, that is, performing or acting a part before a specially assembled audience. Both senses of play are evocatively conjoined in Benjamin's "Program for a Proletarian Children's Theater" (1928/29). In this text, Benjamin intervenes in ongoing debates on "proletarian education" by giving unequivocal priority to the child's imagination and improvisation, declaring the child's gesture a "signal," not so much of the unconscious, but "from another world, in which the child lives and commands" (*SW* 2, p. 203f.). While he grants that an instructor is needed to "release children's signals from the hazardous magical world of sheer fantasy and apply them to materials," Benjamin foregrounds the child's gesture as a model of "creative innervation," one in which receptivity and creativity are in exact correlation. Grounding the performance in a "radical unleashing of play—something the adult can only wonder at" (p. 205), children's theater could become "truly revolutionary," as "the *secret signal* of what is to come that speaks from the gesture of the child" (p. 206).

9.   Jeffrey Mehlman, *Benjamin for Children: An Essay on His Radio Years* (Chicago: University of Chicago Press, 1993), p. 5. For Benjamin's antifunctionalist and antinaturalist position on toys, see also "Cultural History of Toys," p. 115f. Also see Adorno's remarks on children's play, obviously inspired by Benjamin, in *Minima Moralia: Reflections from Damaged Life* (1951), trans. E. F. N. Jephcott (London: Verso, 1978), p. 228.
10.   Benjamin, *The Arcades Project*, trans. Howard Eiland and Kevin McLaughlin (Cambridge, Mass.: Harvard University Press, 1999), p. 390 (K1a,3); p. 461 (N2a,1); *GS* 5, p. 576; also see p. 855 (M^e, 20). Hereafter cited in the text as *AP*. On the significance of children's play for Benjamin's theory of cognition and approach to history, see Susan Buck-Morss, *The Dialectics of Seeing: Walter Benjamin and the Arcades Project* (Cambridge, Mass.: MIT Press, 1989), pp. 261–75.

At first sight, this vision of acting appears to differ from Benjamin's notions of adult acting within a rule-governed artistic institution, be it the traditional stage, the experimental one of epic theater, or the cinema.[11] In both versions of the Artwork essay, Benjamin elaborates at length on the screen actor, who faces his/her audience ("the masses") in their absence, performing instead before the apparatus and a group of specialists. The discussion of the actor's performance before the camera foregrounds the connotation the word has in English, that is, performance as an achievement or *Leistung*, which is being "tested" at both the level of production and that of reception; in other words, it becomes an object of controlled exhibition or, one might say, dis-play. Yet, as I will show, in the earlier version of the essay Benjamin still links the success of that performance to the transformative and apotropaic dimensions of children's play. What is more, he extends the concept of play to the behavior of the spectating collective in front of the screen, including involuntary, sensory-motor forms of reception.

The third meaning in the complex of *Spiel* is that of gambling, the game of chance or, to use Benjamin's preferred term, *Hasardspiel*. His reflections on the figure of the *Spieler* or gambler are familiar primarily from his essay "On Some Motifs in Baudelaire" (1939/1940), where they conform to that essay's generally critical, pessimistic tenor regarding the decline of experience—*Erfahrung* in Benjamin's emphatic sense—in capitalist-industrial modernity. As a symptom of that decline, the gambler exemplifies a mode of attention ever ready to parry mechanical shocks, similar to the reflex reaction required of the worker on the assembly line and, like the latter, no longer relying on experience in the sense of accumulated wisdom, memory, and tradition.[12]

Conceptually, however, Benjamin's interest in gambling belongs to a series of earlier efforts, beginning with *One-Way Street* and continuing into *The Arcades Project*, to theorize an alternative mode of apperception, assimilation, and agency which would not only be equal to the technologically changed and changing environment, but also open to chance and a different future. If experience had fallen in value, proven useless by trench warfare, hunger, inflation, and massive

11.   I am bracketing here another sense of *Spiel* associated with dramatic art, the noun that forms part of the composite term *Trauerspiel*, literally play of mourning, which is the subject of Benjamin's treatise on *The Origin of Baroque Tragic Drama* (1928). Martin Jay reads Benjamin's "saturnine attraction to *Trauerspiel*, the endless, repetitive 'play' of mourning (or more precisely, melancholy)" as a rejection of *Trauerarbeit*, the "allegedly 'healthy' 'working through' of grief"; see Jay, "Against Consolation: Walter Benjamin and the Refusal to Mourn," in Jay Winter and Emmanuel Sivan, eds., *War and Remembrance in the Twentieth Century* (Cambridge: Cambridge University Press, 1999), p. 228. Benjamin's antitherapeutic insistence on repetition in the endless play of melancholia has a structural counterpart, as we shall see, in his later efforts to redeem repetition as an aesthetic, comedic, and utopian category.
12.   "On Some Motifs in Baudelaire" (1940), *Selected Writings*, vol. 4, ed. Michael W. Jennings et al. (Cambridge, Mass.: Harvard University Press, 2003), pp. 329–32; crucial to Benjamin's analysis of the decline of experience is of course the distinction between the concept of *Erfahrung*, experience accumulated over a lifetime and through generations, and that of *Erlebnis*, the isolated, incidental experience that corresponds to a mode of perception governed by shock; see ibid., p. 319.

social and political changes, it was nonetheless imperative to conceptualize some contemporary equivalent to that mode of knowledge.[13] A reinvention of experience—experience under erasure—was needed above all to counter the already "bungled reception of technology" and with it the spiral of anaesthetics (the numbing of the sensorium in defense against shock) and aestheticization which, in Benjamin's (and Susan Buck-Morss's) analysis, was key to the success of fascism.[14]

A crucial term in this project, entwined with the multiple meanings of *Spiel*, is the already mentioned concept of *innervation*.[15] This term broadly refers to a nondestructive, mimetic incorporation of the world—which Benjamin explored, over the course of a decade, through exemplary practices such as writing and reading, yoga, eroticism, children's play, experiments with hashish, Surrealism, and cinema. In an unpublished fragment written around 1929–30, "Notes on a Theory of Gambling" (. . . des *Spiels*), Benjamin states that the decisive factor in gambling is "the level of motor innervation" (*SW 2*, p. 297). The successful contact of the gambler's motor stimuli with "fate" requires, before all else, a "correct physical predisposition" (*SW 2*, p. 298), a heightened receptivity that allows "the spark [to leap] within the body from one point to the next, imparting movement now to this organ, now to that one, concentrating the whole of existence and delimiting it. It is condensed to the time allowed to the right hand before the ball has fallen into the slot."[16] Benjamin insists on the neuro-physiological character of such innervation, which is all the more decisive "the more emancipated it is from optical perception" (*SW 2*, p. 297).

13.   Benjamin's most radical, New-Objectivist rejection of "experience" can be found in "Experience and Poverty" (1933), *SW 2*, pp. 731–36; relying to some extent on the same analysis and even repeating a key passage verbatim, he tactically reverses his position in "The Storyteller: Observations on the Works of Nikolai Leskov" (1936), *SW 3*, pp. 143–66; also see the fragment "Experience" (1931 or 1932), *SW 2*, p. 553. In a note written ca. 1929, he refers to his early critique of (bourgeois) experience, "Experience" (1913/1914), *SW 1*, pp. 3–5, as a "rebellious" act of youth with which, given the centrality of a theory of experience in his ongoing work (one may think of the essays on Surrealism, Proust, and Kafka), he had nonetheless remained faithful to himself: "For my attack punctured the word without annihilating it" (*GS 2*, p. 902). On Benjamin's theory of experience, see Marleen Stoessel, *Aura: Das Vergessene Menschliche: Zu Sprache und Erfahrung bei Walter Benjamin* (Munich: Carl Hanser, 1983); Martin Jay, "Experience without a Subject: Walter Benjamin and the Novel" (1993), reprinted in Jay, *Cultural Semantics: Keywords of Our Time* (Amherst: University of Massachusetts Press, 1998); and Howard Caygill, *Walter Benjamin: The Colour of Experience* (London: Routledge, 1998), a study that productively brings to bear Benjamin's early writings on perception and color on his theory of experience but fails to see that Benjamin's concept of aura, developed in conjunction with his shift of attention (rather than simply in opposition) to urban-industrial modernity, is indispensable to his project of reconceptualizing the possibility of experience in modernity.
14.   Susan Buck-Morss, "Aesthetics and Anaesthetics: Walter Benjamin's Artwork Essay Reconsidered," *October* 62 (Fall 1992), pp. 3–41. Benjamin's characterization of the nineteenth century's reception of technology as failed, miscarried, or bungled [*verunglückt*] appears in "Eduard Fuchs, Collector and Historian" (1937), *SW 3*, p. 266. Also see his earlier elaborations of this argument in *One-Way Street* ("To the Planetarium"), *SW 1*, pp. 486–87, and a more classically Marxist version of it in "Theories of German Fascism: On the Collection of Essays *War and Warriors*, edited by Ernst Jünger" (1930), *SW 2*, pp. 312–21, esp. p. 319ff.
15.   On Benjamin's concept of "innervation," see my essay "Benjamin and Cinema: Not a One-Way Street," *Critical Inquiry* 25, no. 2 (Winter 1999), pp. 306–43; reprinted in *Benjamin's Ghosts: Interventions in Contemporary Literary and Cultural Theory*, ed. Gerhard Richter (Stanford: Stanford University Press, 2002).
16.   Benjamin, "Short Shadows," subheading "Gambling" (*Spiel*), *SW 2*, p. 700.

In other words, rather than relying on the master sense of vision, say, by "reading" the table, let alone an "'interpretation' of chance" (*AP*, p. 513), gambling turns on a "*bodily* presence of mind," a faculty that Benjamin elsewhere attributes to "the ancients."[17] In marginal cases of gambling, this presence of mind becomes "divination—that is to say, one of the highest, rarest moments in life" (*SW* 2, p. 298). The ability to commune with cosmic forces, however, is mobilized in the register of play, of simulation: "gambling generates by way of experiment the lightning-quick process of stimulation at the moment of danger" (*SW* 2, p. 298); it is, as it were, "a blasphemous test of our presence of mind."[18] The moment of accelerated danger, a topos in Benjamin's epistemology and theory of history, is defined in the realm of roulette by a specific temporality: "the tendency of gamblers to place their bets . . . at the very last moment" (*AP*, p. 513). Accordingly, the danger is not so much one of *losing* than one of "*not winning*," of "missing [one's] chance" or "arriving 'too late'" (*SW* 2, pp. 297–98).[19]

With a view to Benjamin's concept of cinema, it is significant that he seems less interested in pursuing analogies with assembly-line work or the stock market than in linking the game of chance to the gambler's ability to seize the current of fate, related to ancient practices of divination that involve the human being in his or her material entirety. Whether or not we are persuaded by this linkage, it represents one of Benjamin's more daring (and, as history would demonstrate, most desperate) efforts to trace an archaic, species-based faculty within a modern, industrial-capitalist context in which mimetic relations (in Benjamin's sense) seem to have receded into "nonsensuous similarity."[20] The rare gift of proper gambling, pursued—and misused—by individuals in a hermetically isolated manner and for private gain, becomes a model of mimetic innervation for a collective that seems to have all but lost, literally, its senses; which lacks that bodily presence of mind that could yet "turn the threatening future into a fulfilled 'now'" (*SW* 1, p. 483). At this

17.   Benjamin, "Madame Ariane: Second Courtyard on the Left," *One Way Street*, *SW* 1, p. 483 (emphasis added). The isolation of the successful gambler from the other gamblers as prerequisite to a telepathic contact with the ball is emphasized—and illustrated with a drawing—in the fragment "Telepathie" (1927/28), *GS* 6, pp. 187–88.
18.   "Die glückliche Hand: Eine Unterhaltung über das Spiel" (1935), *GS* 4, pp. 771–77; 776. Also *AP* 513 (O13,3).
19.   This temporality, Benjamin speculates in *The Arcades Project*, is a crucial dimension of what constitutes the "authentic 'intoxication'" of the gambler (*AP*, p. 512), a state of passion, of delirious trance, an obsession not unrelated to eroticism. Thus, he compares the winner's happiness of having "seized control of destiny" to a man's receiving the "expression of love by a woman who has been truly satisfied by [him]" (*SW* 2, p. 298); he complicates this analogy in Convolute O 13,4, which questions the ability of the gambler as a type to ever "satisfy the woman. Isn't Don Juan a gambler?" (*AP*, p. 513). Benjamin justifies the pairing of prostitution and gambling in the same Convolute with the claim that casino and bordello have in common "the most sinful delight: to challenge fate in lust" (*AP*, p. 489). Also see the fragment, "In Parallel with My Actual Diary" (1929–31), trans. Rodney Livingstone, *SW* 2, pp. 413–14.
20.   This does not mean that the category of "nonsensuous similarity" is a lapsarian one; on the contrary, it allows Benjamin to link the "earlier powers of mimetic production and comprehension" to his own medium—language and writing. "Language may be seen as the highest level of mimetic behavior and the most complete archive of nonsensuous similarity" (*SW* 2, p. 722; also p. 721).

point in history, with traditional political organizations on the left failing to mobilize the masses in their own interest (that is, against fascism and war), Benjamin wagers that the only chance for a collective, nondestructive, playful innervation of technology rests with the new mimetic technologies of film and photography—notwithstanding their ongoing uses to the contrary. As early as 1927, Siegfried Kracauer had designated the turn to the photographic media as the "go-for-broke game" [*Vanbanque-Spiel*] of history.[21] By 1936, the political crisis had forced the literary intellectual himself into the role of a gambler, making his play, as it were, in the face of imminent catastrophe.

*

Benjamin's reflections on *Spiel* belong to a genealogy that he was clearly aware of. In one of his articles on children's toys, for instance, he makes a plea "to revive discussion of the theory of play" that had its last major contribution in Karl Groos's 1899 work *Die Spiele der Menschen* (*The Play of Man*).[22] For a recent contribution to such a revival he cites the "*Gestalt* theory of play gestures" by Willy Haas, founding editor of the journal *Die literarische Welt* in which Benjamin's own article was published. The far more significant touchstone for him, however, is Freud's 1920 essay *Beyond the Pleasure Principle*, a thread I will resume later.[23]

Freud's essay discusses infantile play, famously the "*fort/da* game," in the context of traumatic neurosis as precipitated by mechanically caused, life-threatening accidents, an illness that considerably increased due to the barely concluded

21.   "Photography" (October 28, 1927), in Siegfried Kracauer, *The Mass Ornament: Weimar Essays*, ed., trans. and introduction by Thomas Y. Levin (Cambridge, Mass.: Harvard University Press, 1995), pp. 47–63; 61.
22.   In the following, I will not attempt to relate Benjamin's concept of play to the wider canon of play theory of both earlier and later provenance. For the sake of focus, rather than historicist principle, I will touch only on sources roughly within Benjamin's intellectual habitat. For the revalorization of "play" from the 1950s on, see, for instance, David Riesman, *The Lonely Crowd* (New Haven, Ct.: Yale University Press, 1950); Herbert Marcuse, *Eros and Civilization: A Philosophical Inquiry into Freud* (1955; Boston: Beacon Press, 1966); Eugen Fink, *Oase des Glücks: Gedanken zu einer Ontologie des Spiels* (Freiburg: Karl Alber, 1957); Eugen Fink, *Spiel als Weltsymbol* (Stuttgart: Kohlhammer, 1960); and, in particular, Jacques Ehrman, ed., *Games, Play, Literature*, a special issue of *Yale French Studies*, no. 41 (1968), which introduced European philosophies of play, including Mikhail Bakhtin and Roger Caillois, to an American audience. For a discussion of play theory in aesthetic and literary theory, see Mihai Spariosu, *Literature, Play, Mimesis* (Tübingen: Narr, 1982); and, more recently, Ruth Sonderegger, *Für eine Ästhetik des Spiels: Hermeneutik, Dekonstruktion und der Eigensinn der Kunst* (Frankfurt a.M.: Suhrkamp, 2000). For an attempt to introduce Derrida's concept of play into film theory, see Peter Brunette and David Wills, *Screen/Play: Derrida and Film Theory* (Princeton, N.J.: Princeton University Press, 1989). Finally, for a brilliant interrelation of sociological, philosophical, literary, and aesthetic perspectives on play, see Bill Brown, *The Material Unconscious: American Amusement, Stephen Crane, and the Economies of Play* (Cambridge, Mass.: Harvard University Press, 1996).
23.   *Beyond the Pleasure Principle* of course figures prominently in Benjamin's "On Some Motifs in Baudelaire," where he reads Freud's hypothesis on traumatic shock through Theodor Reik's and Proust's concepts of memory, generalizing it into an etiology of the decline of experience in industrial-capitalist modernity (*SW* 4, pp. 316–18). See Kevin Newmark, "Traumatic Poetry: Charles Baudelaire and the Shock of Laughter," in *Trauma: Explorations in Memory*, ed. Cathy Caruth (Baltimore: Johns Hopkins University Press, 1995), pp. 236–55, esp. pp. 236–41.

"terrible war"; accordingly, his more general speculations on the repetition compulsion and his assumption of a death drive are often read in light of that recent catastrophe and its legacy.[24] Two of the most widely known theories of play, Johan Huizinga's *Homo Ludens* and Roger Caillois's *Man, Play, and Games*, were written in the shadow of the following war, shortly after the French publication of Benjamin's Artwork essay.[25] Since the configuration of play, technology, and war will have some bearing on our understanding of the latter, let me briefly sketch the relevant positions of the former.

For Huizinga, World War II only culminates the decline of the "play-element" in contemporary civilization. "Until quite recently"—that is, in preindustrial, premass society in which play was linked to the sacred—"war was conceived as a noble game—the sport of kings," an agonistic ritual in which fighting was bound by rules and international law. Without these limitations, warfare deteriorates into "barbaric," "criminal violence": "It remained for the theory of 'total war' to banish war's cultural function and extinguish the last vestige of the play-element."[26] In other words, the fascist war is cast as an aberration that is both symptom and executor of the decline of the ludic dimension in modern culture. Caillois goes along with Huizinga's narrative of decline to some extent, but draws a clearer line between earlier forms of ritualized agon and modern, unbounded war: "War is far removed from the tournament or duel, i.e., from regulated combat in an enclosure, and now finds fulfillment in massive destruction and the massacre of entire populations."[27] More than Huizinga, Caillois stresses a causal link between the decline of play—which he describes as a "corruption of games" (chapter four)—and the emergence of total, genocidal war.

Both Huizinga and Caillois define play as a free activity—and source of freedom—inasmuch as it is separated from "ordinary" or "everyday life" ("reality"), diametrically opposed to work, drudgery, necessity, and associated with leisure and a life of luxury. Huizinga in particular stresses the "disinterested character" of play, its lack of material purpose, which he considers necessary for play to fulfill its civ-

24.   Sigmund Freud, *Beyond the Pleasure Principle* (1920), in *The Standard Edition of the Complete Works of Sigmund Freud*, vol. 18, trans. and ed. James Strachey in collaboration with Anna Freud (London: Hogarth, 1955), p. 12. See also Cathy Caruth, *Unclaimed Experience: Trauma, Narrative, and History* (Baltimore: Johns Hopkins University Press, 1996), ch. 3; and the critique of Caruth's reading of Freud in Ruth Leys, *Trauma: A Genealogy* (Chicago: University of Chicago Press, 2000), ch. 7.
25.   *Johan Huizinga, Homo Ludens: A Study of the Play Element in Culture* (1950; Boston: Beacon, 1955). The Dutch original appeared in 1938; the English edition is based on a German version published in Switzerland, 1944, and the author's own translation, which he undertook shortly before his death in 1945. Caillois's study, which responds to Huizinga's, began as an essay written in 1946 and was published in book form by Gallimard in 1958; the English version, *Man, Play, and Games*, trans. Meyer Barash, did not appear until more than two decades later (New York: Schocken, 1979). For a critique of both studies, see Jacques Ehrman, "Homo ludens revisited," trans. Cathy and Phil Lewis, *Yale French Studies* 41 (1968), pp. 31–57; see also Spariosu, *Literature, Mimesis and Play*, pp. 35–40. Benjamin repeatedly quotes Huizinga's magnum opus, *Herbst des Mittelalters* [*The Waning of the Middle Ages*] (1928), in *The Arcades Project*.
26.   Huizinga, *Homo Ludens*, pp. 208, 90; the whole of chapter 5 is devoted to "Play and War."
27.   Caillois, *Man, Play, and Games*, p. 55.

ilizing function. Not surprisingly, he accounts for play's tendency to create a perfect order—"to [*be*] order"—in the language of idealist aesthetics, "terms with which we try to describe the effects of beauty: tension, poise, balance, contrast, variation, solution, resolution, etc."[28] Again, Caillois follows Huizinga up to a point, but takes him to task for viewing play "as action denuded of all material interest," thus effectively excluding bets and games of chance.[29] He amends this omission not only by offering a detailed discussion of gambling and lotteries and their function in Western societies, but by delineating gambling within a differential typology of games, in which chance, *alea*, figures in relation to—and partial combination with—forms of *agon* (competition, test), *mimicry* (simulation), and *ilinx* (vertigo).

Unlike Huizinga, Caillois admits economic and social factors into the discussion of play, yet ultimately he too blames them for the "corruption of games." The professionalization of sports, the pathological, obsessive character of gambling that deteriorates into speculation on the stock market, and the overall commercialization of leisure represent an intrusion into the closed universe of play—its "[contamination] by the real world."[30] Still, if Callois to some extent shares Huizinga's elitism and idealism, he differs from the latter's techno-pessimism. In a passage that echoes a more radical argument in the Artwork essay, he observes that "industrial civilization has given birth to a special form of *ludus*, the hobby." He classifies the hobby with a number of other occupations that function primarily as "a compensation for the injury to personality caused by bondage to work of an automatic and picayune character." By engaging machinery in playful ways (by building models, collecting, inventing gadgets, etc.), "the worker-turned-artisan . . . avenges himself upon reality, but in a positive and creative way." The hobby thus responds to "one of the highest functions of the play instinct." Caillois concludes, "It is not surprising that a technical civilization contributes to its development, even to providing compensations for its more brutal aspects."[31]

28. Huizinga, *Homo Ludens*, pp. 7–10.
29. Caillois, *Man, Play, and Games*, p. 5.
30. Ibid., pp. 44–45.
31. Caillois, *Man, Play, and Games*, p. 32; see also his positive remarks about technological contraptions inducing vertigo at amusement parks and traveling carnivals (p. 50) and his inclusion of the cinema among legitimate forms of mimicry to be found at the margins of the social order (p. 54). These are not the only affinities between Benjamin's and Caillois's theories of play. Indeed, it is striking how Benjamin's elaboration of the various meanings of *Spiel* parallels Caillois's fourfold classification of games in terms of *agon, alea, mimicry,* and *ilinx*. While not aiming at classification, Benjamin traverses the whole range of play from what Caillois calls "paidia," the spontaneous and inventive type of play, to the more calculating, rule-governed "ludus." As certain as it is that Benjamin was familiar with, and ambivalent about, Caillois's work on *mimicry* or *mimétisme*, it is more than likely that Caillois had firsthand or secondhand knowledge of Benjamin's Artwork essay and perhaps even his work on Baudelaire. (The French translation of the Artwork essay's original version, though, does not contain the footnote in which Benjamin develops his concept of play in relation to semblance, and the concept of *Spielraum* [room or scope for play; field of action] is translated as *champ d'action*.) The two men were introduced by Pierre Klossowski, the essay's translator and member of the famous Collège de Sociologie, organized by Georges Bataille, Michel Leiris, and Callois from 1937 to 1939. According to Klossowski, Benjamin "assiduously" attended meetings of the Collège and was scheduled to present a lecture on Baudelaire (or, as Hans Maier claims, on "fashion") in the fall of 1939 which was preempted by the outbreak of the

The imbrication of play with technology, along with the large-scale industrialization of leisure and amusement (in the West) since the mid-nineteenth century, complicates any clear-cut opposition of play and work or, rather, play and (alienated) labor. As play became an object of mass production and consumption, as sports and other recreational forms grew into technologically mediated spectacles (not unlike war), the ideal of play as nonpurposive and nonproductive frequently came to serve as an ideological cover for its "material correlative, commodified amusement."[32] At the same time, this development produced, in the words of Bill Brown, "conflicting economies of play, conflicting circuits through which play attains new value"—in which the transgressive, transformative potential of play and the transformation of such excess into surplus value cannot always be easily distinguished.

For Benjamin (and, for that matter, his friend Kracauer), that very ambiguity presented a point of departure, rather than a token of decline—a chance (to paraphrase Kracauer) to determine the place of the present in the historical process.[33] In the "*Ur*-text" of the Artwork essay Benjamin transposes his reflections on *Spiel* from the children's room and gambling hall to the public arena of history. More precisely, the essay spells out the political and cultural constellation that motivated his interest in the category of play in the first place—a constellation defined, on the one hand, by the rise of fascism and the renewed threat of a technologically enhanced military catastrophe and, on the other, the false resurrections of the decaying aura in the sphere of art (aestheticism), the liberal-capitalist media (star cult), and the spectacularization of political life.

*

The category of *Spiel* figures in this constellation as an aesthetic alternative to *Schein* or semblance, in particular the concept of "beautiful semblance," which finds its fullest elaboration in Hegel. However, Benjamin argues, the German idealist version of "beautiful semblance" already had some "derivative qualities," having relinquished the "experiential basis" that it had in classical antiquity—the

---

war. See Klossowski, "Entre Marx and Fourier," *Le Monde*, May 31, 1969, reprinted in *The College of Sociology* (1937–39), ed. and introduction by Denis Hollier, trans. Betsy Wing (Minneapolis: University of Minnesota Press, 1988), pp. 388–89; Hollier's "Foreword: Collage," p. 21; and Hans Maier, *Der Zeitgenosse Walter Benjamin* (Frankfurt a.M.: Jüdischer Verlag, 1992), p. 66. See also Michael Weingrad, "The College of Sociology and the Institute of Social Research," *New German Critique* 84 (Fall 2001), pp. 129–61.
32.   Brown, *Material Unconscious*, pp. 11–12; see also pp. 106–08.
33.   Kracauer, "The Mass Ornament" (1927), in *Mass Ornament*, p. 75. For Kracauer on commercialized forms of play and leisure, see, for instance, "Boredom" (1924), "Travel and Dance" (1925), "Calico World" (1926), all in *Mass Ornament*; "Roller Coaster" (1928), "Specter in the Amusement Hall" (1930), "Luck and Destiny" (1931), trans. Courtney Federle and T. Y. Levin, *Qui Parle* 5, no. 2 (Spring/Summer 1992), pp. 53–60. While these texts treat new forms of amusement and play with dialectically staged ambivalence, Kracauer was unequivocally critical of the contemporary cult of sports; see, in particular, his deadpan satire, "Sie sporten," *Frankfurter Zeitung*, January 13, 1927, reprinted in Kracauer, *Schriften* 5, no. 2, ed. Inka Mülder-Bach (Frankfurt a. M.: Suhrkamp), pp. 14–18; and his more straightforward critique of the ideological function of sports in *The Salaried Masses: Duty and Distraction in Weimar Germany* (1929/30), trans. Quintin Hoare (London: Verso, 1998), pp. 76–80.

aura. He proposes a genealogy of both terms, "semblance and play" [*Schein und Spiel*], by projecting them back, past Hegel, past Goethe and Schiller (and even past classical antiquity) onto ancient practices of mimesis, the "*Ur*-phenomenon of all artistic activity" (*SW* 3, pp. 137, 127; *GS* 7, p. 368).[34] In mimetic practice, semblance and play were two sides of the same process, still folded into one another: "The mime presents what he mimes merely as semblance [*Der Nachmachende macht, was er macht, nur scheinbar*]," which is to say he evokes the presence of something that is itself absent. But since the oldest forms of imitation, "dance and language, gestures of body and lips," "had only a single material to work with: the body of the mime himself," he does not merely evoke an absent other, but enacts, embodies what he mimes: "The mime presents his subject as a semblance [*Der Nachmachende macht seine Sache scheinbar*]. One could also say, he plays [or performs] his subject. Thus we encounter the polarity informing mimesis." In mimesis, he sums up, "tightly interfolded like cotyledons, slumber the two aspects of art: semblance and play" (*SW* 3, p. 127).[35]

In a related fragment, Benjamin observes that in traditional art and aesthetics semblance and play continue to be entwined in varying proportions; he even postulates that the polarity of semblance and play is indispensable to *any* definition of art: "Art (the definition might run) is a suggested improvement on nature: an imitation which is, in its hidden core, a demonstration," a model or instruction to the original. "In other words, art is a perfecting mimesis" (*SW* 3, p. 137; *GS* 7, pp. 667–68). Yet to the dialectician, Benjamin asserts, the polarity of semblance and play is of interest only if historicized. In his genealogy of Western art, this polarity has been tipped toward semblance, autonomized and segregated in the aesthetics of beautiful semblance which has dead-ended in aestheticism (phantasmagoria, false resurrections of the aura). By the same token, however, he discerns an increase of "elements of play" in recent art: "futurism, atonal music, *poésie pure*, detective novel, film" (*GS* 1, p. 1048; Marcel Duchamp might be added to that list, cf. ibid., p. 1045f.).[36]

34.   See also draft notes for the second version, *GS* 7.2, pp. 667–68, partly translated in *SW* 3, pp. 137–38. The concept of *Schein* is central to Benjamin's major essay on Goethe's *Elective Affinities* (1919–1922; 1924–25), *SW* 1, pp. 297–360, a novel that, unlike idealist aesthetic theory, "is still entirely imbued with beautiful semblance as an auratic reality" (*SW* 3, p. 127). See also the fragments "On Semblance," *SW* 1, pp. 223–25, and "Beauty and Semblance," *SW* 1, p. 283.
35.   This formulation strikingly illustrates the difference between Benjamin's concept of mimesis, which includes anthropological, language-philosophical, epistemological, as well as aesthetic strands of argument, and the traditional usage of the term, which more narrowly pertains to standards of verisimilitude. For a discussion of Benjamin (and Adorno) in relation to other revivals of the concept of mimesis (notably Erich Auerbach's), see Gunter Gebauer and Christoph Wulf, *Mimesis: Culture, Art, Society*, trans. Don Reneau (Berkeley: University of California Press, 1995). On Benjamin's concept of mimesis (in relation to Adorno's), see Josef Früchtl, *Mimesis: Konstellation eines Zentralbegriffs bei Adorno* (Würzburg: Königshausen + Neumann, 1986), pp. 17–29; also see Martin Jay, "Mimesis and Mimetology: Adorno and Lacoue-Labarthe," *Cultural Semantics*, pp. 120–37, and Michael Opitz, "Ähnlichkeit," in *Benjamins Begriffe*, vol. 1, pp. 15–19. Michael Taussig reanimates Benjamin's concern with the mimetic from an anthropological perspective; see his *Mimesis and Alterity: A Particular History of the Senses* (New York: Routledge, 1993), and *The Nervous System* (New York: Routledge, 1992).
36.   A similar observation, which more explicitly seeks to bridge the gap between "art" and mechanically mediated "arts," can be found in an earlier text, "Moonlit Nights on the Rue La Boétie" (1928), in which Benjamin emphasizes the "dimension of play" as the point in which the so-called practical arts—

Benjamin correlates these two developments through an economy of loss and gain (see epigraph): "What is lost in the withering of semblance, or decay of the aura, in works of art is matched by a huge gain in room-for-play [*Spiel-Raum*]. This space for play is widest in film. In film, the element of semblance has been entirely displaced by the element of play" (*SW* 3, p. 127; *GS* 7, p. 369).

Of course, there is a rather basic, if not trivial, association between film and play in the period's term for cinema—*Lichtspiele*, or games of light—and one should not underestimate Benjamin's penchant for literalizing abstract compound nouns into their elements. But there is clearly more at stake in his decision to situate film on the side of play, rather than the cult of illusion. In view of major tendencies in actual film practice of the early 1930s, whether fascist, liberal-capitalist, or socialist-realist, this move appears, at the very least, counterintuitive. The argument begins to make sense, however, in the context of the Artwork essay (which, at any rate, rather refers itself to early cinema as well as montage or otherwise nonclassical, marginalized film practices), if we consider it in relation to Benjamin's larger effort to theorize technology.

In the essay's familiar version, technology primarily figures in its destructive, "liquidating" effect on traditional art, summed up in the erosion of the aura, and its concomitant potential for democratizing culture, based on a structural affinity between the new reproduction technologies and the masses. In the "*Ur*-text," however, the concept of technology is grounded more fully in the framework of what Benjamin refers to as "anthropological materialism." In his 1929 essay on Surrealism, he had invoked that tradition (Georg Büchner, Johann Peter Hebel, Nietzsche, Rimbaud) as an alternative to more orthodox Marxist, "metaphysical" versions of materialism in the manner of Vogt and Bukharin.[37] It is indicative that Adorno, in a letter of September 1936, chose the term "anthropological materialism" to sum up all points on which he found himself disagreeing with Benjamin. The bone of contention for Adorno was what he considered Benjamin's "undialectical ontology of the body."[38] While Benjamin's concept of the body no doubt has roots in theology and mysticism, this does not prevent him from thinking about the body in both historical and political terms.[39] He does so, however, by situating the

---

ranging "from early techniques of the observer [magic lantern shows, dioramas] right down to the electronic television of our own day" (*SW* 2, p. 108)—converge.
37.   "Surrealism: The Last Snapshot of the European Intelligentsia" (1929), *SW* 2, p. 217; see also *The Arcades Project*, Convolute p [Anthropological Materialism, History of Sects], pp. 807–17, and the discussion of French and German versions of that tradition (W8,1), p. 633. On the significance of "anthropological materialism" in Benjamin's work, see Norbert Bolz and Willem van Reijen, *Walter Benjamin* (New York: Campus, 1991), ch. 6; see also Burkhardt Lindner, "Benjamins Aurakonzeption: Anthropologie und Technik, Bild und Text," in *Walter Benjamin, 1892–1940: Zum 100. Geburtstag*, ed. Uwe Steiner (Bern: Peter Lang, 1992), pp. 217–48; and Lindner, "Zeit und Glück: Phantasmagorien des Spielraums," *Benjamin Studies* 1: *Perception and Experience in Modernity*, ed. Helga Geyer-Ryan et al. (Amsterdam: Editions Rodopi, 2002), pp. 127–44.
38.   Adorno and Benjamin, *Complete Correspondence*, pp. 147, 146.
39.   For Benjamin's theologically oriented speculations on the body, see "Outline of the Psychophysical Problem," *SW* 1, pp. 393–401. In this early fragment, he makes a distinction between *Leib* and *Körper* (not quite convincingly translated as "body and corporeal substance") which has important implications

fate of the individual body (and the bodily sensorium) in bourgeois society within a larger history of the human species, and this entails thinking about humans in relation to all of creation and about human history in relation to that of the cosmos.[40] Likewise, as we shall see, he relates the temporal individual body to the constitution of a—metaphoric—collective body, or bodily collective, which is both agent and object of the human interaction with nature. Within this anthropological-materialist framework, then, technology endows the collective with a new *physis* that demands to be understood and re/appropriated, literally incorporated, in the interest of the collective; at the same time, technology provides the medium in which such reappropriation can and must take place. Such a reflexive under-standing of technology makes visible a different logic—a logic of play—in Benjamin's conception of the historic role of film.

This role is determined, along with the polarity of semblance and play, by what he calls "the world-historical conflict between the first and second technologies" (*SW* 3, p. 127). The distinction between first and second technology is developed in the Artwork essay's original section six, which sets up the distinction in art between "cult value" and "exhibition value." Like art, Benjamin states, the first technology emerges in the context of ancient magical procedures and rituals. In the effort to make an overpowering nature serve human needs and ends, the first technology "made the maximum possible use of human beings"; the second technology, by contrast, involves the human being as little as possible. Hence, he asserts, "the achievements of the first technology might be said to culminate in human sacrifice; those of the second, in the remote-controlled aircraft which needs no human crew" (*SW* 3, p. 107). Yet, where a contemporary reader might associate the latter with the latest in American-style electronic warfare (drones, cruise missiles), Benjamin makes an amazing turn. If the first technology is defined by the temporality of "once and for all" and "the irreparable lapse or sacrificial death," the second technology oper-ates in the register of "once is as good as never" since it works "by means of experiments and endlessly varied test procedures" (*SW* 3, p. 107; *GS* 7, p. 359).[41] Its

---

for his conception of politics up and through the 1930s. *Leib* refers to the body as it belongs to and augments "the body of humankind" and as such is able, thanks to technology, partly to include even nature—the inanimate, plant, and animal—into a unity of life on earth. *Körper*, by contrast, refers to the individuated, sentient, and finite being whose "solitariness is nothing but the consciousness of its direct dependence on God" (p. 395; *GS*, p. 6, pp. 80–81). On the significance of this distinction, particularly in conjunction with technology, for Benjamin's understanding of the political, see Uwe Steiner, "The True Politician: Walter Benjamin's Concept of the Political," *New German Critique* 83 (Spring-Summer 2001), pp. 43–88.

40.   The most striking example of this juncture—or, at this point in time, disjuncture—between human and cosmic history can be found in the eighteenth and last of his theses, "On the Concept of History," *SW* 4, p. 396. The idea appears in other contexts as well; see especially his essay on Franz Kafka (*SW* 2, pp. 794–818) and work relating to Fourier (*Arcades Project*, convolute W and passim). See also Beatrice Hanssen, *Walter Benjamin's Other History: Of Stones, Animals, Human Beings, and Angels* (Berkeley: University of California Press, 1998).

41.   I have retained a literal translation of the German proverb, *Einmal ist keinmal*, not only because of its pairing with *Ein für allemal*, but also because of Benjamin's fascination with the phrase; see his short piece "Einmal ist keinmal" (1932), *GS* 4, pp. 433–34.

origin is to be sought at the point where, "by an unconscious ruse, human beings first began to distance themselves from nature. In other words," he concludes, "[its origin] lies in play" (*SW* 3, p. 107).

Unlike Frankfurt School critiques of technology from *Dialectic of Enlightenment* through the work of Jürgen Habermas, Benjamin does not assume an instrumentalist trajectory from mythical cunning to capitalist-industrialist modernity. Instead of "mastery of nature," which the first technology pursued out of harsh necessity, the second "aims rather at an interplay between nature and humanity."[42] Rehearsing this interplay, Benjamin contends, is the decisive "social function of art today." Hence, the particular significance of film: "*The function of film is to train human beings in the apperceptions and reactions needed to deal with a vast apparatus whose role in their lives is expanding almost daily*" (*SW* 3, p. 108).

We could easily read this statement as a behaviorist conception of adapting the human sensorium to the regime of the apparatus or, in the tradition of play theory, as a version of training theory or *Einübungs-Theorie* (Groos).[43] And there is no reason not to, considering Benjamin's interest, thanks in part to Asja Lacis, in the Soviet avant-garde discourse of biomechanics (Eisenstein, Kuleshov, Meyerhold) and his strategically belated endorsement of Productivism and Operativism (Tretyakov).[44] But it would be a mistake to read the statement as simply an inversion of an idealist or aristocratic hierarchy of play and work (such as Huizinga's), to the effect that film, as a "play-form" of technology, would be instrumental to the goal of increasing industrial productivity, albeit on behalf of a socialist society. Notwithstanding Benjamin's advocacy of positioning art in the relations of production of its time, he was interested in *labor* primarily within the larger (anthropological-materialist) frame of humanity's interaction with nature,

---

42.   This notion echoes the famous last section of *One-Way Street*, "To the Planetarium," where Benjamin qualifies the notion of "mastery of nature" by comparing it to education: "Is not education, above all, the indispensable ordering of the relationship between generations and therefore mastery (if we are to use this term) of that relationship and not of children? And likewise technology is the mastery not of nature but of the relation between nature and man. Human beings as species completed their development thousands of years ago; but the development of humankind as a species is just beginning. In technology, a *physis* is being organized through which humanity's contact with the cosmos takes a new and different form from that which it had in nations and families" (*SW* 1, p. 487; *GS* 4, p. 147). See also Lindner, "Zeit und Glück," pp. 137–40.

43.   Karl Groos, *Die Spiele der Menschen* (Jena: Gustav Fischer, 1899), p. v.

44.   On Benjamin's reception of biomechanics, see Hansen, "Benjamin and Cinema," pp. 317–18; see also Alma Law and Mel Gordon, *Meyerhold, Eisenstein, and Biomechanics: Actor Training in Revolutionary Russia* (Jefferson, N.C.: McFarland, 1996). For his endorsement of Tretyakov, see "The Author as Producer" (1934), *SW* 2, pp. 768–82; on the significance of this essay in relation to both the Soviet and German politics of socialist realism (made official doctrine in 1934) and the (Communist-front) Paris Institute for the Study of Fascism (INFA), to which it was originally addressed, see Maria Gough, "Paris, Capital of the Soviet Avant-Garde," *October* 101 (Summer 2002), pp. 53–83. Benjamin's polemically belated invocation of Tretyakov (whose experimental, modernist aesthetics was anathema to the champions of proletarian art and cultural heritage [Becher, Bihalji-Mérin, Lukács] and who was to die in the Gulag in 1939) is echoed by a similar gesture in the third version of the Artwork essay—his positive invocation of Dziga Vertov years after the latter had been denounced as formalist and constrained in his ability to work.

negotiated in the medium of technology. If he understands (children's) play as "the canon of a labor no longer rooted in exploitation," this notion is less indebted to Lenin than to (early) Marx and Charles Fourier. The latter's notion of "work inspirited by play," Benjamin asserts, does not aim at the "production of values" but at a more radical goal: "the amelioration of nature" (*AP*, p. 361; *GS* 5, p. 456). And lest we think here of gradual improvement, let alone progress, the idea of a "better nature" for Benjamin entails another Fourierist maxim, at once more violent and more humorous—the idea of the "cracking open of natural teleology," which dislodges anthropocentric hierarchies (*AP*, pp. 631, 635).[45]

What this might mean becomes a little clearer in a remarkable note elaborating on the statement quoted above concerning film's social function in the adaptation to—innervation of—technology. It is the aim of revolutions, he argues, "to accelerate this adaptation."

> Revolutions are innervations of the collective—or, more precisely, efforts at innervation on the part of the new, historically unique collective which has its organs in the new technology. This second technology is a system in which the mastery of elementary social forces is a precondition for playing [*das Spiel*] with natural forces. Just as the child who is learning to grasp stretches out his hand for the moon as it would for a ball, so humanity, in its efforts at innervation, sets its sights as much on presently still utopian goals as on goals within reach. [*SW* 3, p. 124; *GS* 7, p. 360][46]

In other words, as they seek to resolve the problems of second nature through the systematic transformation of social, economic, and political conditions (as in the Soviet case), revolutions also assert a "different," more species-oriented "utopian will" (*SW* 3, p. 134). The utopian impulses that manifest themselves (qua excess, as it were) in historical revolutions concern the still unresolved revolutionary demands "of the first, organic nature (primarily the bodily organism of the individual human being)"; they give voice to the "vital questions affecting the individual—questions of love and death which had been buried by the first technology" (*SW* 3, pp. 135, 124). (Since Benjamin, in a related fragment, cites de Sade along with Fourier as instantiating these impulses, I would suggest translating the word *Liebe* here as eros, if not sex.)

Two arguments seem to be in play here. One concerns the reconfiguration of the relation between collective and individual made possible by the second

45.   Benjamin's examples are hybrid creatures such as Fourier's "long-tailed men" and Mickey Mouse, "in which we find carried out, entirely in the spirit of Fourier's conceptions, the moral mobilization of nature. Humor here puts politics to the test" (*AP*, p. 635, W8a,5). See also Hansen, "Of Mice and Ducks: Benjamin and Adorno on Disney," *South Atlantic Quarterly* 92, no. 1 (Winter 1993), pp. 27–61; 47.

46.   See also "A Different Utopian Will," fragments associated with the composition of the Artwork essay, *SW* 3, pp. 134–36; and Benjamin's invocation of early Marx in the *Arcades Project*: "On the doctrine of revolutions as innervations of the collective: 'The transcendence of private property is . . . the complete emancipation of all human senses. . . .'" (*AP*, p. 652, X1a,2).

technology. Vis-à-vis more orthodox Marxist concepts of revolution ("metaphysical" materialism), Benjamin insists on the interdependency of, on the one hand, the constitution of the masses, as the "historically unique" collective that has a chance to innervate the second technology as "its organs," and, on the other, the fate of the individual, whose bodily, sensorial, psychosexual being is more than ever an object, witting or unwitting, willing or unwilling, of transformation. The other argument, folded into the former, concerns the disjunctive temporalities of the utopian imagination and the actual state of development, which is not least a question of how to mediate species-historical politics with a contemporary crisis that has its origins in the nineteenth century.[47] Here Benjamin, as so often, resorts to an image. The utopian aim of the second technology—"the unfolding of work in *play*" (*AP*, p. 361)—functions not unlike the moon for which the child reaches as it learns to grasp. The child's gesture may be based in motor-perceptual miscognition; but for Benjamin (unlike Piaget or Lacan, for instance), that miscognition is a creative one, anticipating an alternative organization of perception that would be equal to the technologically changed environment. The child may not reach the moon, at least not in its own generation, but it nonetheless learns to grasp.[48]

Benjamin elaborates the contemporary implications of this cognitive hiatus with recourse to the term *Spielraum*, which has to be read in both its literal and figurative, material and abstract meanings.[49] "Because [the second] technology

47.   Much has been written about Benjamin's concept(s) of history and temporality; particularly relevant here are discussions of Benjamin's experimental intersecting of modern (social, political, cultural) history with "other" histories, be they mythical (*Ur*-history), "natural," cosmic and/or messianic; see, for instance, Hanssen, *Walter Benjamin's Other History*; Buck-Morss, *Dialectics of Seeing*, esp. chs. 5 and 8; Irving Wohlfarth, "Re-Fusing Theology: Some First Responses to Walter Benjamin's Arcades Project," *New German Critique* 39 (Fall 1986), pp. 3–24; Peter Osborne, "Small-scale Victories, Large-scale Defeats: Walter Benjamin's Politics of Time," in *Walter Benjamin's Philosophy: Destruction and Experience*, ed. Andrew Benjamin and P. Osborne (London: Routledge, 1994), pp. 59–109.
48.   In *The Arcades Project*, Benjamin refers to "the idea of revolution as innervation of the technical organs of the collective (analogy with the child who learns to grasp by trying to get hold of the moon)" as one of "two articles of my 'politics,'" the other being "[Fourier's] idea of the 'cracking open of the teleology of nature.'" The image of the overreaching child has a less sanguine precursor in a fragment written ca. 1920/21, where he illustrates the problem of the discrepancy between corporeal motor ability and visual perception with reference to "the case of a child who would develop his visual world without prehensile organs and marooned in one place: different hierarchy of distances" ("Wahrnehmung und Leib," *GS* 6, p. 67). Gertrud Koch persuasively brings this fragment to bear on the Artwork essay in a commentary that elucidates Benjamin's messianic investment in cinema as a "technical apparatus which permits one to forget anthropological lack." "Cosmos in Film: On the Concept of Space in Walter Benjamin's 'Work of Art' Essay," trans. Nancy Nenno, in Benjamin and Osborne, eds., *Walter Benjamin's Philosophy*, pp. 205–15; 209.
49.   Benjamin himself suggests as much when he hyphenates the word, "*Spiel-Raum*," in the note on semblance and play (*SW* 3, p. 127). A similarly self-conscious use of the term can be found in a techno-pessimistic piece by Karl Wolfskehl, member of the George circle and the Munich "Kosmiker" group, whom Benjamin admired notwithstanding ideological differences; see "Spielraum" (1929), in Wolfskehl, *Gesammelte Werke*, vol. 2 (Hamburg: Claassen, 1960), pp. 431–33. Also see Karl Kraus's 1912 statement that the ability to distinguish "between an urn and a chamber pot" is what provides culture with "Spielraum"; lacking this distinction contemporary culture is "divided into those who use the urn as a chamber pot and those who use the chamber pot as an urn," that is, in Hal Foster's reading, "Art

aims at liberating human beings from drudgery," he asserts, "the individual suddenly sees his scope for play, his field of action [*Spielraum*], immeasurably expanded." In this new space, however, "he does not yet know his way around" (*SW* 3, p. 124). In the note on semblance and play cited above and in the section on the "optical unconscious," Benjamin explicitly links this expanded space to the emergence of film. But this linkage does not take a direct route. It mandates a detour through another set of terms, "image-space" [*Bildraum*] and "body-space" [*Leibraum*], in particular Benjamin's effort to theorize the increased imbrication of both as a signature of urban-industrial modernity.

Beginning with *One-Way Street*, Benjamin traces the emergence of a new type, and different organization, of space in both art and everyday life. In the transformations of writing and the changed economy of distance and nearness in the new media of advertising and film, he discerns a paradigmatic reconfiguration of physical space—the space of the body, the space of lived experience—in relation to perceptual space, the space of images. Just as script has entered a new phase of "eccentric pictoriality" and graphic mobility, he argues, images, instead of hanging on museum and collectors' walls, have come to inhabit a three-dimensional and public space, the space of the collective. The gigantic objects touted by advertisements, cars careening out at us from the screen and hitting us between the eyes, the fiery-red pool reflecting a moving neon sign—such things place the perceptual subject not vis-à-vis the image as object but within a dynamic visual, sensorial environment.[50]

The cinema in particular, with its techniques of variable framing and montage, exemplifies this new regime of perception defined by nearness, shock, and tactility. It also brings home the fact that the reconfiguration of body- and image-space is inextricably tied to the interpenetration of human physiological and mental functions with heteronomous, mechanical structures. In this regard (as well as others), the film that one might expect to have provided a touchstone for Benjamin is Dziga Vertov's *Man with a Movie Camera* (1929). Discussing Vertov briefly in a 1927 article on Russian film, he begins to develop a para-Vertovian film aesthetics (with a distinct Surrealist inflection) in a companion piece devoted to Eisenstein's *Battleship Potemkin* (1925), a work that does not exactly belong to the

---

Nouveau designers who want to infuse art (the urn) into the utilitarian object (the chamber pot)" and, conversely, "functionalist modernists who want to elevate the utilitarian object into art." Foster, *Design and Crime* (London: Verso, 2002), pp. 16–17. This is precisely why Marcel Duchamp, "trump[ing] both sides with his dysfunctional urinal" (Foster), provides a case in point for Benjamin's observation of an increase of "elements of play in recent art."

50.   See, for instance, "Attested Auditor for Books" and "This Space for Rent," *OWS*, *SW* 1, pp. 456–57, 476. The reconfiguration of corporeal and perceptual space under the sign of technology reaches a troubling climax in the closing piece of *One-Way Street*, "This Way to the Planetarium" (*Zum Planetarium*), *SW* 1, pp. 486–88; *GS* 4, pp. 146-48. Here Benjamin shifts the scene from urban modernity to the "immense wooing of the cosmos" (or "unprecedented mating with cosmic powers") that he perceives to have fueled, albeit disastrously misguided and miscarried, in World War I. See Irving Wohlfarth's magisterial discussion of this piece, "Walter Benjamin and the Idea of a Technological Eros: A Tentative Reading of *Zum Planetarium*," *Benjamin Studies* 1, pp. 65–109.

city film genre Benjamin evokes in its defense.[51] Film is "the only prism," he argues, "in which the spaces of the immediate environment—the spaces in which people live, pursue their avocations, and enjoy their leisure—are laid open before their eyes in a comprehensible, meaningful, and passionate way." This prismatic work of film involves a *double* structure of technological mediation: it refracts a world that is already shaped by heteronomous structures that have become second nature to us. By bringing this world into visibility, film creates a "*new realm of consciousness*"; it enables human beings to represent to themselves their technologically altered *physis*. By doing so, it "explode[s the] entire prison-world"—our "offices, furnished rooms, saloons, city streets, train stations, and factories" which, in themselves, "are ugly, incomprehensible, and hopelessly sad"—and makes their scattered ruins available for "journeys of adventure"; in other words, for play (*SW* 2, p. 17; *GS* 2, p. 752). When he resumes this passage, almost verbatim, in the Artwork essay's section on the "optical unconscious," the preceding sentence spells out the dual, at once cognitive and liberating function of film in more specific terms: "On the one hand, film advances insight into the necessities governing our lives by its use of close-ups, by its accentuation of hidden details in familiar objects, and by the exploration of commonplace milieus through ingenious movement of the camera; on the other, it manages to assure us of a vast and unsuspected field of action" (*SW* 3, p. 117; *GS* 7, pp. 375–76).

Benjamin's writings on the reconfiguration of space in urban modernity range from the phenomenological register through constructivist enthusiasm to an anthropological-materialist, if not messianic, vision of the revolutionary potential of that reconfiguration. The latter dominates in the 1929 essay on Surrealism, whose visionary language harks back to the final section of *One-Way Street* and still animates parts of the original Artwork essay. In the poetic and political practices of the Surrealists, Benjamin discerned the discovery of a "one hundred percent image-space" as the site for political action (*SW* 2, p. 217). In contrast with the cultural politics of the organized left, the Surrealists acted on the recognition that this site, the habitat of the masses, was being crucially redefined by the expanding image-space (no less, one might add, a space of sounds, scripts, and things) that had opened up with modern technologies of reproduction. This image-space,

---

51.   Benjamin discusses the opening montage sequences of Vertov's *The Soviet Sixth of the Earth* in "On the Present Situation of Russian Film" (1927), *SW* 2, p. 13; for his defense of Potemkin see "Reply to Oscar A. H. Schmitz," *SW* 2, pp. 16–19. Also see his reference to Vertov's *Three Songs of Lenin* (1934) in the third version of the Artwork essay (*SW* 4, p. 262). Major concerns of the Artwork essay—the reflexivity of (second) technology, playful innervation, an experimental aesthetics of self-conscious repetition, the optical unconscious—seem to call out for *Man with a Movie Camera* as an intertext. I have not been able to ascertain whether or not Benjamin saw *Man with a Movie Camera*, but it is more than likely that he had read Kracauer's remarkable review of that film, "Mann mit dem Kinoapparat," *Frankfurter Zeitung*, May 19, 1929, reprinted in Kracauer, *Kino*, ed. Karsten Witte (Frankfurt a.M.: Suhrkamp, 1974), pp. 88–92. Benjamin's affinity with Vertov also suggests itself by reading Jean-Louis Comolli, "Mechanical Bodies, Ever More Heavenly," trans. Annette Michelson, *October* 83 (Winter 1998), pp. 19–24.

Benjamin observes, is no longer separate from the "space of the body"; it cannot be grasped from a position of contemplative distance characteristic of bourgeois high culture ("what we used to call art begins at a distance of two meters from the body").[52] In their artistic and living experiments, the Surrealists at once act upon and enact, if not embody that transformation: "where an action puts forth its own image and exists, devouring and consuming it, where nearness looks at itself with its own eyes, this long-sought image space opens up, the world of universal and integral actuality" (*SW* 2, p. 217; *GS* 2, p. 309).[53]

This convulsive collapsing into each other of body- and image-space assaults traditional boundaries between subject and object, making both into elements of an at once perceptual and material environment. It also short-circuits the dialectics of distance and nearness which is so crucial to Benjamin's thought elsewhere, in particular the concept of the aura and the speculations on the mimetic faculty. By the same logic, it entails a "dialectical annihilation" of the individual: in the new image space "political materialism and physical creatureliness share the inner man, the psyche, the individual . . . with dialectical justice, so that no limb remains untorn." But the demolition of the autonomously, organically conceived individual remains incomplete without an analogous transformation of the collective. "The collective is a body, too. And the *physis* that is being organized for it in technology can, in all its factual and political reality, be generated only in that image space to which profane illumination initiates us" (*SW* 2, p. 217; *GS* 2, p. 310). It is at this point that Benjamin first formulates the notion of revolution as "innervation of the collective," and as contingent upon the collective innervation of technology.

> Only when in technology body and image space so interpenetrate that all revolutionary tension becomes bodily collective innervation, and all the bodily innervations of the collective become revolutionary discharge, has reality transcended itself to the extent demanded by the *Communist Manifesto*. For the moment, only the Surrealists have understood its present commands. They exchange, to a man, the play of human features for the face of an alarm clock that in each minute rings for sixty seconds. [*SW* 2, pp. 217–18]

The closing image of the essay, which fuses human face and mechanical device, "mimetically performs" (in Sigrid Weigel's reading) the "leap into the apparatus," the idea of a radical crossing of the human bodily sensorium with the new *physis*

---

52. "Dream Kitsch: Gloss on Surrealism" (1927), *SW* 2, p. 4. This new economy of distance and nearness is of course one of the major threads in the Artwork essay, leading up to the discussion of "tactile" reception and Benjamin's valorization of "distraction."

53. The last phrase no doubt assimilates the Surrealists to the messianic tradition. Here as elsewhere, Benjamin "superimposes," in Irving Wohlfarth's words, "two opposing actualities—historical and theological—on one another"; see "The Measure of the Possible, the Weight of the Real and the Heat of the Moment: Benjamin's Actuality Today," in *The Actuality of Walter Benjamin*, ed. Laura Marcus and Lynda Nead (London: Lawrence & Wishart, 1998), pp. 13–39.

organized by technology.[54] And the incessant striking of the alarm which culminates the accelerating movement of the text performs the very transformation of avant-garde revolt into revolution that the essay seeks to produce—or, to resume the language of the Artwork essay, the realization of the expanded perceptual-aesthetic *Spielraum* as a space of political action.

*

In the Artwork essay, the imbrication of body- and image-space, of human perceptual-physiological impulses and mechanical structures, and the related logic linking the *démontage* of the individual to the idea of collective innervation are exemplified in the figure of the screen actor. Like many early writers on film, Benjamin contrasts the screen actor's performance with that of the stage actor. Not only does the former forfeit the aura of live performance, as well as the rapport with a corporeally present audience; his or her performance or accomplishment is to a much greater degree determined by a team of experts, from the director and cinematographer to the sound engineer and editor. The morcelization and recomposition of the actor's being, the welding of his body into image-space, requires on his part a total bodily presence of mind (not unlike that of the successful gambler). For the screen actor faces a unique kind of mechanized test, similar to the aptitude tests to which the capitalist labor process subjects individuals daily and without public accountability. By exhibiting the actor's test performance, by turning the very ability to be exhibited into a test, film becomes an allegory of the social (mis)adaptation of technology:

> To perform in the glare of arc lamps while simultaneously meeting the demands of the microphone is a test performance of the highest order. To accomplish it is to preserve one's humanity in the face of the apparatus. Interest in this performance is widespread. For the majority of citydwellers, throughout the workday in offices and factories, have to relinquish their humanity in the face of an apparatus. In the evening these same masses fill the cinemas, to witness the film actor taking revenge on their behalf not only by asserting *his* humanity (or what appears to them as such) against the apparatus, but by placing that apparatus in the service of his triumph. [SW 3, p. 111]

In other words, inasmuch as the screen actor's composite performance achieves an *individual* innervation of technology at the level of *production*, it may spark *collective* innervation at the level of *reception*, in the corporeal space of the audience assembled in the theater, through processes of mimetic identification specific to cinema. (This conception, as one may recall, is diametrically reversed in the

54.   Weigel, *Body- and Image-Space* (see n. 3, above), p. 16. In this otherwise highly perceptive study, film and other technological media are hardly ever mentioned.

canonic version of the essay, in which the audience is assumed to side, in a more Brechtian fashion, with the testing gaze of the camera.)[55]

Benjamin's conception of the screen actor is not as heroic as it may seem. The triumph of the actor's "humanity" is, after all, that of an "eliminated" human being, as he writes elsewhere, the human being "as the fifth wheel on the carriage of its technology."[56] Benjamin's efforts to imagine a different relationship between humans and technology are motivated, fundamentally, by the insight that the reception of technology had already failed on a grand scale: the nineteenth century's dream of technology, fettered by capitalist relations of production, had met a terrible awakening in World War I, the "slave rebellion" of advanced technology.[57] War, inflation, and capitalist rationalization have aggravated the human being's self-alienation, a Marxian category (derived from Hegel) that Benjamin updates by emphasizing the effects of the "bungled" reception of technology on the human sensorium and capability of experience (the spiral of shock and anaesthetics). Importantly, however, he gives that concept a dialectical twist that distinguishes his use of it from merely pessimistic critiques of modernity. For one thing, grounded in secular Jewish messianism and literary gnosticism (Kafka, Freud), Benjamin's concept of self-alienation does not involve the assumption of an originary unalienated condition or a more identical, unified self.[58] For another, he valorizes film for making self-alienation materially and publicly perceivable, in other words, quotable and available for action: "*In the representation of the human being by means of an apparatus his self-alienation has found a highly productive utilization*" (*SW* 3, p. 113; *GS* 7, p. 369).

The screen actor whom Benjamin extols as a preeminent performer of self-alienation is, not surprisingly, Charlie Chaplin.[59] A descendant of the figure of the

55.   Benjamin, "The Work of Art in the Age of Its Technological Reproducibility: Third Version" (1939), *SW* 4, p. 269. A remnant of the earlier pathos survives in the later version in section 11, where Benjamin extols the highly artificial production of the "vision of immediate reality" in film as the "Blue Flower in the land of technology": "The presentation of reality in film is incomparably the more significant for people of today, since it provides the equipment-free aspect of reality they are entitled to demand from a work of art, and does so precisely on the basis of the most intensive interpenetration of reality with equipment" (*SW* 4, pp. 263, 264).

56.   "Theater and Radio" (1932), *SW* 2, p. 585. The image of the "eliminated" or exiled human being also appears in the Artwork essay, where it is attributed to Luigi Pirandello (*SW* 3, p. 112).

57.   "Theories of German Fascism" (1930), *SW* 2, p. 312. See also above, n. 14.

58.   Notwithstanding Benjamin's complicated fetishization of the mother-child relation (see, for instance, *AP*, p. 391, Convolute K2,2), he shared Gershom Scholem's kabbalistic assumption of a "primal and fundamental Galut [exile] in which "all existence, including, 'as it were,' God, subsists," constituting the "state of Creation after the breaking of the vessels" (*The Messianic Idea in Judaism* [New York: Schocken, 1971], p. 45); see Anson Rabinbach, "Introduction," *The Correspondence of Walter Benjamin and Gershom Scholem, 1932–1940*, ed. G. Scholem, trans. Gary Smith and Andre Lefevere (Cambridge, Mass.: Harvard University Press, 1992), pp. vii–xxxviii. On the significance of Kafka for Benjamin's notion of self-alienation, see ibid., pp. xxx–xxxii, and Hansen, "Of Mice and Ducks," pp. 44–46. On literary Jewish gnosticism, specifically Kafka, see Harold Bloom, *The Strong Light of the Canonical: Kafka, Freud and Scholem as Revisionists of Jewish Culture and Thought* (New York: City College, 1987), pp. 1–25.

59.   In draft notes relating to the Kafka essay, Benjamin repeatedly paired Chaplin with Kafka. As a figure of self-alienation, diasporic displacement, and historical ambiguity, "Chaplin holds a genuine key to the interpretation of Kafka" (*GS* 2, p. 1198); see also *GS* 2, pp. 1256–57.

eccentric, Chaplin ranks as one of the first provisional dwellers in the "new fields of action [*Spielräumen*] that emerged with film" (*SW* 3, p. 118; *GS* 7, pp. 377–78). Chaplin's exercises in fragmentation are a case in point:

> He dissects human expressive movement into a series of minute inner-vations. Every one of his movements is composed of a series of chopped-up bits of motion. Whether you focus on his walk or the way he handles his little cane or tips his hat—it is always the same jerky suc-cession of tiny movements, which applies the law of the filmic sequence to that of human motorics.[60]

By mimicking technology's fragmenting effects on the human body—a signature celebrated by the contemporary artistic avant-garde, famously Léger and Soupault—Chaplin "interprets himself allegorically" (*GS* 1, p. 1047). This is to say, he renders self-alienation productive by making it visible, thus enabling, in Michael Jennings's words, "the mass of humans to *see* their own alienation, to rec-ognize the fragmented, oppressive character of history."[61] Such cognition, however, depends upon a double process of *bodily* innervation—the interpenetra-tion of the performer's physiological impulses with the structures of the apparatus, and the audience's mimetic, visceral assimilation of the product in the form of collective laughter.[62] (In terms of film practice, such innervation can of course work through widely varying styles: stoic, whimsical, hysterical—think of performers as diverse as Buster Keaton, Jerry Lewis, and Jacques Tati.)

For Benjamin, the preferred genre of second technology is comedy (the other being science fiction, as evidenced by his lifelong enthusiasm for the writer Paul Scheerbart).[63] Already in his defense of *Potemkin*, Benjamin had attributed the superiority of American slapstick comedy, like that of Soviet revolutionary cin-ema, to its engagement with technology.[64] "This kind of film is comic, but only in

---

60.   Draft notes relating to the Artwork essay, *GS* 1, p. 1040; *SW* 3, p. 94.
61.   Michael W. Jennings, *Dialectical Images: Walter Benjamin's Theory of Literary Criticism* (Ithaca, N.Y.: Cornell University Press, 1987), p. 172. Also see Buck-Morss, *Dialectics of Seeing*: "Chaplin rescued the capacity for experience by mimicking the fragmentation that threatened it" (p. 269).
62.   For a different reading of Chaplin, see Tom McCall, "'The Dynamite of a Tenth of a Second': Benjamin's Revolutionary Messianism in Silent Film Comedy," *Benjamin's Ghosts*, pp. 74–94; p. 85.
63.   Benjamin read Scheerbart's novel *Lesabéndio* (1913) in 1917 and subsequently wrote a review that he never published, "Paul Scheerbart: Lesabéndio," *GS* 2, pp. 618–20; his second, major text on Scheerbart, which was planned as the conclusion to a large-scale work on politics (beginning with two sections respectively entitled "The True Politician" and "The True Politics"), is unfortunately lost; see Steiner, "Benjamin's Politics," pp. 61, 75–77. Benjamin returned to Scheerbart, who had also written a book on the architecture of glass, *Glasarchitektur* (1914) and worked with the Bauhaus architect Bruno Taut, in the 1930s; see "Short Shadows (II): To Live without Leaving Traces" (1933), *SW* 2, pp. 701–02, and his celebration of the new "culture of glass" in "Experience and Poverty," pp. 733–34. In a late text written in French, Benjamin resumed Scheerbart's utopian politics of technology, aligning him with Fourier's cosmic fantasies and mockery of contemporary humanity; "On Scheerbart" (late 1930s or 1940), *SW* 4, pp. 386–88.
64.   In his *Moscow Diary* (December 30, 1926), Benjamin is less sanguine about Soviet cinema's reflexive possibilities: more than for the stage, he observes that censorship of films considerably restricts the range of subject matter and criticism. There is not even room for American slapstick comedy

the sense that the laughter it provokes hovers over an abyss of horror" (*SW* 2, p. 17). Such language still harks back to Bergson, whose famous essay links laughter to the dread of the mechanical, the threatening loss of the *élan vital*.[65] In the Artwork essay, however, anything resembling a techno-pessimistic, lapsarian stance is dialecticized by the paradigm of play. Comedy and play are linked through their antonym—*Ernst*, in its double meaning of both seriousness and earnestness.[66] Ernst corresponds to the logic of once-and-for-all (the irreversible human sacrifice, the discus or shot that kills, tragedy, fascism). *Spiel*, on the other hand, enacts the logic of "*Einmal ist keinmal*," drawing on the "inexhaustible reservoir of all the experimental procedures" of second technology (*SW* 3, p. 127). We can easily think of a wide range of film comedies, not necessarily all silent (consider the Marx Brothers), which exemplify that logic by playing games as much with the order of things as with the order and meaning of words.

Comedy and play have in common the principle of repetition. As many writers have pointed out, comic modes—irony, parody, satire, sight gags—work through quotation and reiteration. Benjamin considers it essential for a new theory of play "to explore the great law that presides over the rules and rhythms of the entire world of play: the law of repetition." For the child, "repetition is the soul of play"; nothing makes him happier than "'doing the same thing over and over again.'" Benjamin invokes Freud—only to depart from him in a crucial way. Comparing the child's compulsion to repeat with the sexual drive in erotic passion, both "powerful" and "cunning," he agrees with Freud's claim that there is indeed an "impulse 'beyond the pleasure principle.'" But he proceeds to read that "beyond" rather ambiguously, if not deviously, through Goethe. "In fact, every profound experience longs to be insatiable, longs for repetition and return until the end of time, and for the restitution of an original condition from which it sprang." Repetition thus understood is not only an effort to domesticate trauma; "it also means enjoying one's victories and triumphs over and over again, with total intensity" (*SW* 2, p. 120). Freud dismisses repetition in pursuit of the pleasure principle as infantile (adults don't laugh at a joke the second time around) and attributes the neurotic compulsion to repeat in the adult to the drive inherent in the living organism to restore a prior state of equilibrium, in other words, the death drive.[67] While Benjamin retains the linkage of repetition and trauma—play as "the transformation of a shattering experience into habit" (*SW* 2, p. 120)—he reconfigures it in terms of a utopian notion of repetition as difference, one that does not privilege traumatic experience as a primal event but makes it

---

inasmuch as "it is based on an uninhibited play with technology. Here, however, all things technological are sacred, nothing is taken more earnestly than technology" (*GS* 6, p. 340); *Moscow Diary*, ed. Gary Smith, trans. Richard Sieburth (Cambridge, Mass: Harvard University Press, 1986), p. 55.

65.   Henri Bergson, *Laughter: An Essay on the Meaning of the Comic* (1900), trans. Cloudesley Brereton and Fred Rothwell (London: MacMillan, 1911).

66.   See Huizinga, *Homo Ludens*, pp. 5–6, 8, 44–45, for an extended reflection on the interrelations between seriousness or earnestness and play.

67.   Freud, *Beyond the Pleasure Principle*, *Standard Edition*, vol. 18, pp. 35–36; 38–41.

productive of a future. Whether fueled by trauma or triumph, the emphasis is on the nexus of play and habit and, conversely, an understanding of habits as "petrified forms of our first happiness, or our first dread, deformed to the point of being unrecognizable" (*SW* 2, p. 120; *GS* 3, p. 131).

In Benjamin's philosophy of history, repetition belongs to those ambivalent, if not antinomic categories that he nursed so stubbornly, and it is inseparable from his politics of happiness and historical redemption.[68] Reductively speaking, Benjamin's concept of repetition oscillates between two extremes: one, Nietzsche's eternal return congealed in the law of the commodity, with fashion as both disguise and perpetuation of the ever-same (Baudelaire); two, dialectically embedded in the former, repetition as the striving for a past happiness that Proust pursued to the point of asphyxiation—a repetition that Deleuze has taught us to read as the production of that past in the very movement of repetition.[69] The latter, turning on *similarity* and hence difference, also recalls Kierkegaard's notion of repetition as a memory in the direction of the future—or, in Benjaminian terms, repetition in the mode of the "yet-once-again" (it might work this time) linked to the messianic idea of repairing a history gone to pieces.[70]

When we turn to cinema as a medium of repetition, we find both poles of the antinomy present though not elaborated or, rather, submerged in the assumption of an *Umschlag* or transformation of quantity (sameness, massness) into quality (similarity, difference). In a quite basic sense, Benjamin regarded film as the medium of repetition par excellence on account of its *technical structure:* mechanical reproduction as replication that lacks an original; infinite reiterability and improvability at the level of production (numerous takes) as well as that of reception, that is, the seemingly unlimited distribution and exhibition of prints of the same film (an argument that, we would argue today, ignores the variability

68.   See Giorgio Agamben, "Walter Benjamin and the Demonic: Happiness and Historical Redemption" (1982), in *Potentialities: Collected Essdays in Philosophy,* ed. and trans. Daniel Heller-Roazen (Stanford: Stanford University Press, 1999), pp. 138–59, esp. p. 155f.

69.   In addition to the *The Arcades Project,* especially Convolutes B, D, and J, see the condensed version of Benjamin's late reflections on repetition in "Central Park" (1939), *SW* 4, pp. 161–99, esp. pp. 184. In his earlier essay on Proust, Benjamin links "eternal repetition" to the "eternal restoration of the original, first happiness," and the writer's pursuit of *mémoire involuntaire* as an "impassioned cult of similarity," his "homesickness . . . for the world distorted in the state of similarity, a world in which the true Surrealist face of existence breaks through"; significantly, Benjamin illustrates this quest with the image of children's repetitive play with a rolled-up stocking. "On the Image of Proust" (1929), *SW* 2, pp. 237–47. On that passage in particular, see Irving Wohlfarth, "Walter Benjamin's Image of Interpretation," *New German Critique* 17 (Spring 1979), pp. 70–98, esp. pp. 79–82. Also see Buck-Morss, *Dialectics of Seeing,* pp. 97–109; Osborne, "Small-scale Victories," pp. 83–84; and Lindner, "Zeit und Glück." Gilles Deleuze develops his concept of repetition with recourse to Proust in *Repetition and Difference* (1968), trans. Paul Patton (New York: Columbia University Press, 1994), pp. 17, 84–85, 122–26 and passim.

70.   On Benjamin's concept of *Ähnlichkeit,* resemblance or similarity, see Opitz, "Ähnlichkeit," and Weigel, *Body- and Image-Space,* ch. 8 and passim, as well as *Entstellte Ähnlichkeit: Walter Benjamins theoretische Schreibweise* (Frankfurt: Fischer, 1997). On Kierkegaard, see Heike Klippel, "Wiederholung, Reproduktion und Kino," *Frauen und Film* 63 (2002), pp. 84–94.

of both exhibition practices and demographically diverse, public events of reception). At the same time, and *because* of both its technological and collective status,
he invested the cinema with the hope that it could yet heal the wounds inflicted
on human bodies and senses by a technology bent on the mastery of nature; the
hope that film, as a sensory-reflexive medium of second technology, that is, rooted
in play, offers a second, though perhaps last, chance for reversing sensory alienation, the numbing of the human sensorium in defense against shock and the
concomitant splitting of experience. "In the cinema," Benjamin writes in *One-Way
Street*, "people who are no longer moved or touched by anything learn to cry
again" (*SW* 1, p. 476; *GS* 4, p. 132).

The Artwork essay resumes this motif and gives it a more concrete—and
rather more violent—elaboration. In the section on the "optical unconscious,"
originally entitled "Micky-Maus," Benjamin tries to make a case for film as the
form of play that could at the very least neutralize, on a mass basis, the traumatic
effects of the bungled reception of technology. Echoing and complicating his earlier statement about it being film's task to train human apperceptions and
reactions for dealing with the apparatus, he asserts: "*The most important social function of film is to establish equilibrium between human beings and the apparatus*" (*SW* 3, p.
117). Film is capable of doing so not only because of its technological foundation
but also because it addresses itself to a collective subject; more precisely, because it
makes psychic states that are normally confined to individual experience (dreams,
fantasies) available to publically shared perception. This is the case, he argues, less
with literal representations of dreams "than by creating figures of collective
dream, such as the globe-encircling Mickey Mouse." The dream world that Mickey
innervates, however, is more likely one of nightmares, in particular modern ones
induced by industrial and military technology. In the transference between the
electrified subject on screen and the audience, Benjamin locates an antidote to
the violent return of modernity's repressed pathologies—through a "therapeutic
detonation of the unconscious":

> If one considers the dangerous tensions which technification and its conse-
> quences have engendered in the masses at large—tensions which at critical
> stages take on a psychotic character—one also has to recognize that this same
> technification has created the possibility of psychic immunization against
> such mass psychoses. It does so by means of certain films in which the forced
> articulation of sadistic fantasies or masochistic delusions can prevent their
> natural and dangerous maturation in the masses. Collective laughter is
> one such preemptive and therapeutic eruption of such mass psy-
> choses. [*SW* 3, p. 118; *GS* 7, p. 377]

The films provoke this laughter not only with their "grotesque" actions, their
metamorphic games with animate and inanimate, human and mechanical traits,
but also with their precise rhythmic matching of acoustic and visual movement—
through a series of staged shocks or, rather, countershocks that effect a transfer

between film and audience and, hopefully, a reconversion of neurotic energy into sensory affect.[71]

*

The rest is history: Mickey Mouse disappeared from the final version of the Artwork essay and with him the concepts of innervation and play. Benjamin may have dropped them not only at Adorno's insistence that the collective laughter at the cartoons was nothing but petit-bourgeois sadism; he also might have lost the courage of his convictions in the face of an increasingly grim reality. (Besides, in a note to the passage above, he himself observed a growing tendency, in the more recent Disney films, to put up comfortably with "bestiality and violence as inevitable concomitants of existence," a tendency that renews the old "tradition inaugurated by the dancing hooligans to be found in depictions of medieval pogroms, of whom the 'riff-raff' in Grimm's fairy tale of that title are a pale indistinct rearguard" [*SW* 3, p. 130].)[72] Still, even if Benjamin, for understandable reasons, withdrew from imagining film as a play-form of technology and cinema as a site for collective and homeopathic innervation, he was willing to wager the possibility of a technologically mediated aesthetics of play capable of diverting the destructive, catastrophic course of history.

The significance of this moment, if not its aberrancy, is thrown into relief by a brief glance at the ways in which the key terms of Benjamin's wager—play versus semblance, film as (second) technology, collective innervation—are configured in two other critical theorists, Herbert Marcuse and Adorno. Marcuse's 1937 essay "The Affirmative Character of Culture," published in the *Zeitschrift für Sozialforschung* (the journal in which the French version of the Artwork essay had appeared the previous year), has often been read, not only as an effort to redeem the idealistic substratum of bourgeois culture against its affirmative reality, especially in its fascist-heroic version, but also as a response to—or, rather, evasion of—the issues raised in—Benjamin's essay.[73] Like Adorno, Marcuse attempts to rescue an aesthetics of semblance or *Schein* (translated here as "illusion"), as the only mode in which a nexus between art and happiness can be maintained, and both invoke Nietzsche quoting Stendhal's statement that beauty is "une promesse de

71.   See Hansen, "Of Mice and Ducks," pp. 41ff. See also Lawrence Rickels, *The Case of California* (Baltimore: Johns Hopkins University Press, 1991), pp. 51–52, and the more recent survey by Esther Leslie, *Hollywood Flatlands: Animation, Critical Theory and the Avant-Garde* (London: Verso, 2002), pp. 104–7.
72.   This observation points to Caillois's more systematic analysis of the dangerous combination of *mimicry* or imitation with *ilinx* or vertigo: in the fusion of mimetic identification with vertiginous ecstasy, Caillois discerns symptoms of split personality and self-alienation which, as mass phenomena, link the medieval Children's Crusade to the "orchestrated vertigo of the Nazi rallies at Nuremberg" (*Man, Games and Play*, p. 126).
73.   A first systematic comparison of the two essays can be found in Jürgen Habermas, "Consciousness-Raising or Redemptive Criticism: The Contemporaneity of Walter Benjamin" (1972), trans. Philip Brewster and Carl Howard Bucher, *New German Critique* 17 (Spring 1979), pp. 30–59.

bonheur."[74] Unlike Adorno, Marcuse does not deal with modernist art, nor does he engage the historical crisis of "beautiful semblance" within the institution of art itself. Where he criticizes the affirmative function of the aesthetic illusion of happiness in the present—the fact that the satisfaction produced by "happiness in illusion" has entered "the service of the status quo"—he remains at the level of a critique of ideology grounded in political economy; except for the latter, there is no discussion of the material—technological, social, cultural—transformations that have rendered the status of art as beautiful semblance, its aura, problematic.[75]

Marcuse returns to the concept of semblance in *Eros and Civilization* (1955), where he attempts to rescue what he considers the political radicality of Schiller's notion of the *play impulse*, with its objective of beauty and its goal of freedom.[76] Aesthetic semblance or *Schein* (here rendered as "dis-play" or "show") is the utopian mode of a reality of scarcity and labor transformed in and through play. This transformation is enacted in the freedom of the imagination to "[trace and project] the potentialities of all being." Marcuse correlates the projected liberation of human beings (into sensuousness or *Sinnlichkeit*) with that of nature (into abundance and an object of aesthetic contemplation); but he says little about the historical interaction between humans and nature, let alone the role of technology in that interaction. The liberation and "self-sublimation" of human "sensuousness" and the concomitant "de-sublimation of reason" (which Marcuse considers one element in his own project of a "reconciliation between pleasure principle and reality principle") remain the object of a classical "aesthetic education," in Schiller's ahistorical humanist sense, rather than an education of the senses in modernity.[77]

Where Marcuse does take on the question of technology, as in his 1941 essay "Some Social Implications of Modern Technology," he presents a critique of the instrumentalist conception of technological rationality as spreading across the whole of society and "almost" the whole realm of thought—a critique that, in one version or another, runs through much of Frankfurt School thought.[78] Like Benjamin, though, Marcuse also invokes the Marxian axiom that the same social apparatus that ties technology to the perpetuation of scarcity has as well "released forces which may shatter the special historical form in which technics is utilized."

74. Marcuse, "The Affirmative Character of Culture," in *Negations: Essays in Critical Theory*, trans. Jeremy J. Shapiro (Boston: Beacon Press, 1968), p. 115.
75. Ibid., p. 121.
76. Marcuse, *Eros and Civilization*, p. 187; Friedrich Schiller, *On the Aesthetic Education of Man, In a Series of Letters*, ed. and trans. Elizabeth M. Wilkinson and L. A. Willoughby (Oxford: Clarendon Press, 1967), in particular letters 14 and 15.
77. *Eros and Civilization*, pp. 88, 189, 193.
78. Marcuse, "Some Social Implications of Modern Technology," in *Technology, War and Fascism*, ed. Douglas Kellner (London: Routledge, 1998), pp. 39–65; 49, 56. Drawing on Lewis Mumford and Thorstein Veblen, Marcuse's critique of technology is motivated rather more by the "terroristic technocracy" of the National Socialists than by American industrial capitalism, in contrast with Horkheimer and Adorno, whose critique of instrumental (scientifically, technologically based) rationality in *Dialectic of Enlightenment* (1944) includes and draws certain parallels between both.

Among other things, he speculates that technology may one day lead to "new forms of individualization," which, in contrast with individualism grounded in property, are grounded in physiological functions: "the machine . . . allocates the work to finger, hand, arm, foot, classifying and occupying men according to the dexterity of these organs." By "meet[ing] a 'natural' individuality" in the human being, the external mechanisms of standardization come to "lay bare the ground on which a hitherto suppressed individualization might develop." It is "insofar as this natural uniqueness molds his thoughts, instincts, emotions, passions, and desires" that the technological process "may become the foundation for a new form of human development."[79] It would not be farfetched to consider this process a form of innervation, albeit a more functionalist one based strictly in production, yet compared to innervation in the Benjaminian sense, it lacks the dimensions of mimetic reciprocity and play—as well as the dialectical relation between a rediscovered, reconfigured individuality and a technologically constituted new collectivity—which Benjamin saw as the potential of second technology.

It is not until *An Essay on Liberation* (1969), written in the wake of the protest movements of the 1960s, that Marcuse can imagine an alliance or "union of liberating art and liberating technology."[80] The utopian concept of socialism he evokes "envisages the ingression of freedom into the realm of necessity" (that is, of play into work), which entails "passing from Marx to Fourier," as well as a "union between causality by necessity and causality by freedom," which entails passing "from realism to surrealism." He considers the Surrealists a model for "the new sensibility" of the 1960s inasmuch as they projected an aesthetically transformed world that "could (in a literal sense!) embody, incorporate, the human faculties and desires to such an extent that they appear as part of the objective determinism of nature," an imbrication for which Breton's concept of "objective chance" provides the nodal point. Such reconstruction of reality requires "the help of a *gaya scienza*, a science and technology released from their service to destruction and exploitation, and thus free for the liberating exigencies of the imagination"— in other words, for play. Beyond the Surrealist model, however, the alliance between liberating art and liberating technology remains limited to either the practical arts—"the art of preparing (cooking!), cultivating, growing things"—or is sidetracked into questions of aesthetic *technique* and form. Significantly, for Marcuse, the "collective *practice of creating an environment*," which alone could accomplish the *Aufhebung* or sublation of art into life, does not include technologically mediated and mass-oriented art forms such as cinema—which it certainly did for the Surrealists.[81]

79.   "Some Social Implications of Modern Technology," pp. 63–64.
80.   Marcuse, *An Essay on Liberation* (Boston: Beacon Press, 1969), p. 48. Also see Hauke Brunkhorst and Gertrud Koch, *Marcuse zur Einführung* (Hamburg: Junius Verlag, 1987), pp. 16, 18.
81.   Ibid., pp. 21–22: 31–32. More precisely put, Marcuse subsumes all technologically mediated aesthetic practice under its capitalist form, the "commercial unification of business and beauty, exploitation and pleasure" (p. 32), or the absorption and neutralization of the desublimating negativity of "black music" by "the market" (pp. 46–47). On the significance of cinema and moviegoing for the

If play for Marcuse remained untouched by technological and aesthetic transformations, and technology in turn did not include the arts of technological reproduction, Adorno engaged both terms at a more concrete level and in conversation with Benjamin. Throughout his work, he again and again returned and—directly or indirectly—responded to the Artwork essay, that is, to the original version (rather than the 1939 version which he himself published in *Illuminationen*). In his posthumously published *Aesthetic Theory*, Adorno explicitly takes up Benjamin's argument on the historical differentiation of semblance and play, in particular the contention that the "withering" of semblance, or aura, is accompanied by an increase of play elements in contemporary avant-garde art and film.

> The rebellion against semblance did not . . . take place in favor of play, as Benjamin supposed, though there is no mistaking the playful quality of the permutations, for instance, that have replaced fictional development. The crisis of semblance may engulf play as well, for the harmlessness of play deserves the same fate as does harmony, which originates in semblance. Art that seeks to redeem itself from semblance through play becomes sport.[82]

Adorno in no way denies the basic affinity of art and play, that "element of play without which there is no more possibility of art than of theory" (*AT*, p. 39). Nor does he contest Benjamin's observation concerning the increase of the play element in modern art, whether in self-referential permutations or in the greater emphasis of art on its own agency, from Debussy to Beckett (*AT*, p. 198). It is rather that Adorno turns the "powerful lesson," which, as Martin Jay rightly insists, he had learned from Benjamin's essay—"a lesson about the impossibility of reversing the decline of . . . 'aura'"—against Benjamin himself.[83] Insofar as art qua play abdicates its responsibility to engage with an antagonistic, heteronomous reality, it merely sidesteps the crisis of semblance that "engulfs" all Western art. In rejecting semblance in the same breath as instrumental rationality, it either regresses into harmlessness ("*fun*") or degenerates into sport.

Within the framework of his aesthetic theory, Adorno assimilates Benjamin's concept of play to a tradition of experimental art and, more generally, to art that, qua play, "seeks to absolve itself of the guilt of its semblance" yet, doing so, results in a "neutralization of praxis" (*AT*, pp. 39, 317). To be sure, semblance, for Adorno (and no less for Benjamin) is more than referential illusionism; he considers most striking the extent to which the crisis of semblance, qua harmony, has affected music, the most nonrepresentational of arts. Still, semblance is the very

Surrealists, see, to begin with, Paul Hammond, ed., *The Shadow and Its Shadow: Surrealist Writings on the Cinema* (London: British Film Institute, 1978).
82.   Theodor W. Adorno, *Aesthetic Theory* (1970), ed. Gretel Adorno and Rolf Tiedemann, trans., ed., and introduced by Robert Hullot-Kentor (Minneapolis: University of Minnesota Press, 1997), p. 100. Hereafter cited in the text as *AT*.
83.   Martin Jay, "Taking on the Stigma of the Inauthentic: Adorno's Critique of Genuineness," unpublished manuscript, p. 4.

condition of possibility for art to engage with reality at all. "The difference of art-works from the empirical world, their semblance character, is constituted out of the empirical world and in opposition to it" (*AT*, p. 103).

Crucially, for Adorno, this dialectics of semblance turns on the mediation of the unformed material within the internal structure of the work of art, its claim to wholeness, however problematic that claim may have become. Hence, in his view, the weakness of an aesthetics of play consists not only in its alleged refusal to engage with reality but, at a formal level, in its regressive evasion of fictive closure in favor of repetition.[84] In one of the paralipomena of *Aesthetic Theory*, largely a commentary on Huizinga's *Homo Ludens* (and to some extent Schiller), Adorno spells out the psychoanalytic reservation against the notion of art as play. Looking back toward childhood, "if not animality," art conceived as play can only be regressive and "inevitably stands in the service of restorative and archaizing social tendencies." The mark of ludic forms in art is repetition, inseparable from the (internal) compulsion to repeat, which Adorno reads unequivocally as the (internalized) "compulsion toward the ever-same" and which he, more literally true to Freud than Benjamin, associates with the death drive (*AT*, p. 317).

The earliest published reference to Benjamin's thesis on play and semblance appears in Adorno's essay "On the Fetish Character in Music and the Regression of Listening" (1938), his polemical response to the Artwork essay. Although he rejects the idea that there might be "new possibilities" in regressive listening, he still accepts (albeit in the subjunctive mood) Benjamin's basic claim: "One might be tempted to redeem [regressive listening] if one were to imagine it as [a phenomenon] in which the 'auratic' character of the work of art, its elements of semblance, gave way to the playful ones." While he allows for at least the possibility that this might be the case in film, he hastens to assert that nothing of the sort has happened in music: "today's mass music shows little of such progress in [the process of] disenchantment. Nothing survives in it more steadfastly than illusion, nothing is more illusory than its reality." Nonetheless, Adorno still shares Benjamin's valorization of play by insisting that the "infantile play" of mass music "has scarcely more than the name in common with the productivity of children." What is more, he sets off genuine play against the bourgeois business of sport which, in its "beastly seriousness" and purposiveness, surrenders the "dream of freedom" to the treatment of "play as a duty."[85]

Four years later, in the context of the chapter on the "culture industry" in *Dialectic of Enlightenment*, Adorno has entrenched himself in the position he was to take in *Aesthetic Theory*, that is, a critique of Benjamin's aesthetics of play as an evasion of the problematic of semblance—and, worse, as a degradation of art to a form of sport. In the unpublished continuation of that chapter, "The Schema of Mass Culture" (completed in October 1942), Adorno analyzes the mechanisms of mass cul-

84.   See, for instance, his remarks on Proust's attempt to "outwit art's illusoriness" by evading the appearance of closure (*AT*, p. 102).
85.   Adorno, "On the Fetish Character in Music and the Regression of Listening," trans. Maurice Goldbloom, in Adorno, *The Culture Industry: Selected Essays on Mass Culture*, ed. with an introduction by J. M. Bernstein (London: Routledge, 1991), pp. 49–50; trans. mod.

ture in relation to sporting events from which it borrows certain features, in particular its emphasis on virtuosity of performance and its ostensible abstention from meaning.

> Thus sportification plays its part in the dissolution of semblance. Sport is the imageless counterpart to practical life, and aesthetic images increasingly partake of such imagelessness the more they turn into a form of sport themselves. One might well perceive in this the anticipation of a kind of play which, in classless society, would sublate semblance along with the principle of utility whose complement it is.[86]

Again, although Adorno does not mention Benjamin by name, he clearly responds to claims made in the Artwork essay. After all, Benjamin himself links sports and film repeatedly, most memorably when he evokes the "newspaper boys leaning on their bicycles and discussing the outcome of a bicycle race" to illustrate the way in which film technology makes everyone in the audience a semi-expert (*SW* 3, p. 114). Given Adorno's animus against sport under whatever political flag or economic system it might be propagated, Benjamin's admittedly somewhat uncharacteristic nod to sportivity was just one more of those "Brechtian motifs" that Adorno had recommended for "total elimination."[87]

Adorno here distorts Benjamin's larger argument about film as a "play-form" of technology in two ways. First, he reduces Benjamin's concept of play, grounded in the latter's theory of the mimetic faculty and philosophy of technology, to one aspect—that of performance under the conditions of a test, developed in relation to the figure of the screen actor. Then he implicitly takes up Benjamin's argument about the cinema as a site of actually *ongoing* collective innervation—and innervation of collectivity—(the question being the direction, quality, and usurpation of that process); but Adorno transposes this argument into a utopian "anticipation of a kind of play which, in classless society, would sublate semblance along with the principle of utility whose complement it is." It is only in a utopian key that Adorno can fathom his friend's view of technology's actual reconfiguration and reconstitution of collectivity. Where Benjamin (and, for that matter, Kracauer) traced signs of change in the present and could imagine some mode of mediation toward a different future, Adorno dichotomizes that temporality into one of utopia and the present as hell. Thus, he dismisses any alterity within the notion of play, first by reducing it to sport, and then by reducing both sport and mass culture to their ideological function in monopoly capitalism: "Sport itself is not play, but a ritual in which the subjected celebrate their subjection. They parody freedom in the voluntary character of the service which

---

86.   [Max Horkheimer and] Theodor W. Adorno, "Schema der Massenkultur" (continuation of the chapter on the culture industry completed 1942), *Gesammelte Schriften*, vol. 3: *Dialektik der Aufklärung: Philosophische Fragmente*, ed. Rolf Tiedemann (Frankfurt a.M.: Suhrkamp, 1981), p. 328; "The Schema of Mass Culture," trans. Nicholas Walker, in *The Culture Industry*, p. 77; trans. mod.
87.   Adorno, letter of March 18, 1936, *Complete Correspondence*, p. 131.

the individual forcibly exacts from its own body a second time."[88] As for the spectating collective, the goal is neither semi-expertise nor emulation, let alone an education in solidarity: "mass culture is not interested in turning its consumers into athletes but only into screaming fans in the stands." By conflating life with a "system of open or covert sportive competition, it . . . even eliminates the tension between the Sunday devoted to sports and the wretchedness of the working week that used to make up the better part of real sport." This is, Adorno concludes, how mass culture enacts the "liquidation of aesthetic semblance."[89]

To be sure, Adorno's conception of semblance and play, especially with regard to experimental art and modern music, is more complex than can be elaborated here.[90] What is curious, however, is that he treats Benjamin's argument as if the relation between semblance and play were one of those binary oppositions that dominate the Artwork essay's later version (aura versus masses, distance versus nearness, etc.)—which it is precisely *not*. When, in his famous epistolary response, Adorno takes Benjamin to task for a supposedly undialectical concept of semblance, he reads the two terms as if they were conceptually independent of each other.[91] In other words, he ignores Benjamin's insistence on a dialectical relation *between* play and semblance—a tension in the polarity that persists, through the historical crisis and polemical erasure of aura, in a Benjaminian aesthetics of film.

*

Adorno's critique of Benjamin's theses, skewed as it may be, urges us to take a closer look at how a theory of film as play translates into not only general

88.   "Schema of Mass Culture," p. 77; "Schema der Massenkultur," p. 328. The passage continues by linking this self-subjectification to the unrecognized sadomasochistic structure of mass-cultural subjectivity and to repetition compulsion: "One can play the master by inflicting the original pain upon oneself and others at a symbolic level, through compulsive repetition."
89.   "Schema of Mass Culture," p. 78; "Schema der Massenkultur," p. 329. As for the "screaming fans in the stands," also see the already cited fragment in *Aesthetic Theory:* "The putative play drive has ever been fused with the primacy of blind collectivity" (p. 317). In their discussions surrounding *Dialectic of Enlightenment* (written up by Gretel Adorno), Max Horkheimer remarkably dissents from Adorno's indictment of sport for its tendency to lapse into manifest brutality: "In sport, there is something of play, and in play there is something of the dream. Athletic accomplishment and gambling. Mass culture has grasped play. Play has something of unrepressed mimesis.—Your concept of mimesis is probably incorrect since real regression is repressed. . . . Repressed mimesis is identical with controlled regression." Max Horkheimer, *Gesammelte Schriften, Band 12: Nachgelassene Schriften 1931–1949*, ed. Gunzelin Schmid Noerr (Frankfurt a.M.: Suhrkamp, 1985), p. 592.
90.   See, for instance, Adorno's chapter on Schönberg in *Philosophie der neuen Musik* (1949; written between 1940 and 1948), in particular the section "Schönberg's critique of semblance and play"; in the same chapter, he invokes Benjamin's argument to address twelve-tone music's relation to gambling and fate. See *Philosophy of Modern Music*, trans. Anne G. Mitchell and Wesley V. Blomster (New York: Continuum, 2003), pp. 37–41; 66. It would also be interesting to consider Adorno's late essays on music, for instance, his effort to come to terms with Cage and Stockhausen, with serial and postserial music, in light of Benjamin's aesthetics of play; see "Vers une musique informelle" (1961). On Adorno and experimental aesthetics, see Robert Kaufman, "Aura, Still," *October* 99 (Winter 2002), pp. 45–80.
91.   "I cannot see why play should be dialectical, while semblance—the semblance you once salvaged in the figure of Ottilie [in Goethe's *Elective Affinities*] . . . —is supposed not to be" (*Correspondence*, p. 129).

assumptions about the medium, but also a consideration of particular aesthetic practices in the context of the cinematic institution. This discussion will lead me, in conclusion, to reflect upon the significance of Benjamin's wager beyond its historical moment, both from the perspective of film and cinema in the age of the digital and with a view to contemporary media politics.

First, Adorno's critique highlights an important difference in the very concept of play: whether in avant-garde art or film, play for Benjamin remains linked to the mimetic faculty, key to his effort to theorize a nondestructive, imaginative innervation of the changed, and ever more rapidly changing, technological environment. As we saw earlier, he is careful to locate the origin of both play and semblance in mimesis, the "*Ur*-phenomenon of all artistic activity," emphasizing their interdependence as much as their polarity (*SW* 3, p. 127; *GS* 7, p. 368). This genealogy diverges from accounts that place the concept of play, in both its idealist and modernist versions, in an antithetical relation to mimesis, more narrowly understood as illusionist imitation or representational realism.[92] If Benjamin's aesthetics of play retains its roots in mimesis, it does so by assuming a wider—anthropological, epistemological, language-philosophical—understanding of the phenomenon, which may manifest itself as much in art as it does in the behavior of the playing child and the gambler, in astrology as well as graphology.[93]

As a kind of play that both draws on and redefines the mimetic faculty—the ability to perceive and produce similarities—film engages with the material world, though not inevitably in a manner that simply reflects its familiar features. If one speaks with regard to Benjamin of photography and film as "new mimetic technologies,"[94] it has to be with the caveat that this does not refer to the (audio-)visual media's ability to resemble the real, their analogue mode of reference—an ability that used to subtend ideological claims to both documentary authenticity and representational realism in mainstream narrative cinema. Benjamin's theory of the mimetic faculty is concerned primarily with "nonsensuous" similarities—correspondences that unconsciously or imperceptibly permeate our lives. The mimetic gift that enabled the ancients to read such correspondences from stars, entrails, dances, chance occurrences—"to read what was never written"—has migrated into language and writing, "the most perfect archive of nonsensuous similarity" (*SW* 2, p. 697); it persists as a physiognomic mode of reading for which

92. Spariosu, for instance, traces the restoration of *play* ("to its pre-Platonic high cultural status") beginning with Kant and German idealism as a process of divorcing it from and opposing it to mimesis (*Literature, Mimesis and Play*, p. 9). See also n. 35, above.
93. See Benjamin, "Doctrine of the Similar" (February 1933) and "Mimetic Faculty" (September 1933), *SW* 2, pp. 694–98; 720–22. For a genealogy of the two versions of Benjamin's essay in relation to, on the one hand, his early philosophy of language and theory of "magic reading" and, on the other, his stance against the totalitarian reduction of mimetic practice in fascist aesthetics (and, I would add, Socialist Realism), see Opitz, "Ähnlichkeit"; also see Josef Fürnkäs, "Aura," in Benjamin's *Begriffe*, pp. 95–146.
94. Buck-Morss, *Dialectics of Seeing*, p. 267; Taussig, *Nervous System*, pp. 143–48; and *Mimesis and Alterity*, ch. 2.

similarity "flashes up" and "flits past," as an aspect of language in excess of, though not isolated from, its semiotic aspect (*SW 2*, p. 722).[95]

While tracing a connection between archaic and contemporary, "profane" modes of reading, Benjamin considers the mimetic faculty a profoundly historical category: it comes into view only at the moment of its decline, when the perceptual world of modern human beings contains far fewer encrypted similarities or "magical correspondences" (*SW 2*, p. 695): "The question is whether we are concerned with the decay of this faculty or with its transformation" (*SW 2*, p. 721). It is in light of this question that Benjamin explores the aesthetic—formal, stylistic, perceptual, experiential—possibilities of the technological media, in particular, how film might "read" similarities that are no longer, or perhaps not yet, sensuously perceivable, and how such a reading might translate into collective and public experience in the cinema.

He pursues these questions through the much discussed notion of an "optical unconscious," which adds a psychoanalytic dimension to the anthropological, language-philosophical, and mystical underpinnings of the mimetic faculty. Introduced in his "Little History of Photography" (1931), this term refers to the idea that the apparatus might record and store aspects of reality invisible to the unarmed human eye, or moments of contingency and indeterminacy that were neither perceived nor intended by the photographer but might at some later point be released to the searching gaze of the beholder (*SW 2*, pp. 510–12). When Benjamin resumes the notion of an "optical unconscious" in the Artwork essay, his examples shift from the still to the moving image and from the world of plants and bourgeois portraiture to the collective everyday shaped by capitalist-industrial technology. If in photography the optical unconscious harbored a revelatory and cognitive function, in film the cinematic procedures of framing and editing augment this possibility with a destructive, liberating, and transformative function in relation to the depicted world. To recall the famous passage from the Artwork essay, first formulated in his defense of *Potemkin*:

> Our bars and city streets, our offices and furnished rooms, our railroad stations and our factories seemed to close relentlessly around us. Then came film and exploded this prison-world with the dynamite of the split second, so that now we can set off calmly on journeys of adventure among its far-flung debris. [*SW 3*, p. 117]

The "prismatic" work of film at once unveils and refracts the everyday, thus making it available for play—for a mimetic appropriation and reconfiguring of its ruined fragments.

95.   See Opitz, "Ähnlichkeit," pp. 31–41, and Weigel, *Entstellte Ähnlichkeit* 9–10; *Body- and Image-Space* xvii, p. 130 and passim, in particular on the distinction between "nonsensuous" and "distorted" similarity. Benjamin borrows the phrase, "to read what was never written," from Hugo von Hofmannsthal's 1906 play *Der Tor und der Tod* (*Death and the Fool*). On Benjamin's theory of reading, also see Irving Wohlfarth, "'Was nie geschrieben wurde, lesen': Walter Benjamin's Theorie des Lesens," in Steiner, ed., *Walter Benjamin*, pp. 296–344.

The image evoked in this passage—which could itself appear in a city film in the manner of Vertov or Vigo—recalls another, equally cinematic, image: Kracauer's Surrealist vision of a vast general archive of outdated photographic images, the jumbled fragments of "a nature alienated from meaning." "The disorder of the detritus reflected in photography cannot be elucidated more clearly than through the suspension of every habitual relationship among the elements of nature. The capacity to stir up the elements of nature is one of the possibilities of film." If "the game that film plays with the pieces of disjointed nature is reminiscent of *dreams*," its historic significance is the task of consciousness (which Kracauer sees fulfilled in the works of Kafka) "to establish the *provisional status* of all given configurations, and perhaps even to awaken an inkling of the right order of the inventory of nature."[96] For both Benjamin and Kracauer, it is crucial that film's game with the fragments of nature destroy the spell of facticity, of naturalness, that maintains the given order. But this idea is inseparable from their messianic belief in photography's material bonding with the "far-flung debris" of modern life, as the condition for its eventual, though unimageable, redemption. So *pace* Adorno, the game that film plays suggests a strong engagement with the empirical world, though that engagement consists precisely in rupturing medium-specific expectations of semblance by means of (in the Benjaminian sense) allegorical procedures.

This type of film aesthetics obviously depends upon the practice of montage—the composing and assembling of shots on the principle of contrast and discontinuity, which creates meanings the individual shots would not have on their own and that is capable of presenting a world that has no referent in empirical reality. Yet, as we have seen with both Benjamin and Kracauer, this is only half the story. The disruption of the naturalized time-space continuum, its allegorical mortification and disfigurement, already resides in the photographic procedure, beginning with the technical fact of split-second exposure. For Benjamin, this mechanically mediated moment may preserve a "tiny spark of contingency," an element of alterity that speaks to another—and "other"—in the future beholder (*SW* 2, p. 510).[97] In other words, the meaning of the image is determined less by its claim to resemblance than by its material bond with the depicted object (the

---

96.   Kracauer, "Photography," pp. 62–63.
97.   The technologically based disjunction between storage and release allows for an unconscious element to enter at two levels, the moment of inscription and the time of reading. In the case of the photograph, this disjunction may involve an uncanny sense of futurity (as in Benjamin's example of the wedding picture of the photographer Dauthendey and his wife who was to commit suicide after the birth of their sixth child)—something that was not visible or knowable at the time speaks to the later beholder of his own form of death (one, however, that Benjamin had been contemplating quite intensely during the period [1931–32] in which he wrote the "Little History of Photography"; see Bernd Witte, *Walter Benjamin* [Hamburg: Rowohlt, 1985], pp. 96–100). It is no coincidence that this particular staging of the optical unconscious has invited comparison with Roland Barthes's notion of the "punctum," the accidental mark or detail of the photograph which "pricks," stings, wounds the beholder; *Camera Lucida: Reflections on Photography*, trans. Richard Howard (New York: Hill and Wang, 1981), pp. 26–27.

camera having been there at a particular point in time, light rays having linked the object with the photochemical emulsion for fractions of a second)—in semiotic terms, its indexicality. As an "imprint of a once-present and unique moment," in Mary Ann Doane's words, the indexical sign is thus essentially a "signature of temporality."[98] Benjamin's investment in the indexical dimension of photographic imaging turns on the element of temporality that characterizes the mimetic faculty: the disjunction between the moment of contiguity and the time of reading as well as the fleeting nature or "flashing up" of the perception of similarity. In the case of film, the opportunities for such temporal disjunction—as the pathway for unconscious modes of perception and cognition—are doubled, at the very least, by the mechanical mediation not only of production but also, qua projection, of reception.[99]

By now it should be obvious that this type of film aesthetics, or conception of film as play, cannot be easily adapted, let alone applied, in the age of the digital. Among other things, the transition from photographic to digital modes of image production has challenged the significance of the indexical, whether as an ideological support for the truth claims of the visual or as an aesthetic point of entry for contingency, unpredictability, and memory. Suffice it here to say that the possibility not only to efface or "correct" unplanned side effects in postproduction but also to "composite" images from innumerable layers of different origins, including purely computer-generated ones, has put into question the epistemology of the material trace and imprint, especially in its traditional association of the photographic record with truth and authenticity.[100] Suffice it also to note that televisual standards of simultaneity have, already prior to digital and satellite delivery, affected the complex time-space relations of cinematic experience, the fictional evocation of a "here and now" in a medium that is "always already a 'there and then.'"[101]

98.   Mary Ann Doane, *The Emergence of Cinematic Time: Modernity, Contingency, The Archive* (Cambridge, Mass.: Harvard University Press, 2002), p. 16. Also see Philip Rosen, *Change Mummified: Cinema, Historicity, Theory* (Minneapolis: University of Minnesota Press, 2001). Centering, respectively, on Charles S. Peirce and on André Bazin, both these studies offer the most thorough and illuminating discussion to date of indexicality in the context of film and the photographic media.
99.   This idea—along with other aspects of Benjamin's aesthetics of film—had already been articulated, more explicitly, by Jean Epstein in "Le Sens 1 (b)," from *Bonjour cinéma* (1921), trans. Tom Milne, in *French Film Theory and Criticism*, ed. Richard Abel (Princeton: Princeton University Press, 1988), vol. 1, pp. 241–46; also see Epstein, "Magnification" (1921), trans. Stuart Liebman, ibid., pp. 235–41. On Epstein's version of the mimetic (physiognomic, animistic) potential of film, elucidated with recourse to Wittgenstein's concept of "aspect-dawning," see Malcolm Turvey, "Jean Epstein's Cinema of Immanence: The Rehabilitation of the Corporeal Eye," *October* 83 (Winter 1998), pp. 25–50.
100.   See, for instance, William J. Mitchell, *The Reconfigured Eye: Visual Truth in the Post-Photographic Era* (Cambridge, Mass.: MIT Press, 1992), esp. ch. 4. On "compositing," see Lev Manovich, *The Language of New Media* (Cambridge, Mass.: MIT Press, 2002), pp. 136–60; see also Thomas Elsaesser, "Digital Cinema: Delivery, Event, Time," in Elsaesser and Kay Hoffmann, eds., *Cinema Futures: Cain, Abel or Cable? The Screen Arts in the Digital Age* (Amsterdam: Amsterdam University Press, 1998), pp. 201–22. The notion that the advent of digitality renders the indexical dimension irrelevant is often expressed in a triumphalist mode, as when Manovich speaks of film being able to "overcome its indexical nature" ("To Lie and to Act: Cinema and Telepresence," *Cinema Futures*, p. 192). For dissenting positions, see Rosen, *Change Mummified*, ch. 8, and Doane, *Emergence of Cinematic Time*, ch. 7.
101.   Elsaesser, "Digital Cinema," pp. 208–09.

The point of such observations cannot be to measure Benjamin's "actuality" in terms dictated by the advance of media technology—an idea that he himself would have suspected of an unreflected ideology of progress that distracts us from the things that stay the same (such as, for instance, the persistence of documentary truth claims or, for that matter, of a good deal of classical-narrative verisimilitude within, if not by means of, the digital).[102] Still, to remain with this type of argument for a moment: I don't think Benjamin would have gone Luddite in the face of digital technology, inasmuch as it opens up for human beings another, dramatically enlarged *Spielraum*, a virtual space that significantly modifies the interrelations of body- and image-space and offers hitherto unimaginable modes of playful innervation.

After all, there is Mickey Mouse. By invoking an example from animated film, that is, graphic cinema that does not require, or need to pretend to, a preexisting, stable referent, Benjamin bypasses the traditional hierarchy of life-action film over animation. If, during the reign of photographic cinema, animation had been considered a marginal genre, associated with cartoons (thus films made for children) and abstract modes of experimental film, the digital paradigm makes photographic cinema a subcategory of animation.[103] For Benjamin, Mickey Mouse not only undermines the hierarchy of genres but, by defying the laws of gravity along with the boundaries between animate and inanimate, organic and mechanical, disrupts the entire "hierarchy of creatures culminating in mankind" (*SW* 2, p. 545), thus realizing Fourier's "idea of the cracking open of the teleology of nature" (*AP*, p. 635): it/he/she "proves that the creature continues to exist even when it has shed all resemblance to a human being" (*SW* 2, p. 545; *GS* 6, p. 144). It could well be said that, as a figure of technologically generated, artificial subjectivity, Benjamin's Mickey Mouse points toward the general imbrication of physiological impulses with cybernetic structures which, no longer limited to the imaginative domain of cyber-fiction, has become common practice in science and medicine, architecture and design, and a host of other areas.

102. On Benjamin's complex notion of "actuality," grounded in Jewish messianism, see Wohlfarth, "Measure of the Possible" (n. 53, above), especially pp. 18–25. As Sigrid Weigel elaborates (*Body- and Image-Space*, pp. 3–9), ever since the commemoration of Benjamin's eightieth birthday in 1982, there has been a tendency to conflate Benjamin's concept of actuality with the question of (his own) contemporary relevance; cf. Siegfried Unseld, ed. *Zur Aktualität Walter Benjamins: Aus Anlaß des 80. Geburtstags von Walter Benjamin* (Frankfurt a.M.: Suhrkamp, 1972). The latest example—and nadir—of this genre is Hans Ulrich Gumbrecht and Michael J. Marrinan, eds., *Mapping Benjamin: The Work of Art in the Digital Age* (Stanford: Stanford University Press, 2003).
103. See, for instance, Manovich, "To Lie and to Act," p. 205. Such medium-specific claims tend to ignore that, at the level of film history, mainstream animated films, in particular Disney cartoons, already by the mid-1930s were cultivating a naturalistic look patterned on the (life-action) Hollywood continuity style, relegating the destabilizing, metamorphic, and fantastic possibilities of animation to experimental cinema. See Kristin Thompson, "Implications of the Cel Animation Technique," in Teresa de Lauretis and Stephen Heath, eds., *The Cinematic Apparatus* (New York: St. Martin's Press, 1980), pp. 106–120; 108ff.; and Eric Smoodin, ed., *Disney Discourse: Producing the Magic Kingdom* (New York: Routledge, 1994). See Eisenstein's critical remarks about "the crude naturalism" of the landscapes in Bambi, against the background of his enormous enthusiasm for earlier Disney films, *Eisenstein on Disney*, ed. Jay Leyda, trans. Alan Upchurch (New York: Methuen, 1988), p. 99.

If Benjamin's Mickey Mouse is a figure of both simultaneity and futurity, it is not merely on account of the figure's technical—and relative semiotic—independence from photographic indexicality. Mickey Mouse belongs to the modernist "culture of glas" (Brecht, Le Corbusier, Adolf Loos, Scheerbart), in which Benjamin saw the potential for a "new, positive concept of barbarism" that would replace a moribund tradition of experience.[104] In the world of the (early) Disney films, "it is not worthwhile to have experience." Enacting the fairy-tale "motif of leaving home to learn what fear is," Mickey Mouse relies on imaginative improvisation rather than memory. It is the figure's absolute contemporaneity that accounts for the appeal of these films: "the fact that the audience recognizes its own life in them" (*SW* 2, p. 544; *GS* 6, pp. 144–45).

This potentially paradoxical claim once again demonstrates (*pace* Adorno but also vis-à-vis an unproblematic genealogy of the digital) that Benjamin's notion of film as play, even in the form of animation, turns on a relation of reference with the material, historical world. But that referentiality is mediated, not only at the level of cinematic inscription but crucially by the dimension of *collective reception*. In the Artwork essay, as we have seen, the claim that in certain films the audience recognizes its own life is linked to the cinema's therapeutic and, as Benjamin hopes, apotropaic function vis-à-vis technologically induced violence. Insofar as in the movie theater the reactions of the individual are a priori determined by the matrix of mass reception, collective reception entails the possibility of mutual self-regulation: "No sooner are these reations manifest than they regulate one another" (*SW* 3, p. 116). Benjamin's discussion of Mickey Mouse as a figure of collective dream spells out the psycho-perceptual prehistory that makes this self-regulation politically imperative. By articulating the repressed pathologies of technological modernity, his speculation suggests, these films could preemptively diffuse, through collective laughter, an otherwise destructive potential. In other words, by activating these (individually based) mass-psychotic tendencies in the space of collective sensory experience, in the mode of aesthetic play, the cinema might prevent them from being acted out in reality, in the form of organized mob violence, genocidal persecution, and war.

Three years earlier, Benjamin had presented a more benign vision of Mickey Mouse as a figure of collective dream, a dream that offered "tremendous relief" to "people who have grown weary of the endless complications of everyday living and to whom the purpose of existence seems to have been reduced to the most distant vanishing point on an endless horizon." Here the emphasis is on the "miracles" that seem to have been "improvised out of the body of Mickey Mouse"—"miracles that not only surpass the wonders of technology, but make fun of them." In that dream, "nature and technology, primitiveness and comfort, have completely merged" (*SW* 2, pp. 734–35). In the Artwork essay, Mickey's dream work is cast as a far more dangerous game, and the dreaming collective—"the people"—as an

---

104.   Benjamin, "Experience and Poverty" (1933), *SW* 2, pp. 731–36.

extremely volatile, "compact mass."[105] In both cases, however, Benjamin was able to imagine that the cinema, as a site of collective reception, constituted a sensory-reflexive horizon in which the liberating as well as pathological effects of technological modernity could be articulated and engaged.[106] This is to say that, despite the fact that he was not exactly a moviegoer (unlike Kracauer, for instance), Benjamin understood that cinema as a play-form of technology crucially entailed the interaction between films and audience in the public theater space, the aesthetic mobilization of affective and cognitive processes that both depend upon and shape the viewer's memory, imagination, and mimetic capacity.

Benjamin's vision of Mickey Mouse as a cheerful barbarian countering the violence unleashed by capitalist technology with games of innervation fell prey to the all-too-realistic fear that the therapy, for now, had failed; that the collective laughter of the mass audience might indeed turn out, as Adorno had warned, to be a prelude to catastrophe. He not only dropped the anthropological-materialist and messianic impulses of the Artwork essay in favor of a "general and mild politics of distraction";[107] he also wrote essays such as "The Storyteller" (1936) and "On Some Motifs in Baudelaire" (1940) that cast the historical impact of technology and the media of reproduction in a more critical, if not elegiac, key. Yet, if Benjamin's work goes to the heart of media politics today, in particular the largely unsatisfactory debates on violence in and of the media, it is not because of either his techno-utopian or his media-pessimistic stance, but rather his radical ambivalence, his effort to think both positions through in their most extreme implications. In this sense, the question of his actuality for current debates on film and media may ride less on particular prognostications than on the peculiar structure of his thinking and writing. If he shared with Gramsci the call to a "pessimism of the intellect," he did not link it, like the latter, with an "optimism of the will" but, rather, an experimental will to explore and shift between antithetical if not antinomic perspectives.[108]

105. See Benjamin's long footnote on the concept of "the masses," *SW* 2, pp. 129-30.
106. Benjamin is thus part of the theoretical genealogy for my attempt to understand cinema as a form of "vernacular modernism"; see Hansen, "The Mass Production of the Senses: Classical Cinema as Vernacular Modernism," *Modernism/Modernity* 6, no. 2 (April 1999), pp. 59–77; reprinted in Christine Gledhill and Linda Williams, eds. *Reinventing Film Studies* (London: Edward Arnold; New York: Oxford University Press, 2000), pp. 332–50, and "Fallen Women, Rising Stars, New Horizons: Shanghai Silent Film as Vernacular Modernism," *Film Quarterly* 54, no. 1 (Fall 2000), pp. 10–22.
107. Gillian Rose, "Walter Benjamin—Out of the Sources of Modern Judaism," *New Formations* 20 (Summer 1993), p. 75.
108. For Benjamin this mode of thinking was an existential matter: as he wrote to Gretel Karplus [Adorno] in early June of 1934, "my life as much as my thinking moves in extreme positions. The scope that [my thinking] thus claims, the freedom to move on parallel tracks things and thoughts that are considered incompatible, assumes a face only at the time of danger" (*Gesammelte Briefe*, vol. 4, p. 441). Also see his letter to Gershom Scholem, of May 29, 1926, in which he characterizes his attitude in all things that really matter as "always radical, never consistent"; *The Correspondence of Walter Benjamin*, trans. Manfred R. Jacobson and Evelyn M. Jacobson (Chicago: University of Chicago Press, 1994), p. 300 (trans. mod.). On the antinomic structure of Benjamin's thinking see, in particular, Anson Rabinbach, "Between Apocalypse and Enlightenment: Benjamin, Bloch, and Modern German-Jewish Messianism," *New German Critique* 34 (Summer 1985), pp. 78–124; Irving Wohlfarth, "Et Cetera? The Historian as Chiffonier," *New German Critique* 39 (Fall 1986), pp. 143–68; esp. p. 158ff.; and John McCole, *Walter Benjamin and the Antinomies of Tradition* (Ithaca: Cornell University Press, 1993).

The antinomies in which Benjamin's thinking moved still speak to contradictions in media culture itself, and in a political sphere that cannot be thought of as independent or outside of technological mediation. As far as the ascendancy of an aesthetics of play over one of semblance is concerned, one could well argue that the development Benjamin discerned and valorized has culminated in visual digital genres such as video or computer games, television ads, music videos, and a new cinema of attractions. Andrew Darley, for instance, analyzes the shift manifested in these genres in terms of an aesthetics of play, associated with ephemeral, sensuous, and physical distractions and repetitive forms, which displaces an aesthetics of representational meaning, narrative absorption, and interpretation.[109] Drawing on, among others, Caillois and Huizinga, Darley situates this aesthetics of play at that end of the continuum which Caillois characterizes as *ludus*, a highly regulated, formalized, and institutionalized type of play (in contrast to the opposite pole of *paidia*, the improvisational and imaginative type of play favored by Benjamin). Darley cautions against overestimating the new ludic aesthetics as politically progressive (the shibboleth of "playful resistance"), pointing out contradictions in the allegedly heightened activity attributed to the spectator in these interactive diversions: "it is not a matter of spectators playing *with* these texts (insofar as the expressions at issue *are* texts)"; rather, "play principles are inscribed *already* within their different modes of address.... Indeed, to a great extent it is not incorrect to say that it is the spectator who is 'played with.'"[110] If spectatorial activity is focused on the acquisition of skills and memorizing of moves, would this not vindicate Adorno's verdict against the "sportification of play" as a form of internalized social discipline? Perhaps. But, to stay with Benjamin's point, the genres discussed by Darley also promote a playful innervation of new technologies, albeit with diminished expectations regarding its utopian, liberating, and even apotropaic significance. The question Benjamin might pose today is to what extent the isolated, private circumstances of such play reduce, if not diffuse, its potential for turning the new configurations of body- and image-space into a space for collective action.

With the rise of the Internet and the World Wide Web, we are dealing with a new type of public sphere, at once infinitely expanded and extremely fragmented. At the same time, new forms of alternative and oppositional publicness are confronted by a dominant public sphere—or whatever one might call the powerful alliance between an oligarchically instrumentalized state and the conglomerated media industries—which is becoming ever more fictitious, disconnected from economic, social, and cultural realities on a global scale. Both Benjamin and Adorno knew that the decay of the aura was propelled as much by its technologically enhanced resurrections as by its "liquidation" in technological reproduction.

109.   Andrew Darley, *Visual Digital Culture: Surface Play and Spectacle in New Media Genres* (London: Routledge, 2000), esp. ch. 8.
110.   Ibid., pp. 172–73; see also pp. 176–78.

Today, the "huge gain in room-for-play" inaugurated by the photographic media is more than matched by the industrial production and circulation of phantasmagoria. Techno-aesthetics is not only inseparable from consumer capitalism but ever more essential to political marketing, to say nothing of the marketing of wars. And aesthetic devices honed in film and television do not simply supply phantasmagoric effects to political publicity; they are intrinsic to the very staging of these events. None of this is exactly news, but the degree to which such practices have become naturalized should sound a heightened level of alarm even if the very genre of alarm has long since become part of the game. All the more reason for us, as historians, critics, and theorists, artists, writers, and teachers, to take Benjamin's gamble with cinema seriously and to wage an aesthetics of play, understood as a political ecology of the senses, on a par with the most advanced technologies.

Carleton E. Watkins. The Grizzy Giant. *ca. 1870. Smithsonian American Art Museum. Museum purchase from the Charles Isaacs Collection made possible in part by the Luisita L. and Franz H. Denghausen Endowment.*

They Might Be Giants: Carleton Watkins, Galen Clark, and the Big Tree*

ELIZABETH HUTCHINSON

To mid-nineteenth-century Americans, California was well-known as the origin of many a "tall tale." "The Notorious Jumping Frog of Calaveras County," Mark Twain's classic 1865 fable about a grizzled old-timer whose acrobatic amphibian—"Dan'l Webster"—did not measure up in the final competition, captures the larger-than-life spirit that surrounded the men and women living in the foothills of the Sierra Nevada Mountains.[1] Calaveras County was already known as the home of California's most legendary heroes: the giant sequoia trees. After their "discovery" by European Americans in 1855, the mammoth trees became the immediate subject of national attention. The gigantic scale of these trees, and the implication of age that went with their height, captured the country's imagination.

The summer that Twain published his Californian myth, Carleton Watkins ventured into the area for the third time to make photographs of these giants that would convey their almost unreal greatness. He made several photographs of the "Grizzly Giant," then the largest and oldest known tree in the United States. Watkins split his portrait into two views: a full-scale image that shows the height of the tree and a section that emphasizes its girth.

It is the latter that is the focus of this investigation. An extraordinarily large photograph for the time, the 18-by-22 inch *Section of the Grizzly Giant, 33 Feet Diameter* tries to approximate the scale of its subject. The negative was created with a "mammoth" camera specifically constructed to capture the scale and grandeur of California's overgrown landmarks: waterfalls several times higher than Niagara, rock formations bigger than cathedrals, and trees on an unheard-of scale. The Grizzly Giant seems almost too big to fit into this frame. It stretches nearly to the

* Earlier versions of this essay were presented at Arizona State University on November 17, 1999, and at Columbia University on March 18, 2000. This research was begun for Alexander Nemerov's course on American Art 1840–1914 at Stanford University in the winter of 1993. Further research was supported with a grant from the Research Allocations Fund Committee of the University of New Mexico. The Gilder Fund of Barnard College provided help with reproductions. I would like to thank Geoff Batchen, Alexander Nemerov, Bill Truettner, and Gray Sweeney for their helpful comments on earlier drafts.
1. Mark Twain, *The Celebrated Jumping Frog of Calaveras County, and Other Sketches*, foreword by Shelley Fisher Fishkin, introduction by Roy Blount, Jr., and afterword by Richard Bucci (New York: Oxford University Press, 1996). The story was originally published in a New York newspaper in 1865.

Watkins. Section of the Grizzly Giant.
*1865. Courtesy Department of Special
Collections, Stanford University Libraries.*

sides of the print, the trunk shooting out of the top without beginning to narrow, as if it could go on forever.

If this is not enough to cast the viewer into a state of awe, the vast girth of the tree is underscored by positioning a figure at its base. This man is, physically and symbolically, no slouch himself; he is the six-feet-two-inch Galen Clark, the caretaker of the copse of giant sequoias in which the Grizzly Giant stands. Clark's knowledge and skill as a naturalist and guide were made famous in countless articles and books about the region. The photograph's significance is further underscored by the stature of its photographer. When he exposed the image, Carleton Watkins was already the best-known California landscape photographer of his day.[2]

Susan Stewart has written provocatively about the subject of giants in Western culture. The gigantic, Stewart claims, provides a metaphorical screen through which an individual can work out his or her relationship to the exterior world: "We find the gigantic at the origin of public and natural history. The gigantic becomes an explanation for the environment, a figure of the interface between the natural and the human."[3] Made the year after the Yosemite Valley and nearby Mariposa Grove of Big

2.   For a comprehensive bibliography of works on Carleton Watkins, see Amy Rule, ed., *Carleton Watkins: Selected Texts and Bibliography* (Boston: G. K. Hall & Co., 1993). The most helpful for this study are Nancy K. Anderson, "'The Kiss of Enterprise': The Western Landscape as Symbol and Resource," in William Truettner, ed., *The West as America: Reinterpreting Images of the American Frontier, 1820–1920* (Washington, D.C.: Smithsonian Institution Press, 1991), pp. 237–84; Nanette Margaret Sexton, "Carleton E. Watkins: Pioneer California Photographer (1829–1916): A Study in the Evolution of Photographic Style, During the First Decade of Wet Plate Photography," Ph.D. diss., Harvard University, 1982; and the numerous publications on Watkins by Peter Palmquist.
3.   Susan Stewart, *On Longing: Narratives of the Miniature, the Gigantic, the Souvenir, the Collection* (Durham, N.C.: Duke University Press, 1993), p. 71.

Trees were set aside as national monuments, the juxtaposition of these three "giants" can be seen as a testament to the possibilities of giants, natural and human, to appropriately structure an American relationship to the Western landscape.

The choice to use a work by Watkins to investigate the cultural meanings of images of the West in this period is an obvious one. Long praised for the beauty of his quasi-modernist formal compositions, he has recently been described as a propagandist for the exploitation of California's natural resources, creating aesthetic images that legitimized the commercial development of the region. The debate over how much attention to pay to Watkins's unique vision continues today.[4] However, my focus is not primarily on the artist but on his audience. In what follows I'd like to speculate about the meanings the photographs might have communicated to their viewers by closely examining the prints themselves, the physical contexts in which they were viewed, and the period visual culture they invoke. I do this by examining two prints made from this negative, one produced shortly after the negative was exposed and one printed sometime after 1875.

By grounding this analysis in two products of a single negative, I hope to avoid a common pitfall in writing about photographs, which is to reduce them to unproblematic, virtual illustrations of social forces instead of active players in the field of visual culture. For at least two decades, scholars have called for a turn away from formalist readings of nineteenth-century photographs toward an understanding of the historical changes that were supported by the books, periodicals, and archives in which they appeared.[5] Interestingly, this process of rehistoricizing can take us away from the materiality of the objects being discussed. While many scholars describe the content and even the style of photographs at length, they often look past the details of individual prints.[6] By this I mean the exposing, developing, and printing that are necessary to creating the final illusionistic image, as well as the signs of wear and use that show the unique histories of each object. In other words, historians of photography tend to write about pictures and *not* prints. We discuss what a photograph depicts as if our access to it is uninfluenced by such extraneous visual information. And yet it seems to me that such signs of construction and use directly affect *how* we see *what* we see in a photograph that is the subject of historical investigation. My interest comes from a desire to investigate how close looking allows us to see more clearly how visual culture is the bearer of meaning in specific historical contexts for specific audiences. If we really want to understand photography's role in changing attitudes toward the American West,

4.   This is evidenced by Douglas R. Nickel et al., *Carleton Watkins: The Art of Perception* (San Francisco: San Francisco Museum of Modern Art, 1999).
5.   See, for example, Douglas Crimp, "The Museum's Old/The Library's New Subject," *Parachute* 22 (Spring 1981), pp. 32–37; Rosalind Krauss, "Photography's Discursive Spaces: Landscape/View," *Art Journal* 42, no. 4 (Winter 1982), pp. 311–19; and Allan Sekula, "The Body and the Archive," *October* 39 (Winter 1986), pp. 3–64.
6.   An exception to this might be found in Carol Armstrong's discussion of the variance in prints used in early photographically illustrated books. See Armstrong, *Scenes in a Library: Reading the Photograph in the Book, 1843–1875* (Cambridge, Mass.: MIT Press, 1998).

for example, we can learn a lot from how these two prints invite changing views. As I will argue below, one print—in its internal form and in the contexts in which it was viewed—encourages an attitude of grandeur and reverence toward the Grizzly Giant, while the other, made two decades later and viewed in different contexts, encourages the dispassionate, even commodified attitude of the tourist.

My analysis reinforces Douglas Nickel's theory that Watkins's work contributes to a shared nineteenth-century visuality of modernization. I am particularly interested in tourism as an aspect of the development of modern subjectivity.[7] I use tourism not only in its literal sense of referring to commercial activities set up for actual travelers, but also in terms of what Dean MacCannell explores as the "ideological framing of history, nature, and tradition . . . that has the power to reshape culture and nature to its own needs."[8] At the same time, these two prints expose the conflicts embedded in literal tourism in mid-nineteenth-century America. These conflicts were generated by the tensions between the antimodern ideology with which romantic travelers pursued "scenery" and the commercial processes used to produce this intangible product.[9] As I will suggest, this conflict became exacerbated in the period between the two prints because of things that affected people's relationship to both Watkins's photograph and its subject matter.

1865

The Grizzly Giant is the acknowledged patriarch of the Mariposa Grove of Sequoias. It is not so tall and graceful in general outline, nor is its cubical contents as great as some other trees in the Grove. It is located on more comparatively open and dry ground and has a unique individuality of majestic grandeur all its own, different from any other known Sequoia. It has been very badly injured by fires during unknown past centuries, leaving only four narrow strips of sapwood connecting with its roots. Many of its top branches have been broken down by the weight of heavy winter snows and fierce gales of wind. . . . Dying for centuries, yet still standing at bay, it is probably not only the oldest living tree, but also the oldest living thing on earth.

—Galen Clark, *The Big Trees of California, Their History and Characteristics*

It is useful to remember right at the beginning *where* and *how* early prints of *Section of the Grizzly Giant* were encountered. Carol Armstrong has written powerfully about the need to reinsert nineteenth-century photographs into the albums and

7.   On tourism and modernity, see Dean MacCannell, *The Tourist: A New Theory of the Leisure Class* (New York: Schocken Books, 1989), and James Clifford, *Routes: Travel and Translation in the Late Twentieth Century* (Cambridge: Harvard University Press, 1997).
8.   Dean MacCannell, *Empty Meeting Grounds: The Tourist Papers* (New York: Routledge, 1992), p. 1.
9.   On the "production" of scenery, see Dona Brown, *Inventing New England: Regional Tourism in the Nineteenth Century* (Washington, D.C.: Smithsonian Institution Press, 1995).

books in which they were generally to be found.[10] This is certainly where the mammoth plate *Section* belongs. While 1865 marked the year that Watkins's stereo views began to be marketed nationally, the primary means of encountering his larger pictures that year was in the bound albums he had been publishing since 1863, updating the plates after subsequent trips.[11] To reconstruct the experience of this photograph we might first look at how the image falls within a narrative created by the album of which it was a part. For unlike the personal photograph albums with which we are most familiar, which bring together images garnered from all over and are arranged according to the owner's personal whim, the extant Watkins albums offer to diverse viewers a similar set of images arranged in a similar order.

No one to date has commented on the order of images in Watkins's albums, but the progression followed by them is a logical one, repeating the experiences of visitors to the area from beginning to end, first using horizontal photographs and then vertical ones (so that the viewer did not have to constantly turn the heavy album).[12] The initial picture in most of them is *The First View of the Valley from the*

10.   See Armstrong, *Scenes in a Library*, pp. 15–17.
11.   Nanette Sexton has written that Watkins generally sold the mammoth plates only as sets, binding them into huge, sixty-pound albums. Sexton, "Carleton E. Watkins," p. 231.
12.   This itinerary roughly conforms to that described by visitors from the 1850s to the 1870s. See, for example, Fitz Hugh Ludlow, "Seven Weeks in the Great Yo-Semite," *Atlantic Monthly* (June 1864),

The First View of the Valley
from the Mariposa Trail

Watkins. The First View of the Valley from the
Mariposa Trail. *1865–66. © The J. Paul Getty Museum.*
Courtesy The J. Paul Getty Museum, Los Angeles.

Mariposa Trail; it reproduces a panoramic scene taken from a promontory not far from the Mariposa Trail, which led into Yosemite Valley from the south. The second image, *Best General View of the Yosemite Valley from Mariposa Trail*, marks another view available along this trail. After that, the viewer metaphorically enters the valley, looking first to the left at *El Capitan* and then to right to *The Bridal Veil Fall*. Subsequent pictures take the viewer up the valley toward Cathedral Spires and the Three Brothers, then into the Little Yosemite Valley to view the Vernal and Nevada Falls, and out of the region via the easily climbed Sentinel Dome for some final panoramic views. The final images are of the Mariposa Grove, located over twenty miles southwest of the Valley that was, in 1865, usually visited on both the way in and the way out of Yosemite itself. Subsequent tourist guides reinscribe this itinerary as the standard. In 1868, State Geologist Josiah Whitney published *The Yosemite Book*, designed as a guide to visitors to the area and, according to John Sears, the model for all subsequent nineteenth-century guides to the region.[13] The book not only recommends this same route, it even previews those experiences in twenty-eight photographs made for the publication by Watkins.

Viewing images bound into an album structures not only *what* to look at, but also *how* to view it. While small stereocards might seem like expendable parlor toys, the very act of looking at the weighty tome would encourage a reverential feeling. Guests would have to bend over tables to gaze into the heavy books, a position that would direct their attention away from their pedestrian surroundings "into" the view in a quiet setting that would emphasize a sense of personal contact with the awesome monuments of the West. The idea of contemplation is particularly strongly invoked in the *Grizzly Giant* photographs, which are positioned at the end of the album, with the *Section* following the full view.

This sequence seems to have been important to the artist. Watkins photographed the base of the Grizzly Giant on each of his trips to the Mariposa Grove. His early pictures of the "Section" are horizontal, and thus appear at the end of the first suite of images in the 1863 albums. In 1865, he switched to a vertical composition. This may have been influenced by the fact that he was photographing illustrations for Whitney's *Yosemite Book* at the same time; *The Yosemite Book* photographs are all verticals. In both Whitney's book and albums containing prints from the 1865 negative, Watkins placed the *Section* after a photograph of the entire Grizzly Giant. Moreover, the inclusion of a human figure in the *Section* for the first time (the

pp. 739–54, and Isaac H. Bromley, "The Big Trees and the Yosemite," *Scribners' Monthly* 3 (January 1872), pp. 261–77. My information is based on albums from the 1860s in the collections of the Addison Gallery of American Art, Andover, Massachusetts; the California Historical Society, San Francisco; the Center for Creative Photography at the University of Arizona, Tucson; the Gray Herbarium Library of Harvard University, Cambridge, Massachusetts; Stanford University Library Special Collections, Stanford, California; and the Syracuse University Library Special Collections Research Center, Syracuse, New York. In albums that contained views from more than one series, the *Grizzly Giant* portraits come at the end of the Yosemite and Mariposa photographs.
13.   Josiah D. Whitney, *The Yosemite Book: A Description of the Yosemite Valley and the Adjacent Region of the Sierra Nevada, and of the Big Trees of California* (New York: Julius Bien, 1868); John F. Sears, *Sacred Places: American Tourist Attractions in the Nineteenth Century* (New York: Oxford University Press, 1989), p. 137.

other photographs are pure landscapes) encourages the viewer to consider the relationship of people to the American landscape.

All three of the figures in *Section of the Grizzly Giant* would have been recognized by viewers of mammoth prints. Modern scholars have located only a handful of the albums, suggesting that circulation of the expensive, heavy objects was limited. Several have been traced back to earlier owners, such as the influential minister and California booster Thomas Starr King, the Central Pacific Railroad financier Collis P. Huntington, and the Harvard botanist Asa Gray. Viewers also certainly included Watkins's patrons Josiah Whitney and John Frémont and his wife, Jessie Benton Frémont and, we can assume, other Yosemite promoters such as editor Horace Greeley and House Speaker Schuyler Colfax, both of whom visited the region in the early 1860s. The elite group who saw a mammoth plate image of the *Section* early on thus included many who were directly concerned with the natural, scientific, and economic potential of the region.

These viewers would have interpreted the image in light of their own experiences of the Big Trees. In the mid-nineteenth century, the Mariposa Grove was as important as any other feature of the area. Contemporary accounts by scientists and travelers devote at least as much time to describing the first encounter with the giant sequoias as to rhapsodizing about the domes and waterfalls of the Valley. As Whitney claimed, "No other plant ever attracted so much attention or attained such a celebrity within so short a period."[14] The age of the trees impressed visitors as much as their size. As Greeley over-optimistically noted upon his visit:

> That they were of very substantial size when David danced before the ark, when Solomon laid the foundations of the Temple, when Theseus ruled in Athens, when Aeneas fled from the burning wreck of vanquished Troy, when Sesostris led his victorious Egyptians into the heart of Asia, I have no manner of doubt.[15]

The antiquity of the trees seemed to offer reassurance. Visitors to the Grove even hugged the trees. Trees were frequently personified as models of human greatness in mid-century culture, and descriptions of the giant sequoias frequently treat them as animate beings. Greeley called them "patriarchs"; another visitor described them as "hoary old survivors."[16] The *Section* invites similar associations. As the viewer gazes at the bark of the Grizzly Giant, the tree seems to take on human qualities. Knots and bumps begin to coalesce into faces, especially on the left side.

In *Section* the figure of Galen Clark provides a model of the viewer's communion with the vastness of nature. Clark's tiny body is almost absorbed by

14.   Whitney, *The Yosemite Book*, p. 103.
15.   Horace Greeley, *An Overland Journey from New York to San Francisco in the Summer of 1859* (New York: Alfred A. Knopf, 1964), p. 264.
16.   Greeley, *Overland Journey*, p. 267; Bromley, "Big Trees," p. 266; "The Big Trees of California," *Harper's Weekly* (June 5, 1858), p. 357. For discussions of the personification of trees, see Simon Schama, *Landscape and Memory* (New York: Alfred A. Knopf, 1995), pt. 1.

the tree. The monochromatic photograph adapts the guide's colors to those of the Grizzly Giant, but the affinity between these two runs deeper, so that the wisps of Clark's beard start to look like the leafy fronds of the young trees in the front of the composition. Covered in slouchy layers—checked shirt, cardigan, jacket, with long pants that bunch around his boots, Clark's wrinkled silhouette echoes that of the tree behind him. The caretaker and his charge even share the same posture, seeming to lean back to the left and turn slightly to the right. The resemblance between man and tree is such that we need to labor to pick out the details of Clark's features. In fact, one of Watkins' viewers wrote that his eye was wearied by the work involved in taking in this view.[17]

The wealth of detail has a moral. It forces the viewer to achieve her understanding of the landscape through great effort, causing her to meditate on the complexity of God's creation. Contemporary aesthetic theory encouraged Americans to look for signs of divine and national destiny in representations of nature.[18] Asher Durand's well-known 1848 painting *Kindred Spirits*, which depicts friends Thomas Cole and William Cullen Bryant "reading" a landscape, demonstrates this tradition. The figures are overwhelmed, absorbed, by the view, and in their concentration and gestures demand the viewer's serious visual investigation and interpretation. The almost photographic precision with which Durand renders the rocks and leaves arrests the viewer in studious stillness as her eyes bore deeper into the details.

While there is no evidence that Watkins read Durand's *Letters on Landscape Painting* or other documents of the American Romantic tradition, his photographs conform to the compositional conventions of this school. His understanding of a correct depiction of landscape could have come through his exposure to photographs by Francis Frith and Frederick Langenheim, whose work drew on the conventions of painting, during his early career in the studio of Bay Area photographer R. H. Vance. Moreover, by 1865 Watkins had long been associating socially and professionally with highly educated men and women like the Frémonts, which would have offered opportunities to discuss how to interpret nature.

Aesthetic discussions in nineteenth-century America frequently took on a nationalist tone. Durand and Cole routinely celebrated the nation's wilderness as a sign of the country's unique destiny. A desire to endow the Mariposa Grove (until recently a Mexican territory) with a national identity can be seen in the fact that visitors named the trees after cultural heroes, including "George Washington," "General Jackson," and, with an inadvertent tip of the hat to Mark Twain, "Daniel Webster."[19] The naming of the species itself became an opportunity to demonstrate

17.   Rev. H. J. Morton, "Yosemite Valley," *The Philadelphia Photographer* 11 (1866), p. 377.
18.   See Asher B. Durand, "Letters on Landscape Painting: Letter Two," *The Crayon* 1 (1855), p. 34; J. Gray Sweeney, "The Nude of Landscape Painting: Emblematic Personification in the Art of the Hudson River School," *Smithsonian Studies in American Art* 3, no. 4 (Fall 1989), pp. 43–65.
19.   Whitney, *The Yosemite Book*, p. 103; Greeley, *Overland Journey*, p. 264. The debate over naming is recounted in N. P. Willis, "The Mammoth Trees of California," *Hutchings California Magazine* 8 (March 1857), p. 390.

Top: Asher B. Durand. Kindred Spirits.
1849. Collections of the New York Public
Library, Astor, Lenox and Tilden
Foundations. Bottom: James Otto Lewis.
Col. Daniel Boon. *1820. Courtesy the*
Saint Louis Art Museum.

nationalist pride, with British scientists immediately suggesting the name *Wellingtonia gigantea*, and Americans clamoring for *Washingtonia gigantea*. The final name decided upon was *Sequoia gigantea*, because of the similarity between the new trees and California's other redwoods, the *Sequoia sempervirens*. Clark's pose reinforces an association with American heroes. With his woodsman's garb and gun at the ready he invokes countless nineteenth-century representations of another American cultural hero: Daniel Boone.

Clark himself came to play the role of the heroic American "natural man." Until his friend John Muir began crusading for conservation at the turn of the century, Clark was the man most associated with the Yosemite region. A surveyor and guide who served on the Yosemite Commission and was the official caretaker of the Mariposa Grove, Clark had been personally involved with nearly every group of visitors to the Yosemite area. Most stayed overnight at the ranch he erected in 1857. In subsequent years, he expanded his ranch into a hotel (now called the Wawona) and with his friend Milton Mann developed trails and roads to make traveling easier. Clark used his authority to promote a reverent relationship to nature similar to the one encouraged by the narrative of the album. His books repeatedly describe the Mariposa Grove as an example of "the mighty grandeur and magnificence of the works of God."[20]

If the giants *in* the picture helped structure the viewer's response, the giant outside the picture—Watkins himself—did, too. For viewers of the album were not just looking at pictures of nature's self-evident grandeur, but at *Watkins's* views. The name was embossed on

---

20.   Quoted in Shirley Sargent, *Galen Clark, Yosemite Guardian* (San Francisco: Sierra Club, 1964), p. 129.

the cover and printed on the title page, and often even signed on the plates themselves. Although Watkins wasn't the first photographer to venture into Yosemite and the Mariposa Grove, or even the first to take photographs from many of the points of view included in the album, his is the name that is associated with a definitive understanding of the area. Watkins's photographs even set up expectations for travelers before they came. As Fitz Hugh Ludlow put it in a letter published in the *Atlantic Monthly* while en route to the region, "We were going into the vale whose giant domes and battlements had months before thrown their photographic shadow through Watkins's camera across the mysterious wide continent."[21]

The respect the image confers on these giants would have been particularly appealing for the albums' viewers, as they, too, were interested in the development of the American landscape. Some benefited from the scientific exploitation of the region, contributing to the establishment of an American geology and botany with institutional support. Others gained economically from the idealized perception of the landscape that the three giants created. As George Dimock has pointed out, the celebration of Yosemite as an exceptionally important national natural treasure, and the preservation of the area for public use, facilitated public comfort with the private development of adjacent lands for the mining and lumber companies of John Frémont, Collis Huntington, and others.[22] Finally, setting up Yosemite as America's first Western tourist destination spawned a different kind of lucrative landscape development, including the railroad, hotels, and other kinds of concessions. In her analysis of painters Albert Bierstadt and others, Nancy Anderson has argued that Western landscapes frequently negotiated the new realm of economic development by appealing to older ideas about the elevated value of nature:

> Skillfully crafted and consciously composed for the market interested in the West (often as an investment), most Western landscapes carried a conciliatory message implying that the natural and technological sublime were compatible, that the wilderness landscape Americans had used to define themselves and their nation since the seventeenth century could endure as a cultural icon while being converted to economic use.[23]

The album's viewers didn't see these projects as crass commercialism. They linked their personal view of the West with national necessities. Album owner Thomas Starr King, whose book on the White Mountains of New Hampshire helped spread American landscape tourism, first saw the Big Trees on a trip designed to rally California behind the Union cause. Speaker Colfax saw the Grove after it had been set aside as the nation's first natural area to be protected from private development. The fact that the Senate took time out from war administration to create what was to become the National Park system in 1864 is not a coincidence. Angela Miller

21.   Ludlow, "Seven Weeks in the Great Yo-Semite," p. 740.
22.   George Dimock, *Exploiting the View: Photographs of Yosemite and Mariposa by Carleton Watkins* (North Bennington, Vt.: Park-McCullough House, 1984).
23.   Anderson, "'The Kiss of Enterprise,'" p. 241.

has suggested that representations of the West made around the years of the Civil War attempted to create a harmonious image of a future, reunified America, which provided a temporary escape from the painful rifts and losses in the East.[24] Oliver Wendell Holmes's articles on photography in the *Atlantic Monthly* during the Civil War praise Watkins's "calm," "clear," and "distanced" views. Holmes was particularly intrigued by the ability of photography to transport the viewer to a different time and place: one article, printed in the same month as the South's first major victory at Manassas, invites the reader to join him on a "stereographic trip" to the American landmarks of Romantic travel: New York's Niagara Falls, the White Mountains of New Hampshire, and Virginia's Natural Bridge.[25]

For its early viewers, then, the *Section*, in its visual details and in the contexts in which it was viewed, seemed to endorse a destiny that benefited the nation and themselves. Names like the "Grizzly Giant" and the "Father" and "Mother of the Forest" invite the viewer to think of these trees as superhuman creatures who assure us of the greater plan (and paternal care) of God. Romantic viewers found the Mariposa Grove a sign that this continent was as old as other aspects of God's creation, and that the young republic had something ancient and noble with which to counter Europe's monuments of civilization. In a more presentist light, hopeful Union supporters named other trees after human "giants" such as Ulysses S. Grant and Abraham Lincoln. For viewers from this narrow group, the problems embedded in this endorsement—the contradictory idea of developing public access to a natural preserve, the tenuous proposal that romantic ideas could hold off crass tourism, the questionable belief that nature can solve cultural problems—were hard to see. But as the nation was unable to simply return to a path of progress, so Watkins's photograph ultimately fails in its attempts to perpetuate a vision of America unified through shared values. Visual culture frequently incorporates aspects of the very discourses it would most want to suppress, and hints of the instability of these values can now be found in the same image that proposes them.

Its title referring to the divisive war in a way that "base" or "trunk" never would, the *Section* seems to be as much an appeal for moral leadership as a demonstration of moral authority. The *Section* seems unable to sustain its conciliatory message about the ability to control interpretations of man's relationship to larger forces. The figure of a small human in front of a vast monument recalls Elihu Vedder's *Questioner of the Sphinx*, painted only two years before the *Section* was made in a New York City that was torn by riots. Vedder described his painting as showing "the hopelessness of man before the immutable laws of nature."[26] Clark, too, seems to be searching for solace, modeling the viewer's turn to the landscape for explanations of

24. Angela Miller, *Empire of the Eye: Landscape Representation and American Cultural Politics* (Ithaca, N.Y.: Cornell University Press, 1993), p. 205.
25. Oliver Wendell Holmes, "Doings of the Sunbeam," *Atlantic Monthly* 12 (July 1863), p. 8; Holmes, "Sun-Painting and Sun-Sculpture," *Atlantic Monthly* (July 1861), pp. 16–17.
26. Quoted in Matthew Baigell, *A Concise History of American Painting and Sculpture* (New York: Harper and Row, 1984), p. 171.

Elihu Vedder. The Questioner
of the Sphinx. *1863.*
Bequest of Mrs. Martin Brimmer.
© Museum of Fine Arts, Boston.

the chaotic human world. The pale fissures in the tree's bark even evoke this chaos, as several of the shapes resemble topsy-turvy human bodies. The end of the album thus provides as many questions about the viewer's appropriate relationship to the American land as answers.

1881

> As a result of the great injuries it has sustained from the destructive elements and lack of moisture in the ground during the past few centuries, the wood growth has been very slow, the annual ring increase being as thin as wrapping paper, too fine to be counted with the unaided eye. The inside growth of bark has been equally slow, and has not been equal to the wear and disintegration on the outside by the elements. The bark is now worn down smooth and very thin, and probably the tree does not now measure as much in circumference as it did several centuries ago.
>
> —Clark, *The Big Trees of California*

According to his 1907 book, Clark knew that the stature of the Grizzly Giant was diminishing over time due to natural forces. What he did not realize was the way in which his and Watkins's efforts to preserve the tree contributed to this process. Each facilitated the transmission of information about the Mariposa Grove to a broadening audience that was bound to see the American landscape differently. A later Watkins photograph captures this audience. It shows families relaxing on the porch of Clark's expanded hotel. The women's hoop skirts and the presence of a delicate baby carriage suggest that visitors came for a less rigorous experience of nature than their forebears. The lodge has changed, too. Its original log walls have been replaced by clapboard and the woods surrounding the building have been cleared to create a lawn enclosed by a picket fence. All of these things suggest that tourists of the Gilded Age brought with them a desire for the comforts of home. Tourism in Yosemite was becoming increasingly tied to a spreading middle-class leisure industry.

Susan Stewart has observed that the late nineteenth century witnessed a transformation of the gigantic from a mode associated with individual heroes and community values to the anonymous sphere of commercial advertising.[27] In the case of the *Grizzly Giant*, it is interesting to note the speed with which something revered as a sign of divine and human greatness was reduced to a gimmick to attract the fractured attention of the modern consumer. In particular, the consumers appealed to by advertising images of the Grizzly Giant were tourists. Watkins's photographs cannot be divorced from this transformation. As

Watkins. Mammoth Grove Hotel. ca. 1872. The Metropolitan Museum of Art, gift of Carole and Irwin Lainoff, Ruth P. Lasser and Joseph R. Lasser, Mr. and Mrs. John T. Marvin, Martin E. and Joan Messinger, Richard L. Yett and Sheri and Paul Siegel. © The Metropolitan Museum of Art.

"markers" of a tourist attraction, they participated in a system that was inherently unstable. As MacCannell has argued, within tourism, markers frequently replace, and sometimes even obliterate, the attraction itself, as when a high-rise tourist accommodation destroys the "natural" character of the setting, which attracted the tourists who stayed there.[28]

As I will show, these changes can be seen in a print made from Watkins's negative of the *Section of the Grizzly Giant* sometime after 1875. It suggests the loss

27.   Stewart, *On Longing*, p. 85.
28.   On "markers," see MacCannell, *The Tourist*, pp. 109–17.

of the authority of the Grizzly Giant as a site demanding reverence *and* of Clark and Watkins as interpreters of that experience. While Watkins, Clark, and the Grizzly Giant seem like three giants whose fates are inextricably linked together, the men's names do not actually appear anywhere in later prints made from the negative. This omission coincides with a decline in status for both men. Watkins lost the rights to his early negatives to his competitors John Jay Cook and Isaiah West Taber during the financial crises of 1875 and 1876. By the 1880s, Taber was distributing Watkins's Yosemite photographs under his own name within an ever-increasing tourist market. Travelers who were not interested in or who could not afford an entire album of Watkins's views could purchase an unmounted mammoth print for five dollars—less than an expensive chromolithograph.[29] Rolled up, such an image could easily be carried home and stored with other souvenirs. As a souvenir, it was incorporated into the travelers' own narratives of the trip rather than being integrated into the controlled narrative of Watkins's album.

The challenge of the Taber print of the *Section* is to retain a sense of this giant tree in an image that seems to disappear into the gigantic inventory of tourist photographs of the American landscape. Clark's pose echoes countless tourists posed in front of a landmark. The very title printed on the bottom of the image, with its seemingly random number, implies the existence of countless other photographs in this inventory alone. Without a familiarity with the prints' author or subjects, does the photograph demand the viewer's attention at all?

29.   Prang's print of Albert Bierstadt's *Sunset: California Scenery* was listed in the 1869 catalog for ten dollars. Ron Tyler, *Prints of the West* (Golden, Co.: Fulcrum Publishing, 1994), p. 139.

Watkins. Section of the Grizzly Giant. *ca. 1866,*
published by Isaiah West Taber after 1875.
Metropolitan Museum of Art, the Elisha Whittelsy
Collection, the Elisha Whittelsy Fund, 1972.
© The Metropolitan Museum of Art.

This transfer of authority over the interpretation of the photograph from a socially-connected photographic master to an anonymous consumer can be seen in an important element of this print: the band across the bottom edge that bears the title. Introducing a different kind of representational system into the supposedly indexical transcription of nature, this crisp line of type interrupts the viewer's involvement with the scene depicted. The gray strip behind the words defies the illusion of space created by the image. The viewer is transported not into the scene, but into an imaginary space where the tree is not a physical object but merely a spectacle.

Such an observation recalls the fact that the Mariposa Grove was designated a protected area explicitly to save it from such a fate. By 1864, the Calaveras Grove had already been developed into a crass commercial wonderland where visitors could dance on a tree stump, ride horses through another fallen giant, and climb the scaffolding that entrepreneurs had erected in order to flay the bark of the "Mother of the Forest" for display in the East. But while the Grizzly Giant was protected from such vulgar treatment, it was subjected to photography, which is, in its own way, a method of "skinning."

Later viewers of the *Section* were likely to respond to Galen Clark differently, too. Without the recognition by a viewer who had personally toured the Grove with Clark, the stalwart guide's tiny scale and sideways glance make him almost insignificant. He is so overwhelmed by the tree that he looks freakish, Lilliputian. As in photographs of post-Civil War freak show "professional giants" posed with dwarves, the man's diminuition and the tree's overgrown appearance suggest scale signifies nothing outside its own entertainment value.[30]

Clark's archaic miner's garb makes him a sign of local color, like the picturesque "mule-men" and Indians described in Yosemite guidebooks. This loss of identity was, in many ways, literal for Clark, who suffered a decline in reputation and power in 1880. Losing a political struggle in that year to those who wanted the Park to accommodate more visitors, Clark was removed from the Yosemite Commission and reduced to making a living by offering buggy tours to the growing number of tourists speeding through the region. In posing for such pictures, he encouraged the commodification of Yosemite even as he worked to slow the process.

The imposition of an increasingly market-driven authority over the park is echoed in the Taber print of the *Section*. Although Taber prints are generally of no lower quality than those published by Watkins's studio, late prints of the *Section* suffer because of what seems to be damage to the negative. In this scene, for example, there is an out-of-focus oval "bruise" on the tree trunk above Clark's head, and the dark flecks and glitches that litter the background of the print have gone unspotted. Fingerprints in the upper left corner of the image further signal the printer's carelessness. These dark, greasy-looking marks recast photographic printing as an industrial production. These breaks in the illusionism of the photograph add

---

30.   On "professional giants," see Robert Bogdan, *Freak Show: Presenting Human Oddities for Amusement and Profit* (Chicago: University of Chicago Press, 1988), p. 113.

another screen between the viewer and the scene represented. Calling attention to the surface of the print, they remind the viewer that photographs are objects, even commodities. The materiality of the print reinforces this impression. Printed on paper made from wood pulp, a technology introduced to the United States in 1866, the photograph evokes the sacrifice of California's forests to the lumber industry. Wood pulp paper was much cheaper and easier to produce than the rag paper that preceded it, but it was also less durable. The edges of the photograph show it to be razor thin, absurdly fragile for the support of so substantial a subject, and rather like wrapping paper, the disposable industrial product to which Clark compares the mighty tree's waning rings.

In the development of Yosemite, the symbolic authority of the California landscape as a sign of America's destiny was also shown to be vulnerable. Travelers working through prefabricated itineraries often found themselves unable to re-create the appropriate response to the wonders of nature, as one of the Mariposa Grove's visitors described:

> Alas! There was the first big tree, sunlight sparkling all over its great cinnamon-colored trunk, and I was ready to shout, and, spurring my prosaic beast, to rush with the rest in a graceless scramble to be first to reach his majesty's foot. The charm was broken. I was willing, anxious to be deeply moved, but no answering emotion came—such moods do not come at the bidding. . . . I had built an ideal grove, and at first sight it was demolished.[31]

31.   "The Yosemite," in William Cullen Bryant, ed., *Picturesque America; or, The Land We Live In* (New York: D. Appleton and Company, 1874), p. 471.

Watkins. Sections of the Grizzly Giant. *Enlarged details. ca. 1866. Courtesy Metropolitan Museum of Art.*

The best visual comparison to bring out the disenchanted meanings of the later print of the *Section* might be a popular illustration of P. T. Barnum's star performer Jumbo the Elephant (with his trainer, Matthew Scott) made about the same time. Posters the size of Watkins's prints began to appear on the walls of buildings in cities in the 1870s and 1880s, marking the triumph of commercialism over the landscape.[32] Incorporated into the anonymous tourist experience of a commodified Yosemite, Watkins's once-sublime Giant has lost its punch. Posed against his own charge's trunk, Clark has also become ineffectual. Very early in his career, Clark had prevented local shopkeepers from putting up advertisements on the mammoth trees. The commissioners passed a law prohibiting signs in the Yosemite land grant, but such precautions did not keep the trees' meaning frozen in time. The significance of the Grizzly Giant, like the stature of Clark the wilderness guide and the fame of Watkins the photographer, competes with new kinds of greatness produced in a commodity economy where the heroic stature of an elephant surpasses that of a president.[33]

These days, prints from Watkins's negative are more likely to be found framed on museum walls than in studies or parlors. Album leaves have become separated from one another, and Taber prints have been mounted and interfiled with earlier prints. In this context, the story they seem to tell is one about art. The art-world context has preserved Watkins's gigantic stature even as the passage of time has further erased Clark's and the Grizzly Giant's. While critics have worked hard to recuperate the histories in which nineteenth-century photography played a role by turning away from the form of the images, sometimes the photographs themselves can tell that story in the strongest way.

32.   Taber prints found in museum collections often show wrinkles and rumples similar to those seen in posters, due to poor-quality mounting, frequently by the original owners.
33.   Sargent, *Galen Clark*, p. 76.

Jumbo on his Travels. *ca. 1880. Courtesy Historical Collections, Bridgeport Public Library, from the Elizabeth Seeley Collection.*

Hollis Frampton is widely viewed as one of the most brilliant and important American avant-garde filmmakers to have emerged in the late 1960s. Yet since the publication of an *October* special issue (no. 32, Spring 1985) following his untimely death twenty years ago, his work has received little sustained scholarly attention—this in spite of the enormously rich, complex body of films and writings he left behind, much of which remains unknown or unexplored. *October* is publishing the following cluster of essays, each of which examines hitherto neglected aspects of Frampton's theory and practice, in the hope that his work will once again receive the attention it deserves.* In "Words into Film," Federico Windhausen unearths the considerable influence of Hugh Kenner's version of Romanticism and modernism on Frampton; Melissa Ragona's "Hidden Noise" explores the role of mathematics in shaping Frampton's use of sound in his films; and in his essay, Michael Zryd begins the difficult task of charting Frampton's shifting conceptualizations of his massive, unfinished film project *Magellan.*

October is grateful to Marion Faller and the Whitney Museum of American Art for giving us permission to publish for the first time a lecture Frampton gave at the Whitney in 1979, and to Michael Zryd for editing and annotating this lecture.

—Malcolm Turvey

* Others are also trying to rectify this situation. Keith Sanborn, P. Adams Sitney, and Su Friedrich are hosting a conference on Frampton at Princeton University starting November 5, 2004. For more information, see the advertisement at the back of this issue.

The Invention Without a Future*

HOLLIS FRAMPTON

Hollis Frampton delivered the following lecture on November 17, 1979, at the Whitney Museum of American Art in New York as part of a seven-part lecture and screening series, "Researches and Investigations into Film: Its Origins and the Avant-Garde," organized by John Hanhardt, Curator of Film and Video at the Whitney (the other speakers were Thom Anderson, Nick Browne, Noël Burch, Regina Cornwell, Tom Gunning, Ken Jacobs, and Maureen Turim). The talk exists only as a typed transcript from a cassette tape, now lost. Slight changes have been made in order to clarify the grammar and syntax of the transcription. Punctuation has been modified to preserve Frampton's distinct speech rhythms, and Frampton's asides, digressions, and informal framing remarks have been preserved better to convey the wit, as well as the substance, of his lecture.

—Ed.

My tentative working title was "The Invention Without a Future." As the date has drawn nearer the true title has grown longer and now probably should be "A Partial Disassembling of an Invention Without a Future: Helter-Skelter and Random Notes in Which the Pulleys and Cogwheels Are Lying Around at Random All Over the Workbench." It seems difficult to make this entity congeal into one or a dozen exact representations or exact theses. The more I look at it, in particular the more I look at that diaeresis in the entropy of the arts during the last couple of centuries that we call the early cinema, the more it looks like a kind of goosebaggy monster. So this is all entirely a tentative projection in which I will begin by reciting an epigraph. This epigraph is a quotation that could, it seems, have been written at almost any moment from the beginning of the industrial revolution, or at least its very early years, to within, let's say, not the past week but the beginning of the past decade:

> Our fine arts were developed, their types and uses were established, in times very different from the present, by men whose power of action upon things was insignificant in comparison with ours. But the amazing growth of [our] techniques, the adaptability and precision they have

* Edited and annotated by Michael Zryd.

* Edited and annotated by Michael Zryd.

attained, the ideas and habits they are creating, make it a certainty that profound changes are impending in the ancient craft of the Beautiful.

Well, to use that phrase in the present time I think we would have to strain certain conventions of terminology. "Beautiful" is even capitalized. Nevertheless, one still hears the word used.

> In all the arts there is a physical component which can no longer be considered or treated as it used to be, which cannot remain unaffected by our modern knowledge and power. For the last twenty years neither matter nor space nor time has been what it was from time immemorial. We must expect great innovations to transform the entire technique of the arts, thereby affecting artistic invention itself and perhaps even bringing about an amazing change in our very notion of art.

And from a little farther on in the same essay:

> Just as water, gas, and electricity are brought into our houses from far off to satisfy our needs in response to a minimal effort, so we shall be supplied with visual or auditory images, which will appear and disappear at a simple movement of the hand, hardly more than a sign.

That quotation is of course from Paul Valéry. It is most widely associated with another text for which it serves as the epigraph, and that is a 1932 essay by Walter Benjamin called "The Work of Art in the Age of Mechanical Reproduction."[1] Now I don't think this is the moment to attempt to unpack, repack, explicate, reaffirm, or criticize Benjamin. It is striking though that we still seem to be haunted, almost plagued, by the same concerns, and I mean not only what I might call the anthropological concerns of that essay but as well the political concerns of that essay, which I think we might simply say has aged relatively well in that it continues to irritate us thirty-five or forty years later.

Water and gas and electricity are, it would seem, distinctly allied in Valéry's mind as needs (rather than desires, let's say, or some form of entertainment)—with a need, personal and social, for images, auditory and visual images. That need is one that has been fostered, has assumed its present state of power, by the very inventions that we may imagine Valéry was talking about. It's also striking that Valéry situates the new technologies of which he speaks (and it hardly matters what those technologies are) not only within an arena of desire, but specifically within one of power, one in which he sees power wielded, formed, organized, as it were—and I would simply

---

1.   Quoted in Paul Valéry, "The Conquest of Ubiquity," *Aesthetics*, trans. Ralph Manheim (New York: Pantheon Books, 1964), p. 235. The first two quotations appear as the epigraph to Walter Benjamin's "The Work of Art in the Age of Mechanical Reproduction," published in *Illuminations*, ed. and with an introduction by Hannah Arendt, trans. Harry Zohn (New York: Schocken Books, 1969), p. 217. (The last quotation from Valéry appears on p. 219 of the Benjamin text and p. 226 of the Valéry text.) Benjamin's text was first published in 1936, not 1932.

point out that it is a relatively novel insight. It is still true in this culture that, aside from those poor powers which are wielded in the realm of the purely physical, the supreme arena of power is language, the dominant code of culture, as they are fond of telling us. And I find it quite striking that Valéry at this moment discerns a corresponding arena of power, an extension of the old arena of power of language, a new domain for the wielding of power, if that power only be that of persuasion, within what he refers to as visual and auditory images, one which is furthermore created by the very existence of a reproductive technology, a mechanical technology very much of the scope and somewhat of the kind that had at a much earlier moment made his own craft, that of a public and disseminated literature and criticism, possible.

The essay to which this is an epigraph (well, I guess it still is its epigraph) is one from which I would like to conserve only a single line for the moment. This is Benjamin: "For the first time in world history, mechanical reproduction emancipates the work of art from its parasitical dependence on ritual."[2] The argument with which he prepares and supports that is, I think, quite familiar, and it has been subject to a certain amount of challenge within the past few decades. It is, roughly, that the ancient and traditional arts, or at least the visual arts, began as a kind of sympathetic magic; one painted the elk on the wall of the cave surrounded by little men with bows and arrows in the hope of catching more elk the next day (or what have you). That, I think, now is probably seen as a questionable assertion, but in the 1930s perhaps it was not. And as the thing to be caught, the goal of the sympathetic magic, becomes more intangible, if the game afoot is the trapping not of an elk but of the good will of the Almighty, then the ritual which art serves is translated, becomes somewhat more abstract, becomes, so to speak, the ritual of systemic religious belief and practice.

There are, however, other rituals. The supreme ritual of our time is not probably either that of bagging live meat on the hoof or appeasing the alleged mysterious forces of the universe. It is the ritual of possession, the creation of possessible things, the conservation of the possessible, the ritual process by which the things of the world and then their reproductions or representations are validated so that they can become ownable, so that they can become possessible. I would point out in passing that we are engaged here today in a fairly complex variation on exactly that ritual in an edifice [the Whitney Museum] that houses all manner of validated, possessible works of *art*, I believe they are called.

Benjamin, in his essay, says that the new image-making and reproducing technologies challenge, at the root, the notion of authenticity, or the unique aura of the possessible thing, and thereby tend to subvert, to undermine the vintage, ownable thing. The new work of art, the work made through the agency of the machine, because of at least its alleged infinite reproducibility, escapes, or at least has the possibility of escaping, the problem, or the characteristic uniqueness, by which something that is in potentially finite supply—that is to say, the work of art

---

2.   Benjamin, "The Work of Art," p. 224.

(we can go on making it in one form or another to our heart's content)—is moved laterally in its characteristics to resemble something that is in strictly infinite supply, that is, real estate. The real estate industry, I believe, has never succeeded in manufacturing any more of its commodity. It has only manipulated the manner in which that commodity is valued. So that it is a collateral assertion, or at least suggestion, of Benjamin's that because reproducibility rescues the work of art from the predicament of real estate, it democratizes it. If it is impossible to own the *Mona Lisa* (in fact, it is inadvisable to, since presumably the responsibility is much too large, whether you like the thing or not), nevertheless it is possible to have for free, if you are willing to dispense with its unique aura (*he* uses the word "aura"), with the specific fact of that specific mass of pigment on that particular panel guided by the fine Italian hand of that particular aura-ridden artist—if you are able to dispense with that, if you can give it up, then you can have something like the *Mona Lisa*. You can have it, so to speak, for nothing, or next to nothing. Its cost is low. You don't have to have a palace to house it in; then you don't have to heat the palace; then you don't have to hire armed guards to defend it. And we can ask ourselves whether it's worth it or not to dispense with that aura in the interest of the likeness. I think it is probably in the general vicinity of the arguments with which Benjamin surrounds the notion that the reproducible tends to democratize the work of art that he is most vulnerable. He is, of course, eager in that circumstance, and it is an eagerness that we reaffirm, to produce some tentative proof, if not a fully rigorous one, that *something* has democratized the work of art, that it is not now in that time, and had not been for quite some time, that thing which it had been before.

In fact, something had happened by 1932, indeed had begun to happen a hundred years before, which was not, I think, in the least special. The arts had begun what might be understood from a look at the rest of the culture a process of normalization. By normalization I mean a very, very simple thing. By a particular moment in the seventeenth century, let us say, it was no longer necessary to pump the water out of coal mines and tin mines in England by animal power or by bailing or by complicated processes of drainage and siphoning and so forth. The walking-beam engine had taken over that process. By a very short time later, three or four decades, a large proportion of Western manufacture of all kinds had been, as we say, industrialized, or it had at least been mechanized. The process was a slow and very helter-skelter one. Transportation, for instance, our current plague, only became mechanized very late. In fact, I think we could say that the arts were among the very first generalized activities to undertake that process of normalization, as I will call it, and it is thus the more striking, and in an intelligently managed universe, the more puzzling, that that process of normalization within the arts has been the last—it is now, I think, almost the only—process in which mechanized normalization is still seen as problematical. It was true by 1932, as Gertrude Stein put it, that we have all forgotten what horses are. We seem, however, not to have forgotten to this day what pre-normalized art is like. We even seem to hear still the niggling objection to it.

I was at a conference a week ago in Rochester, which was a different sort of ritual, one in which Xerography, and in particular the color Xerox image, began its process of validation, of valuation, in a museum given over to photography—to, if nothing else, very large holdings of objects, possibly works of art, which definitely have intrinsic value because they're silver prints; if nothing else, you can reclaim the metal. (We'll get to that later on, literally, as well as in my remarks.) Xeroxes are a kind of thing that anyone can make by walking up to a machine and dropping in fifty cents. Not only are Xeroxes made out of paper and a little bit of hydrocarbon but worse, nothing much more than pigmented paraffin, and bad paper at that, at least as far as the standard Xerox goes.

I was experiencing a little trouble, a little pain, in being forcibly jerked up the slopes of Helicon, as if with a winch. In fact, it didn't work. There was constant objection on the part of the Xerox artists themselves. We now have, it seems, a unique class or tribe of artists for every single medium and sub-medium. They found themselves feeling extremely uncomfortable in those circumstances, and finally there came a moment of hysterical crisis, as one might say, an interlude, in which one of the chief exponents of the practice stood up in the audience in the midst of a panel and delivered herself of a twenty-minute encomium to the effect that, as a Xerox artist, she wished to say that Xerox copies, Xerox images, definitely were not works of art, and she hoped that, after the grant from the Xerox Corporation which had created the exhibition and the symposium to begin with had run out, the whole matter would be dropped as quickly as possible because she was not, and she felt no one else was, prepared for the onslaught of yet another art within living memory.

We seem, of course, to have had quite a few of them, but the one that concerns us here—and presumably there are still a few Civil War veterans around who can remember its very beginnings—is that of film. And I think perhaps there a few things after all to be said about film (in fact, I know there are, if I can find out what they are on these pieces of paper here) that are not as they seem, or they are not at least as we are accustomed to think of them. I suppose we could group our discussion under a rubric of contrasts—old and new, *staroe i novoe*[3]—and try to examine the predicament *then*, that is, in that opalescent time before D. W. Griffith had cast the shadow of his mighty bulk upon film, the proto-cinema—and *now*, an extended period, which has seen the growth of that moment that we have called the New American Cinema or the avant-garde (an art paramilitary organization). We are accustomed to think that now we are in possession, in the practice of film, of a high technology. In fact, that is not true. In the 1890s, at a time when every project amounted to a fresh creation under a new logos, everyone who made films did so not only under the re-normalization of a genuinely new technology but one of which they were entirely possessed. That is to say, if you had a camera (or if, like Billy Bitzer, you had a camera that actually made perforations in

3.   The reference is to Sergei Eisenstein's *The Old and the New*, aka *The General Line* (1929, Sovkino, USSR). Ed.

the film at the same time it was making images on it, spitting the one thing out a little chute at the bottom and winding the other up in a roll at the top),[4] and a tripod to put it on more or less, and some way to develop the stuff, you were at that time living at the cutting edge of a new technology, and you were in complete possession of it. That now is simply not so.

Film is probably a high technology. It is, of course, a deeply hybridized, bastard technology as well, as rickety a collection of electromechanical devices as a Model T Ford, of which anyone who engages in film practice has available at any given moment only a very constricted segment. Obviously I'm talking about those practitioners we call filmmakers; I'm not talking here about those practitioners we call Francis Ford Coppola, who presumably believe themselves to be in full possession of the high (and stagnant) technology of film. But in fact, within filmmaker practice, there has been not only a constriction of the available, there has also been a factionalization within that constriction, so that one hears denounced in certain quarters, for instance, all those persons who engage in the impunity of the optical printer. Let us return to old times and simple means, the argument seems to go, and that will be progress. In fact, the early cinema insisted absolutely, as it properly should have, upon the entire possession of its tools, of its materials, if you will, of its means of production. So that within films even at the present time, I think we can see atavistic remnants of the reaction against mechanization, normalization, from which photographers, filmmakers, certain others whom we will not mention—it begins with a "v," or it begins with a "c," and that's a little more rarefied but the juncture's still there[5]—an internal crystallization of a reaction that has so often been brought to bear upon those new image-making arts of which Valéry speaks from without. Again, I don't think this is the moment to unpack the psychological implications of that. Perhaps it is just the hollow and unctuous tones of the cultural superego speaking out of an unexpected mouth, let us say.

Another notion that I think should be challenged has to do with the cost of the work of art. First of all, in general, it's alleged that film is expensive. That probably is open to debate. As far as I know the most expensive art currently practiced in the West in total cost is symphonic music, because you're supposed to hire a hundred and twenty people for six weeks, and put them in a big building, and heat the building, and so forth. It is only for the composer that it's cheap. In an economic environment that tends to demand that nothing can be printed unless you print a hundred thousand copies of it; whole forests fell for Saul Bellow to become a Nobel laureate, for example; vast tracks in Idaho were the raft that floated Mr. Bellow to Sweden on that occasion. Then, the notion of the cost of the work of art was defined to a certain degree—it still may be on a certain

4.   Billy Bitzer (1872–1944) is best remembered today as D. W. Griffith's cameraman. Ken Jacobs's *Tom, Tom, the Piper's Son* (1969), which was one of the first avant-garde films to take up early film, reworks an early film Jacobs claims was made by Bitzer in 1905.
5.   Frampton is referring to video and computers, media viewed with suspicion by many American avant-garde filmmakers in the 1970s and 1980s.

horizon—because it was initially a technology that was a by-product. I would remind you first of all that the old film support, cellulose nitrate, was military fall-out just as surely as microelectronics are today. It was gun cotton, very simply. A large manufacturing technology existed to produce the stuff in quantity. The flexibility and transparency of the stuff were what was at issue in this case, not its explosiveness, but that has continued to be a problem. Nitrate, as we know, still undergoes slow motion explosion, and nineteenth-century military technology is (after all) working its revenge upon the early cinema silently in millions of dark tin cans all over the West.

The emulsifying or suspending agent is gelatin. The Eastman Kodak Company still insists that the very best photographic gelatin is made from selected ear and cheek clippings of Argentinean beef cattle that are fed on mustard greens. How's that for magic? Take one cow—steer, I beg your pardon (that's quite important, too, probably, in some total reckoning of the thing)—five pounds of mustard greens. . . . There's a recipe book for the imagery of a high art. But that gelatin could only become available in quantity after a specific economic moment had been reached in the West. That was the development of vast latifundia for the raising of beef cattle in the Western United States and in the Argentine. The gelatin was, again, a fallout from a process of exploitation of an entirely different kind. And finally there was that brief moment during which the photographic industries fastened upon silver-halide technology as the material basis of the image, which proceeded also from an unusual circumstance and that was the great silver strikes of the 1870s and '80s in Colorado and in Idaho, which released vast quantities of that element into the market within the period of a decade. The total quantity of silver in the world increased by something like three decimal orders of magnitude. Nevertheless, it had always been rare. It was made available again, briefly and in quantity, through a process of real-estate exploitation. So that it would appear, in a way, and there's nothing unusual in this for our arts (if the Romans had not practiced slavery in Spain, the sulfide of mercury called cinnabar would never have been found in quantity in the Mediterranean, and thus certain reds that we treasure in the paintings of the Renaissance would not be around to this day), it is simply and normally that the usual bad commercial karma was settled from the beginning on film just as it had been upon everything else.

Now, however, we have crossed into a temporal domain where the cost is not deferred, and probably we should give momentary attention at least to what a film costs now, or to what something that is called a film, costs now. The sociable presentation of film, which is itself a ritual of the right of free assembly, produces some rather odd side effects. I calculated, in the small town that I live a few miles from upstate, that one single screening of *Apocalypse Now* [1979, Francis Ford Coppola] produced, among other apocalyptic figures, the use of approximately 390 gallons of gasoline to take an audience of 250 people to see it—this is one screening— about seven thousand road miles of travel for those people. If you translate that into the number of times that film will be screened before Francis Ford Coppola gets his money back (it's a process of infinite convergence, of course) and do the bookkeeping on it, you will cease to wonder why the petroleum industry or indeed the manufacturers of automobiles in Detroit seem to approve of the movies and indeed perhaps understand something of the not-very-secret affinities between those manufacturing processes. There are also, of course, movies that teach you how to drive automobiles, you understand, so there's some reciprocation there.... The real competition is from the electronics industry, not from coinage, which was once its only competition, and that is an industry that, if it builds it into the right circuits, can convert two milligrams of silver into a potentially endless series of images. That same two milligrams ends up being about one frame of 35mm camera negative, which is tied up, is, as it were, quarantined forever, or as long as we are quite sure that we wish to hold onto that image. In order to get the material back, we must release the image itself from the culture, we must cast it out.

So what has happened is that what was once seen as a copious popular art is very rapidly becoming paradoxically fragile, rare and bounded in time. The figures that are usually given (and they are not mine, I heard this two weeks ago from Beaumont Newhall who is, at the very least, venerable enough to quote) that the silver print (he was talking about still photography but this means our film process as well) will be all washed up in thirty years, that is to say, within the lifetime of most of the people in this room. So that it probably behooves us—yes, I know, Bucky Fuller: we will make movies out or cornstarch or something like that—it is incorrect, it is inaccurate for us to speak of copiousness, of ready availability of a common product. Ironically, the very fact that film and the photograph escape certain conditions of ritual, the fact of their reproducibility, has virtually assured their disappearance. The more copies of it we can make, the more we are assured we don't have to make any because we can always make them, and eventually, of course, none will have been made, and it will disappear. So it seems that, like the exercises of speech and sexuality, film and its allied arts of illusion are at once limit-lessly plentiful and painfully fugitive.

Unless, of course, we wish to massively intervene, and the cost of that massive intervention is itself something that we had probably better examine pretty care-fully. The industry—that is, that of the Detroit of the image, certain hills around the Los Angeles basin—has managed their share of the problem very nicely, that is to say it has arranged to have its product retrieved, archived, reproduced, cared for at the public expense. But the early cinema that we are talking about, and our present one, are, in that regard, totally vulnerable. It tends to be true of most of the proto-cinema that one print, or two, or half a dozen exist. It tends to be true also now that that an infinitely reproducible artifact exists in one copy or fewer than a dozen. There may be a hundred *Window Water Baby Moving*s [1959, Stan Brakhage] strewn around the planet in various states of disrepair, but that itself is a completely anomalous situation, which will tend to mean, in about the year 2050, for instance, if we're still interested in such things, that *Window Water Baby*

Moving will appear to constitute virtually, in its entirely, thirty-five years of cine-matic arts. Thus, we will seem to have been ground slowly but exceedingly fine.

At the very onset, then, of this tremulous, momentary phenomenon, one of its real inventors—no, I certainly don't mean Edison—said that the cinématograph was an invention without a future. And that remark continues to puzzle me. It puzzled me for a very long time, but after a while I began to construct a tentative reading of it. What did Lumière mean when he said that the cinématograph, and of course he was referring to his machine, had no future? I think there are two possible readings, or I can imagine two at least, of that remark that are neither complementary nor convergent but are coeval, and I will present them in a brief sketch.

There's a story, and I might as well quote it since I always do, a story of Borges—yes, he's going to quote Borges again—in which he speaks of a series of circumstances that surround a project that was never completed, and that project was the pleasure dome or pleasure garden or system of palaces or what have you of Kublai Khan.[6] I think most of us know the circumstances surrounding Coleridge's attempt to say something about that project. He had received, very much in the terms of the times, the entirety of the poem, all its assonances and alliterations, during an opium dream from which he awoke, and, like a good servant of the Muse, he began to transcribe the instructions. This is rhetoric familiar enough, I think, from our own time. And a knock at the door interrupted him. A person from the neighboring village of Porlock, whom he did not know, barged into the house, took up his afternoon, and then vanished back into that Porlock from which that person had proceeded. And when the stranger was gone, Coleridge found that his poem had evacuated along with him. Borges then goes on to point out that not only was the poem never completed, not only was the pretext never built, but the original architect of Kublai Khan's system of palaces received his instructions, his blueprints so to speak, also in a dream, a dream that he, the architect, was never quite able to remember in its entirety either. And Borges closes his brief pseudo-essay with the remark that we may have here a series of events in which a new idea was struggling to come into the world, not necessarily the specific palace perhaps, something glimpsed thus far only in outline. There is, of course, an implied prediction in that, presumably some centuries hence, when we have perhaps changed the forms of our ratiocinations and reserve our dreams for less technical matters, someone may find himself or herself confronted with Kublai Khan's system of palaces, whatever it is, in broad daylight, so to speak, and at that point the idea, heaven help us, will have found its way into the world.

I might conjecture in parallel with that, and this is entirely conjecture, but one whose eventuation will be drastically forced in the near future in any case, that the photograph and then film and now, heaven help us, that thing that begins with "v," may eventually be seen not as a series of separate but somehow

6.   Jorge Luis Borges, "The Dream of Coleridge," *Selected Nonfictons*, ed. Eliot Weinberger (New York: Viking, 1999). Ed.

mysteriously related—what to call them?—in the technical sense perhaps "excre-
ments" would be reasonable—more indeed as parts of something, as tentative
attempts, at once complete and approximate, to construct something that will
amount to an arena for thought, and presumably, as well, an arena of power,
commensurate with that of language.

My other conjecture makes Lumière perhaps a more philosophical figure
than he was. One finds out, I guess, who the philosophers were by a process of
historical Monday-morning quarterbacking. Philosophy is not of the present.
After all, a decade ago, Andy Warhol was a philosopher for five minutes. But in
Lumière's case, he was touched for a moment with an insight, newly implied if
not original, about history. From a certain point of view it was impossible at the
beginning, as Lumière said "let there be light," for the cinematograph to have a
future because it did not have a past. Now the future is, after all, something that
we manufacture. We can be willful about it and perverse, if we wish, but nevertheless even our willfulness, even our perversity is ordinarily understood to be
subsumed by a temporal machine containing and originated and guided by
human beings called historical process. Until such time as there is a past of some
sort, a history, furthermore, of some sort, that is, a past which has been examined,
has been subjected to a critical, a theoretical analysis, there can be no future
because there is no apparatus for prediction and for extrapolation. I do not
mean, of course, that history in any exact sense is something that is guaranteed
by the possession of a past. Only its possibility is guaranteed. But the first work of
the proto-cinema, in that light, was to begin to provide films with a past. Well,
heaven knows, it has done so. In fact, it has quite a few pasts. There is now the
gradual and sketchy discernment of something that we might call a history. There
is also that quite regular past that everything has, which is a big pile of rubbish.
There was a long period in between during which film as a general practice even
has finally managed to acquire its share of guilt by having worked both sides of every
street it could find.

So that it is only now, I think, that it begins to be possible to imagine a future,
to construct, to predict a future for film, or for what we may generically agree to
call film and its successors, because it is only now that we can begin to construct a
history and, within that history, a finite and ordered set of monuments, if we wish
to use T. S. Eliot's terms, that is to constitute a tradition. After a century, nevertheless,
it is still true that no one knows even how to begin to write the sort of thing that
film through its affiliation with the sciences might expect of itself, that is a *Principia
Cinematica*, presumably in three fat volumes entitled, in order: I. Preliminary
Definitions; II. Principles of Sequence; III. Principles of Simultaneity. The wish for
such a thing is somewhat like the wish of a certain aphorist who said—I believe the
last of his aphorisms, or at least the last that I have read—that he would like to
know the name of the last book that will ever be published.

So that finally, there is one last thing we should stop doing. We should stop
calling ourselves new. We are not. They were new. We are old, and we have not

necessarily aged as well as we should. To cite Eliot again: he reports himself as answering someone who objected to, I suppose, Shakespeare, Dante, and Homer on the grounds that we know more than they did by replying, "yes, we do, and they are precisely what we know." We also know more than that very early cinema did. Unfortunately, they are not precisely what we know. We are only beginning to penetrate the phantom, the fiction of the copious and the readily available, to poke around in dusty attics, into the sort of mausoleums guaranteed by a rapacious copyright system, for example, and to retrieve heaven knows what—probably not Shakespeare, Dante, and Homer—it would be nice to know who the Homer of films will ultimately be perceived as, by the way, let alone the Dante—but at least something of the context in which those texts, if they ultimately are exhumed, will be perceived.

To that end, then, I have brought along thirty minutes or so of such rubbish, which presumably contains embedded in it a Stradivarius or a scarab or something priceless. This is simply a roll, upon which I won't comment at all, from the Paper Print Collection at the Library of Congress. I wouldn't be surprised if other such things have been exhumed at this party earlier in the week. My principle of selection is so embarrassing that I don't propose to tell you anything about it at all, but it demonstrates something of that past which, like all pasts, is self-proclaiming, repetitive, redundant, naughty, sometimes astonishing, and, in this case, on the principle that nothing much was made of it at the time, essentially impenetrable to us. It is by that mechanism that this body of material, whatever it is, then imposes upon us the responsibility of inventing it.

FOUNDATION FOR ART IN CINEMA

CINEMANEWS

NOVEMBER/DECEMBER · 1977

VOL. 77-6 $.50

Consider An Avant-Garde
Filmmaker For Your
Lecture Series

an avant-garde filmmaker

Peter Feinstein Associates   36 Shepard Street, Cambridge, MA 02138   617/547-0359

Please help us. We want to know who is interested in avant-garde film. If you complete this form, whether or not you
intend to arrange for a lecture, it would be greatly appreciated.

Name _____   Telephone _____

Title _____

Organization _____

Address _____

City _____ State _____ Zip _____

☐ I wish to book Hollis Frampton.   Dates: 1st Choice _____ 2nd Choice _____ 3rd Choice _____

☐ I am interested in booking Hollis Frampton at a future date: ☐ 6 months ☐ 1 year.

☐ Please send additional information about ☐ Hollis Frampton ☐ Other filmmakers. Names _____

☐ We are interested in film as an art form. Please keep us informed.

☐ We have no interest in avant-garde film. Please take us off your mailing list.

Additional comments: _____

Cover of Cinemanews, *volume 77–6,*
November/December 1977.

Words into Film: Toward a Genealogical Understanding of Hollis Frampton's Theory and Practice*

FEDERICO WINDHAUSEN

> *This whole business of words—the whole sense of tense and complicated problems about knowledge, about making things in relation to all the things that were already made with words—seems to have fallen into film.*
>
> —Hollis Frampton, 1971

That the American filmmaker Hollis Frampton raised objections to critic P. Adams Sitney's term "Structural film," on the grounds that Sitney was giving new life to "that incorrigible tendency to label, to make movements," is notable, but hardly surprising.[1] During a 1976 talk, published the following year in *Cinemanews*, Frampton voices a familiar complaint about modern critical commentary, decrying the manner in which its classifying names and terms tend to "render the work invisible." Presumably, Sitney's grouping was no more popular among the independent filmmakers emerging in the 1960s than Minimalism had been with the painters and sculptors of the same era. But in Frampton's witty discursus (which carries off a transition, on its way to Sitney, from the failure of Cubism and French Structuralism as descriptive labels to the snobbishness of the New York painting scene of 1969), the objection to critical generalizations eventually leads to a more telling point about another topic, the relationship between the postwar American avant-garde cinema and English-language poetry. Addressing himself to fellow filmmaker James Broughton, Frampton claims that in Sitney's book *Visionary Film*, the interpretative framework is

> derived largely from an undergraduate seminar in romantic poetry with Harold Bloom at Yale. That makes something of a Procrustean bed. Brakhage gets to be Wordsworth, by an extraordinary piece of

* First and foremost, I thank Annette Michelson for her counsel. Thanks also to Malcolm Turvey for helpful suggestions, to Edoardo Moretti for an early reading, and to Michael Zryd, Anthology Film Archives, and the Museum of Modern Art Archives for invaluable research assistance.
1. All quotations in this paragraph are from "Hollis Frampton in San Francisco," *Cinemanews* 77–6 (1977), pp. 8-9.

prestidigitation. And Stan professes at least not to be totally uncomfort-able with that; I mean, how one squares the Stan Brakhage one knows and loves up with the notion of emotion recollected in tranquility I'll be goddammned if I understand. And it's mercifully not cartooned out too heavily. I mean, we don't have Harry Smith as Robert Browning and Lord, isn't it wonderful? Peterson as Keats, and who the devil are you, James? But that was the extent of the intellectual tool kit that he had to tinker and unlock this strange device. It worked a little—you can sort of pile a little Freud on top of that, and so forth. Freud according to the American gospel only and the Freud of course of *The Interpretation of Dreams*; not, for instance, of *Civilization and Its Discontents*, but that's it.

Frampton goes on to imply that Sitney's Romantic tool kit leaves him ill-equipped to treat the body of films he labels "Structural," even though the attempt "to square it away and bring it up to the light, and so forth" is the work of an "honest" critic. For dramatic effect (offering a pronounced bodily utterance that the transcriber for *Cinemanews* feels compelled to identify, in brackets, as a sigh), Frampton laments that Sitney's essay "ended with me."[2]

Frampton's characteristically performative critique does not offer us, in any explicit manner, alternative interpretations of the films of either the post-Romantic visionaries or the Structural group. Despite the artist's reluctance to show his hand, however, we are provided with clues to important aesthetic issues. Frampton acknowledges that Sitney was working with "strange" and difficult films and, more importantly, that the young critic sought to make sense of newer work, Brakhage's in particular, by tying it to an older tradition, as interpreted by the elder critic Bloom. Frampton does not attack Sitney for being possessed of a tool kit; he merely suggests that the historical and conceptual connection it constructs is not a convincing one, especially given the evident lack of "tranquility" in an oeuvre as impassioned as Brakhage's. Notice that Frampton is not concerned with disputing the value of criticism and its interpretations; rather, he is intent on questioning the usefulness of frameworks derived from Bloom and from the Americanized Freud, while hinting that other perspectives could serve as more valuable critical instruments.[3] Frampton's public criticism of Sitney is motivated not only by his professed allegiance to modernists who set themselves against the Romantic

2.   Sitney concludes his text by placing Frampton's work within another subcategory of the Structural film, one he calls the "participatory" film, a "form which addressed itself to the decision-making and logical faculties of the viewer." P. Adams Sitney, *Visionary Film: The American Avant-Garde 1943–1978*, 2nd ed. (New York: Oxford University Press, 1979), p. 392.
3.   The nature of Frampton's interest in *Civilization and Its Discontents* is stated more clearly in other texts, where Frampton consistently connects Freud's thesis to the fact that film footage needs to be processed before it can be viewed. Thus, "film-making is an edifice of delayed gratification; by a kind of inversion of Freud's thesis in *Civilization and Its Discontents*, one is constantly reassured in film-making that one is engaged in a civilized activity." Scott MacDonald, "Hollis Frampton," *A Critical Cinema: Interviews with Independent Filmmakers* (Berkeley: University of California Press, 1988), p. 67.

canon, but also by his understanding of the critical and theoretical alternatives to Bloom's views.

One of these alternatives was provided by Hugh Kenner, the influential writer on modernism whose views are often set in opposition to Bloom's in the domain of American literary criticism and scholarship. As Sitney himself has acknowledged, in a text published after the filmmaker's death, Kenner was "one of the few critics Frampton seems to have admired."[4] In what follows, I show how Frampton's ideas, particularly the filmmaker's notion of "epistemological inquiry" and key aspects of his view of modernism, were shaped by Kenner's writings. It was in part due to Kenner's influence, I argue, that Frampton objected to Sitney's characterization of the relationship between the postwar American avant-garde cinema and English-language poetry.[5]

*

None of the earliest available references to Kenner in Frampton's published texts and transcripts were initially intended for publication. In the two most significant early instances, Kenner is cited by name, first in a typed dialogue with Carl Andre, from 1963, and a few months later in a letter to a friend who had been corresponding with Kenner.[6] Both texts suggest a familiarity with Kenner's 1962 article, "Art in a Closed Field," and his book on Beckett, Flaubert, and Joyce, whom he calls "stoic comedians."[7] One indicator of the lasting value of Kenner's writings for Frampton is the length of time he spends citing the critic—he recounts the book's main theses as late as 1976 to an audience at the San Francisco Art Institute.[8] He also paraphrases a passage from the same book in an interview in 1977, albeit without naming Kenner in that context.[9] Only two explicit citations of Kenner appear in writings initially intended for publication, in the essays "For a Metahistory of Film: Commonplace Notes and Hypotheses," from 1971, and "Digressions on the Photographic Agony," from 1972.[10] The texts referenced in those essays are Kenner's *The Counterfeiters: An Historical Comedy* and

4.   P. Adams Sitney, "Re-Viewing Frampton," *American Film* (April 1986), p. 67.
5.   Janissaries and devotees of Frampton esoterica can rest assured that I do not present Kenner's work as the master key that will unlock the filmmaker's project. No such key exists, of course.
6.   Carl Andre and Hollis Frampton, "On Movies and Consecutive Matters," *12 Dialogues: 1962–1963*, ed. Benjamin H. D. Buchloh (Halifax: The Press of the Nova Scotia College of Art and Design and New York University Press, 1980), pp. 53–56; Hollis Frampton, "Letters from Framp 1958–1968," *October* 32 (Spring 1985), pp. 41–42.
7.   Kenner, "Art in a Closed Field," *Virginia Quarterly Review* 38, no. 4 (Autumn 1962), pp. 597–613; Hugh Kenner, *The Stoic Comedians: Flaubert, Joyce, and Beckett* (Boston: Beacon Press, 1962).
8.   "Hollis Frampton interview 4/23/76, SFAI," unofficial tape transcript, Pacific Film Archive, p. 7.
9.   Mitch Tuchman, "Frampton at the Gates," *Film Comment* (September–October 1977), p. 58. The passage from Kenner is from *The Stoic Comedians*, p. 3.
10.   Hollis Frampton, "For a Metahistory of Film: Commonplace Notes and Hypotheses" and "Digressions on the Photographic Agony," *Circles of Confusion: Film, Photography, Video, Texts 1968–1980* (Rochester, N.Y.: Visual Studies Workshop Press, 1983), pp. 108, 185.

his major study *The Pound Era*.[11] Finally, as R. Bruce Elder has pointed out, a passage from Frampton's essay "A Pentagram for Conjuring the Narrative," first published in 1972, bears a strong resemblance to a passage from *The Pound Era*.[12] The process of constructing a genealogy of Frampton's ideas begins with these direct and indirect references.

In January 1963, Frampton and sculptor Andre were continuing their unique exercise in artistic debate, begun in October 1962, with a typed dialogue entitled "On Movies and Consecutive Matters."[13] At a point in the exchange when Frampton is broaching the topic of artistic method, he writes, "Hugh Kenner has said that for the purposes of understanding a work of art, it is often helpful to think of it as though it followed certain rules, like a game."[14] In April of the same year, Frampton writes to his friend Reno Odlin: "Might I paraphrase Kenner thus: 'Poetry (and the arts at large) is not a subject to be studied and certified in, but an enterprise to be inquired into.'" He adds,

> For a working artist, this is the necessary point of view. Otherwise, we must, like the adolescent I once was, believe that art is something done by "other people." We must close the set upon a finite group of monuments that excludes our own work. And that is the viewpoint of those who sd/ of the *Cantos*, ok latin, ok greek and french and italian tags, but no chinese. We wish to develop the sensibilities we already have, not to extend the range of our sensibilities. It seems to me that Kenner wd/ have the reader move his consciousness out of the pathetic and into the operational view of art.[15]

These are primary clues, delivered by an artist in formation, one who has yet to develop the public persona of a playfully erudite man of letters. Frampton articulates, through the prism of his own interests, the belief that a particular set of interrelated practices, namely those of the artist and those of the interpreter, need to be democratized. For Frampton, the young artist who seeks to expand beyond a fixed canon of "monuments" and create work that will "extend the range of our sensibilities," Kenner's concepts will be functional and pliable enough to serve his needs for well over a decade.

The intersecting concepts of the open/closed field and the rule-bound game first appear in Kenner's work in "Art in a Closed Field," and again soon afterward in *The Stoic Comedians*. Given that Frampton refers to the game concept

11.   Hugh Kenner, *The Counterfeiters: An Historical Comedy* (1968; Baltimore: Johns Hopkins University Press, 1985); *The Pound Era* (Berkeley: University of California Press, 1971).
12.   R. Bruce Elder, *The Films of Stan Brakhage in the American Tradition of Ezra Pound, Gertrude Stein, and Charles Olson* (Waterloo, Ontario: Wilfrid Laurier University Press, 1998), pp. 100–02. I shall not review the allusion Elder mentions, but I note here that the passage from the "Pentagram" essay is one of many examples of the ironic essentialism discussed later in this essay.
13.   Andre and Frampton, "On Movies and Consecutive Matters," pp. 53–56.
14.   Ibid., p. 55.
15.   Frampton, "Letters from Framp 1958–1968," pp. 41–42.

prior to the publication of the book, it is likely that he read the 1962 article first. Kenner's article argues that poets and novelists of the modern era redefine the boundaries of their respective practices by selecting specific elements from the culture and ordering them according to self-made laws or rules. Describing this method as the arrangement of a finite set of elements within a closed field, Kenner acknowledges that this "sounds like a game," but the game analogy receives only occasional mention, since the closed field is presented as "the dominant intellectual analogy of our time."[16] Resonating with the modernist interest in science and mathematics, the closed field analogy is said to develop from the theory of fields in general number theory.[17] In the 1962 book, Kenner argues that modern literary practice responds and contributes to a post-Enlightenment culture shaped by a variety of functional systems, "proper to the world of IBM, of probability theory, of concern with modes of short-range and long-range causality, historical, socio-logical, psychological. . . . Inside this analogy The Stoic Comedians elected to imprison themselves, the better, in working out its elaborate games, to mime the elaborate world."[18] In *Bouvard et Pécuchet*, Flaubert parodies the encyclopedists who believe in facts but are not possessed of comprehension; in *Ulysses*, Joyce attempts, impossibly, to exhaust an infinite topic, the city of Dublin, within the confines of a finite book. In contrast, Beckett begins with simple, reduced scenarios that expand beyond their pronounced constraints, toward a "paradoxical fecundity."[19] Kenner's stoic comedian feigns a dual closing—of the practice of writing, through a calculated approach to method, and of the manifest subject matter of the text, through a seemingly systematic or reductive approach to structure and/or content. For the comedian, what is funny here is the high-mindedness of those who would, like the Stoics, present a deterministic and moral picture of a world comprised of harmoniously ordered and readily apprehensible parts. The comic game exposes the Stoic's folly through its deployment of structuring principles, which seem to displace beliefs about the power of empiricism, rational systems, and logical orders into the domain of art.

Before reviewing the historical narrative linked to Kenner's concepts, we can begin to examine how this "deliberately wielded" analogy, used to "lend structure and direction to our thoughts," serves Frampton's practice.[20] Immediately follow-ing the Kenner reference in the 1963 dialogue, Frampton recalls a significant discovery generated by the production of a series of photographic portraits of Frank Stella, from 1959. The photographer's series can be programmed to include elements he considers errors, "imperfections of my invention," created by his own

---

16.   Kenner, "Art in a Closed Field," pp. 599, 605.
17.   It should be noted, however, that Kenner does not offer empirical evidence to support this claim, just as he fails to cite direct references to the analogy in modernist literature, thereby leaving unresolved the issue of whether the critic is creating a new analogy for instructive purposes or identifying an analogy already in circulation.
18.   Kenner, *The Stoic Comedians*, p. 96.
19.   Ibid., p. 101.
20.   Kenner, "Art in a Closed Field," p. 605.

"warning mechanism" or "system."[21] Retrospectively, Frampton's discovery can be seen in Kennerian terms: struggling against the narrow confines of a single "sensibility" or style, Frampton designates imperfect and "dangerous" elements for his field in order to ensure some measure of heterogeneity. The game he plays is most valuable when it is expansive, generating diversity in the field of photographic practice and undermining the viewer's sense of how and why a picture in a series can appear to be "right" or "wrong." By 1970, when Frampton completes a film, *Zorns Lemma*, which is largely predicated upon the viewer's discovery of deliberate errors in an ordered structure, he has considered these issues long enough to add a few masterstrokes: he employs the alphabet, an order that is directly linked to processes of learning, and, through the title, makes reference to set theory, thereby signaling the importance of the elements-field relation.

Tellingly, Frampton first refers to the game analogy when discussing method and practice. Frampton shares Kenner's view that "it is helpful" for artists to think of art as a game because it allows for the reconceptualization of artistic practice as a deliberative act—imaginative, but also selective, purposeful, even practical. The selection of elements for the art work and the creation of rules for the interaction or use of those elements cannot be properly described as merely intuitive activities, since they involve unmistakably cognitive processes of thinking and making. Thus, in an interview from 1980, Frampton maintains that he does not take issue with Sitney's use of the phrase "sumptuous optical rhetoric" in an analysis of his films.[22] "Rhetoric," with its intimations of studied presentations and calculated effects, is an acceptable term for the filmmaker who once joked, "All my intentions are conscious."[23] He goes on, in the interview, to surmise that "Brakhage would be extremely uncomfortable to have it suggested that his cinematography, his diction, his camera vocabulary, was in any sense rhetorical or that it had been deliberately chosen and adopted for a particular reason." The main implication in Frampton's statement is that Brakhage refuses to concede that his expressive visual style entails some measure of rational, deliberative choice. Frampton accepts that his practice could be categorized as poesis, but in this case he uses Brakhage as a foil, as he often does from the early 1970s onward, in order to assert that he is not tied to Romantic notions of individual style. This is not necessarily because he rejects the notion of the artist as an expressive individual, but rather due to his view of the limitations of any one particular style, which would seem to provide only one way of seeing things. One of Frampton's primary models, Pound's *Cantos*, attempts to "turn the closed field inside out, and make it an instrument of possibilities, not foreclosures," in Kenner's words, and as we shall see later, Frampton is

21.   Andre and Frampton, "On Movies and Consecutive Matters," p. 55.
22.   Bill Simon, "Talking About *Magellan*: An Interview with Hollis Frampton," *Millennium Film Journal* 7/8/9 (Fall–Winter 1980–1981), p. 21.
23.   Frampton, "Hollis Frampton. IV," Sound Recording no. 73.6, March 10, 1973, Museum of Modern Art Archives.

highly aware that his own expansive approach, his own version of the open field, has a utopian dimension.[24]

Kenner's broad framework allows an artist such as Frampton the freedom to reconceptualize and revise artistic practice through contemporary methods and concepts that appear to be deeply rooted in the culture. In his discussion of Pound in the final pages of the article, Kenner provides a schematic placement of the poet in an American tradition of independent learning, innovative selection, and perpetual self-invention.[25] Given the fact that American libraries, in their search for material to feed the educational curriculum, have devised their collections with carefully considered choices, in direct contrast to the long-standing European method of expansive accretion, the production of the *Cantos* "parallels the act which for three centuries has constituted the continuing history of the United States: selection, definition, choice, imposed first by frontier circumstances, later by pedagogical necessity, and finally by national habit." In Kenner's view, the inclusions and exclusions in the *Cantos* are decided through a careful process of appraisal, rich with implicit significance. And "what Pound seems to be implying is an adventurous comedy . . . a comedy of discovery." What is funny in this particular comedy is perhaps the lone American autodidact's hubris, his notion that he can build an original curriculum and a new cultural heritage completely on his own, encompassing "any, but any, level of diction, of tone, of subject, personal or public." What is worth taking seriously is the manner in which his deployment of the open field provokes questions—about practices of reading and interpreting, about the self-reliant reformation of tradition, about the relation between structures of order and knowledge, and so on.

It is highly likely that Frampton also read *The Poetry of Ezra Pound*, the 1951 book by Kenner that succeeded in alerting the literary community to the scholarly neglect of Pound. Particular attention is paid to Pound's rhetoric of vision, evident in the poet's championing of the "luminous detail," the distinct poetic "image" that communicates directly to the reader. When addressing this issue, Kenner reminds us that "Looking about the world, we know things" and that "knowledge resides in the particulars."[26] In other words, if something like a theory of knowledge can be gleaned from Pound's anti-Romantic practice, then its base claim would be that we begin not with ideas, as Kenner says Descartes would have it, but rather with the apprehension of particulars, in phalanxes, groups, collections, assemblages. Once the base claim is accepted, the poet needs to determine whether ideas can be communicated, with any sort of immediacy, through carefully ordered combinations of specific, apprehensible words.

24.   Kenner, "Art in a Closed Field," p. 611.
25.   All quotations in this paragraph are from Kenner, "Art in a Closed Field," pp. 611–13.
26.   Hugh Kenner, *The Poetry of Ezra Pound* (Lincoln: University of Nebraska Press, 1985), pp. 77, 84.

With the appearance of these theoretical issues, as well as the reference to Descartes, we encounter the basis for important points of distinction between Kenner's modernists and Bloom's Romantics. Consistently concerned with the inter-related issues of epistemology and communication, Kenner's Pound develops an "Ideogrammic Method" that is valued for its inauguration of an analytic tendency in the writer, who must choose the words most appropriate to the phenomena under consideration, and of a cognitive process in the reader, for whom the world has been presented anew through the language of the modernist text. The experiences of both the writer and the reader are to be heightened or intensified by a revived awareness of the word's ability to reach its recipient with immediacy. In Kenner's view, it is the avowal of this belief in the communicating word that sets the modernists apart from the Romantics. Although Kenner never cites it, the follow-ing statement by Shelley, from his "Defence of Poetry" of 1820, condenses what the modernist critic takes to be an essential Romantic claim: "when composition begins, inspiration is already on the decline, and the most glorious poetry that has ever been communicated to the world is probably a feeble shadow of the original conception of the poet."[27] In *The Poetry of Ezra Pound*, Shelley and the poets of the "post-Cartesian Romantic Movement" are characterized in terms of a collectively shared and deep-rooted skepticism with regard to language. Kenner discerns in Tennyson and Shelley "an identical distrust of the possibility of any communica-tion, especially of emotional states, without constant comment, constant overt appeal to the reader's experience, habits, and day-dreams." Unlike the Romantic who is "conscious of an audience to be influenced rather than of a poem to be made," the modernist poet avoids "exhortation" by situating emotions and ideas "there on the page—there among the images," for our "steady contemplation, there whenever we return."[28]

Almost ten years after the publication of Kenner's book, Bloom begins to present his interpretation of the Romantics in *Shelley's Mythmaking*. In any number of texts by Bloom published from the sixties through the mid-seventies, Frampton would likely have recognized the claim that Shelley distrusts language. Bloom and Kenner both agree that, for Shelley, conception forms the ideal imaginative state, with linguistic composition marking the onset of creative decline. But alongside this standard interpretation, the reader of Bloom finds the contention that Shelley's view of poetic practice constitutes a heroic position. Within Bloom's canon of visionary poetry, the highest rankings belong to those writers who fully embody the value system articulated by Shelley. If Kenner suggests that the Romantics neglect the "poem to be made," then an analogous point is made by critics who have asserted since the early sixties that, in Bloom's work, the emphasis placed on Romantic poems as visionary "commentaries" facilitates the Romantic

---

27.   Quoted in David Fite, *Harold Bloom: The Rhetoric of Romantic Vision* (Amherst: University of Massachusetts Press, 1985), p. 32.
28.   Kenner, *The Poetry of Ezra Pound*, pp. 72, 68.

canonizer's disregard for the complex particulars of "the words on the page" and "the poem-as-object."[29] As literary scholar David Fite and others have noted, Bloom assumes the extremist's position, defending the will of the prophetic poet against not only the textual studies of the New Critics of the fifties but also against the culture of modernity.[30] Bloom's critics see his extended apologia for the Romantic imagination as a rejection of the modernist's standard gestures, in particular the attempted suppression of inspiration and instinct in favor of the demands of the modernist object.

Kenner, acting as the modernist canonizer, goes so far as to propose that Pound's art of cognition is an *advance* over Romantic solipsism and skepticism ("Pound is a far more important figure than Browning or Landor, Eliot than Tennyson or Shelley").[31] Kenner also rejects New Criticism's narrow version of formalism, but without renouncing detailed textual analyses, so long as the words on the page are understood within contextual frameworks, expanding outward to the whole of modern culture. In Fite's view, "the words on the page matter *more than anything else*" for Kenner because "not only are those words the life of the poet" but they also constitute "verbal embodiments of the cultural energy that has helped give them shape."[32] Kenner's critical analyses of Pound's texts are never so insular as to exclude exegetical stories about the culture of modernism, and this feature of his writing likely held substantial appeal for Frampton, who eventually develops, in his mature years, an essayistic combination of formal, conceptual, and historical analysis, and for whom intrinsic structures are so important.[33]

29.   Fite, *Harold Bloom: The Rhetoric of Romantic Vision*, p. 32.
30.   Obviously, a review of the many debates surrounding Bloom's writings on the Romantics would fall beyond the scope of this essay. The relevance of deconstructionist critiques, such as Jacques Derrida's writings on phonocentrism and Paul de Man's texts on Bloom, is addressed in David Fite's chapter "Humanism in the Extreme: The Predicament of Romantic Redemption," *Harold Bloom: The Rhetoric of Romantic Vision*, pp. 162–87.
31.   Kenner, *The Poetry of Ezra Pound*, p. 19.
32.   Fite, *Harold Bloom*, p. 177. See also David Fite, "Kenner/Bloom: Canonmaking and the Resources of Rhetoric," *boundary 2* 15, no. 3/16, no. 1 (Spring/Fall 1988). For overviews of Kenner's criticism that complement Fite's analysis, see Marjorie Perloff, "The Outsider as Exemplary Critic: Hugh Kenner," *William Carlos Williams Review* 19, nos. 1 & 2 (Spring/Fall 1993), and Lawrence Lipking, "kenner," *The Denver Quarterly* 12, no. 1 (Spring 1977).
33.   Revisionist scholarship in this area of modernist studies draws upon but also departs from Kenner's early work on Pound, in which the emphasis lies squarely in the poet's *command* of language. For example, in his study of the complex shifts in doctrine among the canonical writers of the modernist avant-garde, Michael Levenson traces the development of "a persistent ambiguity in early modernism: the desire for the autonomy of form and the claim that the root source and justification for art is individual expression." Scholars such as Levenson argue that Romantic individualism was never fully eclipsed by "the autonomy of art, logic, politics and ethics," by polemical views articulated "from the standpoint of objective truth and objective value." Michael H. Levenson, *A Genealogy of Modernism: A Study of English Literary Doctrine 1908–1922* (New York: Cambridge University Press, 1984), pp. 135, 133. By contrast, Kenner's pioneering work tends to overstate the modernist rejection of individual, psychic authority. As for Frampton, his essays come closest to Levenson's argument when addressing modernist photography. Of Edward Weston, for example, Frampton writes that he attempts, paradoxically, to construe the photograph as both an autonomous, objective record of reality and a product of the artist's perceptual processes and imaginative, constructive practices.

Before encountering Sitney's adjunction of poetic and cinematic traditions in the concept of "visionary film," Frampton would have found in Kenner's book the construction of a unique analogy, one that connects Pound's images-in-movement with the moving image medium of the cinema. Kenner opens a chapter entitled "The Moving Image" as follows: "The 'motion' of the moving image is contained, ultimately, in the word-to-word jostle of language itself. The simplest sentence 'moves.'"[34] Kenner makes clear that when Pound asks his reader to experience and think about the movement from one word to the next, the poet articulates a modernist view of aesthetic experience that includes both sensual apprehension and intellectual processes. In a later chapter, Kenner explicitly connects the "action" of the *Cantos*, by which he means the complex rhythmic development of recurring words, to Sergei Eisenstein's concept of montage, as set out in "A Dialectical Approach to Film Form" (1949). Kenner refers to Eisenstein's famous discussion of a succession of images that would lead the viewer to "the idea of murder—the feeling of murder, as such,"[35] in order to explain how the *Cantos* function as a "plotless" epic of emotions and ideas, constituting a grand revision of linguistic structures and reading practices. Broadly speaking, both autodidacts, American and Soviet, develop radically revisionist projects, seeking formal and cultural transformations of the structural relationships within a text and of the demands placed upon the interpreter of that text; both use an aesthetic of juxtaposition, or montage, to direct the interpreter to specific feelings and ideas. These general points of connection between both artists are familiar to scholars of modernism by now, but in the 1950s, Kenner's treatment of Eisenstein would likely have assisted Frampton with a crucial transition, from the work of a poet to that of a visual artist working with series.[36] Not long after producing photographic series in his post-poetry phase, Frampton begins to work in film. As Christopher Phillips notes, the still photograph could not provide Frampton with the visual equivalent of a "characteristic element of Poundian poetics, *phanopoeia*, the play of successive images."[37] Eisenstein's preferred machines could, however, and Kenner suggests this quite clearly.[38]

34.   Kenner, *The Poetry of Ezra Pound*, p. 62.
35.   Sergei Eisenstein, "A Dialectical Approach to Film Form," in *Film Form: Essays in Film Theory*, trans. Jay Leyda (New York: Harcourt Brace & Co., 1949), p. 61.
36.   Notably, Frampton rejects Eisenstein at an early stage of interest in the cinema. See the letter dated July 18, 1959, in Frampton, "Letters from Framp 1958–1968," p. 32. The nature of Frampton's engagement with Eisenstein's films and writings changes drastically after he commits himself to filmmaking.
37.   Christopher Phillips, "Word Pictures: Frampton and Photography," *October* 32 (Spring 1985), p. 69. In a letter from 1962, Frampton notes that Pound's "*Cantos* rest on continuous articulation, almost continuous 'denouément' . . ." Frampton, "Letters from Framp 1958–1968," pp. 37–38.
38.   According to Frampton's own chronology, he comes to the realization that he will not become a poet following his 1957 visits to Pound at St. Elizabeth's; after trying his hand at classical scholarship, he explores photography intensively from 1958 through 1962, the year when he first picks up a Bolex movie camera. His period of transition, which ends with the production of his first publicly screened films, lasts from the fall of 1962 until the spring of 1966. By 1973, Frampton tells an audience at the Museum of Modern Art that he has "developed such a quantity of still photography antibodies that if I

*

A review of the historical narrative that Kenner develops in *The Stoic Comedians* and *The Counterfeiters* will serve as a point of transition into a key concept in Frampton's writings, namely epistemological inquiry. In *The Counterfeiters*, the counterfeiting gesture embodied in Andy Warhol's Brillo boxes emerges as merely the latest episode in a long trajectory of artists availing themselves of "problems . . . latent in the Western psyche" since art's discovery of itself as art.[39] "That awareness synchronized with, and may have been caused by, the ascendancy of empirical philosophies" that rejected art, in the first moments of its self-realization, on the basis of its disorderly nature. Early in the "Metahistory" essay, the text with which Frampton begins his parallel pursuit of theory and practice in the seventies, a story from *The Counterfeiters* is recounted.[40] A description of a society of radical empiricists who were Jonathan Swift's contemporaries, Kenner's story (and Frampton's gloss) provides an example of the uses and abuses of the experimental science and natural philosophy movements of the seventeenth century. Both Kenner and Frampton intend to remind the reader that the concept of a fact has a history, one that includes periods in which empirical data was intensely fetishized. (In Frampton's "Digressions" essay, the nineteenth-century pursuit of laws, over and above any examination of cultural "assumptions," is attributed to the legacies of Locke and Newton.)[41] According to the narrative endorsed by Frampton, the seventeenth century establishes a tradition of overvaluing the apparent and the sensible, of concentrating exclusively on facts and apprehensible traces while denigrating the imagination.

In the second stage of the narrative, the eighteenth century collects the findings of the new sciences in taxonomic structures. Prominent among these is the encyclopedia, an Enlightenment invention that Kenner calls "a feat of organizing, not a feat of understanding," an allegedly profound and expansive compendium organized according to the reductive and arbitrary method of alphabetization.[42] When Kenner points out that each entry, authored by a particular expert and speaking to a particular implied reader, may have nothing to "say" to the author or reader of another entry, he is pointing to the fragmentary nature of the whole; his depiction suggests that the encyclopedia is not a purely objective record of our world but rather a cultural artifact. In the critical environment to which Flaubert belongs, rationalist, empiricist, and positivist claims about Facts and Things

---

ever tried to inhale it again I would get sick and die." Frampton, "Hollis Frampton. IV," Sound Recording no. 73.6, Museum of Modern Art Archives, March 10, 1973. In more than one interview, he attributes his conversion from photographer to filmmaker to the intensification of his interest in the successive movement of images in time.

39.   Kenner, *The Counterfeiters*, p. 80.
40.   Frampton, "For a Metahistory of Film," *Circles of Confusion*, p. 108.
41.   Frampton, "Digressions on the Photographic Agony," *Circles of Confusion*, p. 188.
42.   Kenner, *The Stoic Comedians*, p. 2.

remain vulnerable to artistic parody.[43] In a magazine interview, Frampton repeats the passage on encyclopedias from *The Stoic Comedians* almost word for word. Instead of citing Kenner, however, he proposes that his musings on encyclopedias developed entirely out of the voracious bibliophilia of his adolescence, thereby transforming a Kenner story into a counterfeit Frampton story.[44]

According to Kenner's interpretation of the canonical literature of modernism, the modernist method places its trust in the power of language, communicating to a cognitive reader through renewed words on composed pages, as the modernist critique questions the culture's faith in empiricism and rational systems. The general appeal of Kenner's work for Frampton would seem to lie in the critic's combination of a rigorously canonical approach to literature with an expansive account of modern ideas and technologies. In Kenner's books, historically significant artifacts and events, such as *Gulliver's Travels* and the conversion of the Babbage Engine into the Turing Machine, are incorporated into a winding narrative of the emergence and transformation of commonly held cultural assumptions. Kenner's network of revelatory historical details, each employed in the analysis of particular assumptions, comprises a conceptual history, and this is the genre of literary criticism that speaks directly to Frampton.[45]

To some interpreters, the critique suggested by Frampton's cinematic parodies of systematic structures may appear to conflict with the implication of a fundamentally metaphysical worldview in some of his essays. As evidenced in his use of terms such as "let us imagine," "let us pretend," and "let us suppose," however, Frampton prefers to explore an ambiguous form of rhetoric, frequently allowing speculations to stand unqualified. By blurring the distinctions between an imaginative conceit, a summary of another writer's theories, and a statement of his own views, Frampton writes himself into the role of a philosophically oriented ironist. Frampton the ironist displays a deep interest in essentialism, of the sort that looks for correspondences between science and transcendental metaphysics,[46] as when

43.   Near the end of *The Counterfeiters*, Kenner asserts, "Empiricism is a game. Its central rule forbids you to understand what you are talking about. The application of this rule, when we remember that we *are* playing a game, yields satire." Kenner, *The Counterfeiters*, p. 173.
44.   Kenner makes his point by asking his reader to consider the differences between encyclopedia articles on quaternions, the Renaissance, and waterfalls. Frampton insists that his favorite entries in the twelfth edition of the *Encyclopedia Britannica* are quaternions and waterfalls, going on to restate Kenner's main thesis. See Kenner, *The Stoic Comedians*, p. 3, and Tuchman, "Frampton at the Gates," p. 58.
45.   Looking beyond the highly serviceable field/game analogy, a number of topics and concepts appear in both Kenner's and Frampton's writings. Due to limitations of space, this essay will not analyze further points of connection. Instead, I refer the reader to the chapter-length version of this essay in my forthcoming dissertation.
46.   Frampton's interest in transcendental ideas is also evident in his references to the work of Jorge Luis Borges. Borges serves as a model for Frampton's writing not only for his interest in idealism, theories of time, and the history of metaphysics, but also for his merging of scholarly criticism and fiction in a profoundly intertextual project. Under the influence of Borges, Frampton develops a writing style that Annette Michelson describes as a "concerted confusion of genres." Annette Michelson, "Poesis/Mathesis," *October* 32 (Spring 1985), p. 6.

Alfred North Whitehead's philosophy of Events and Eternal Objects is somehow confirmed by neurophysiological studies of the "protolinguistic sign" in pheromonal and neuromuscular communication.[47] Irony permits Frampton the freedom to articulate and explore, in any manner he chooses, those positions that are articulated in Kenner's narrative.[48] But he differs from Kenner when he directs his attention to the primary essentialist traditions of the modernist visual arts, as laid out in his essay on Edward Weston: the medium-specific investigations and doctrines of the arts and modernism's subsequent pursuit of broader ontological questions, which moved "to strip the pretext of the visual image or the referent of the linguistic artifact to its own proper set of specifications as well."[49] With an eye to the former tradition, Frampton differentiates between film and video, for example; his appreciation for the latter tradition informs the connections he constructs between the concepts of science and those of idealism.

Perhaps nostalgically, but never naively, Frampton writes *as if* artists were still constructing grand metaphysical or essentialist theories of art and existence in the manner of the modernists. But Frampton's commitments lie elsewhere, in a homegrown combination of sociohistorical, anthropological, and epistemological theories.[50] Throughout the corpus of his published texts, works of art are analyzed in terms of their artifactual status: they are taken to be the material products of the purposeful practices of individuals and collectives, subject to change as values and norms change. He begins applying the term in his essays in 1971, when he conjures up a "class" of artifacts called metahistories. Produced by the artist who searches for the historical elements that will constitute his or her tradition, each metahistory is an active and open rearrangement of historical chronologies and verifiable facts. These imagined artifacts of historical reinterpretation "made things strong in their own immanence," constituting "an open set of rational fictions . . . [that] bid as fairly for our contemplative energy as any other human fabrications. They are, finally, about what it felt like to reflect consciously upon the qualities of experience in the times they expound." Acting as usable frames for cultural history, metahistories "remain events in themselves."[51] If each is "about" the thinking that went into its making, this is not only because they are

47.   Frampton, "Impromptus on Edward Weston: Everything in Its Place," *Circles of Confusion*, p. 152.
48.   David E. James has argued that Structural filmmakers employ "predetermined protocols" in order, in part, to "ironize" such usages, thereby creating "internal tensions" (between opposed practices, formal elements, ideas, and so on), which can be explored and elaborated through film itself. James, *Allegories of Cinema: American Film in the Sixties* (Princeton: Princeton University Press, 1989), p. 244. In Frampton's case, irony allows him to examine opposed epistemic views (such as historicism and essentialism) in his films and writings.
49.   Frampton, "Impromptus on Edward Weston," *Circles of Confusion*, p. 142.
50.   The significance of essentialist and historiographic or historicist perspectives for Frampton's writings was first addressed by Noël Carroll, "A Brief Comment on Frampton's Notion of Metahistory" (1986), reprinted in his *Theorizing the Moving Image* (New York: Cambridge University Press, 1996), pp. 313–17.
51.   Frampton, "For a Metahistory of Film," *Circles of Confusion*, pp. 107–08.

created through a process of conscious deliberation but also because human reflection is embodied in artifacts.

Frampton's continued treatment of embodiment in the artifact finds him adding new terms in his 1972 essay on Paul Strand. "Let us suppose," he writes, that every art work "assumes an entire cosmology," discernible in its "deliberative structure," which is defined as "what is apparent, that is, the denumerable field of elements and operations that constitute the permanent artifact of record"; its "axiomatic substructure," made up of that which is "handed" to the artist by culture or tradition, "implies an entire epistemology."[52] (Combining Frampton's terms with Kenner's schema, we can say that the blind believer in Facts would look only to the deliberative structure, while the axiomatic substructure would be explored by the Stoic comedian.) The photographer becomes an "epistemologist" when investigating the cultural assumptions embodied in photography's appearances (in its prints) and in its "normative" processes. According to this particular photographic sensibility, as articulated in Strand's early essays, "the least discernible modification (from a conventionalized norm) of contrast or tonality must be violently charged with significance, for it implies a changed view of the universe, and a suitably adjusted theory of knowledge."[53] (Frampton parodies his own formulation in his 1974 essay on video, when he writes that he is "tempted" to view each family's calibration of the image-adjustment knobs on the household television set as "an adequation of the broadcast image to the family's several notions of the universe.")[54]

Two years later, the axiomatic substructure concept is developed further in a published lecture on composition, which draws upon Pound's 1931 text "How to Read." The depiction of Pound resembles that of Strand in the earlier essay, insofar as each becomes a representative of the idea that the autonomy of art lies in its materials, which Frampton compares to the Symbolist "notion that language . . . should, of its own nature, tend to secrete poems."[55] The autonomy issue is tangential, however, to the problem of how aesthetic texts and practices are interpreted and, more specifically, to the question of what can actually be learned from epistemological inquiry. Expanding upon the claim, made first in the essay on Strand, that axioms (by which he seems to mean both the implicit assumptions and the explicit principles that inform the production of an art work) are "subject . . . to change on very short notice,"[56] Frampton gives us a sense of how complex the

52.   Frampton, "Meditations around Paul Strand," *Circles of Confusion*, p. 131.
53.   Ibid., pp. 132–33.
54.   Frampton, "The Withering Away of the State of the Art," *Circles of Confusion*, p. 169.
55.   Frampton, "Notes on Composing in Film," *The Stoic Comedians*, p. 118. This Symbolist idea is referenced again in Frampton, "Impromptus on Edward Weston," *Circles of Confusion*, p. 145. Frampton's interpretation of Symbolism is consistent with the views articulated in Hugh Kenner, "The Poetics of Error," *MLN* 90 (1975), pp. 738, 740, and in Kenner's chapter "The Persistent East," in *The Pound Era*, passim.
56.   Frampton, "Meditations around Paul Strand," *Circles of Confusion*, p. 131.

practices of composition and reception have become in the contemporary climate. Interdisciplinary influences and interests abound, intentional misinterpretations and the Cagean negation of deliberate decisions have acquired a heightened value, and any new axiom can be superseded once it becomes readable, thereby assuming "the historical role of all norms."[57] In Frampton's strategic response to this labyrinth of motives, assumptions, and contexts, he advances the theory that "one learns to write mainly by reading those texts that embody 'invention,'" since "what we learn when we read a text is how it was written."[58] This Poundian premise can be restated to bring out its fundamentally prescriptive point: writers must be critical readers if they are to learn their practice, and while each and every reader does not always read in order to write, all critical readers must take into consideration the practice of writing. The initial identification and isolation of works belonging to the artist's "immediately apprehensible" tradition falls under the heading of reading; "unlearning," as Pound calls it, follows reading with an "excernment, castigation, and transvaluation" of the axiomatic substructure of those works.[59] Unlike the artist, whose misreading is sanctioned if it leads to an imaginative reinterpretation of an axiomatic substructure, the critical interpreter faces a "predicament," a cultural imperative to understand the artist's readings and misreadings simultaneously. Somewhat less directly than in his earlier advancement of the artist who acts as an epistemologist, Frampton suggests that the active, critical interpreter must recognize both the individual and the more broadly based cultural perspectives, or worldviews, embodied in the innovative work of art and situate it in a complex historical field, or "open set."[60]

Clearly, Frampton finds emblematic practitioners of epistemological inquiry in modernism, especially among its writers and photographers. Yet if Eisenstein emerges as one of only a few filmmakers discussed directly in the writings, this can be attributed to Frampton's assessment of film history. For if Eisenstein is the cinema's first committed epistemologist, as Frampton suggests, decades will pass before the art form witnesses the effects of his legacy, in the New York film scene of the 1960s. As the North American revival of intellectual cinema gains prominence, Frampton finds that the response of contemporary criticism and theory is falling wide of the mark; soon enough, he begins to publish his views on theoretical and historical issues in aesthetics. And while he tends to refrain from criticizing the critics in print, he remains vocal and opinionated in public discussions and private correspondence. To our opening quotation, from the 1976 talk, we might add another, taken from the corrective suggestions sent by Frampton to film critic Wanda Bershen, in response to an early draft of her 1971 *Artforum* article on *Zorns Lemma*. After dividing earlier filmmakers such as Maya Deren and Kenneth Anger along Freudian and Jungian lines, he asserts that

57.   Frampton, "Notes on Composing in Film," *Circles of Confusion*, p. 121.
58.   Ibid., p. 118.
59.   Ibid., p. 119.
60.   Ibid., p. 122.

The most striking break that the cinema of structure makes with previous *genera* is in its repudiation of *psychology* in favor of *epistemology*. One effect this has is to widen both the field of reference (*vide* Snow's interest in Valery, mine in mathematics) and the comprehensible "Tradition" (Landow's 'found' footage; Jacobs' *Tom Tom* which proceeds from pre-psychological, even autobiographical interests in physiognomy and gesture).[61]

The Structural filmmaker is a metahistorian and an epistemologist, best understood as yet another version of the American artist as self-inventing autodidact. Rejecting the clichés of feeling and conventions of form associated with the psychology model, Frampton's filmmaker-epistemologist seeks to expand the tradition of cinema on deliberative (formal, material) and axiomatic (conceptual) levels. The new tradition follows Eisenstein in its dual exploration of the nature of the cinema and of the nature of our perceptual and cognitive experiences in general. Ken Jacobs's *Tom Tom the Piper's Son* (1969), for example, allows the viewer to reflect upon cinematic spectatorship, cinematic narrative, cinematic illusionism, cinematic tableaux, cinematic history, and so on; but it is also a film that attempts to convey a primary fascination with the human body and its movements as visible phenomena.

*

Frampton the filmmaker places himself "very clearly on the side of Eisenstein [as opposed to André Bazin], drastically and, again, utopianly so," employing montage in the service of an investigation of the "special place of the spectator and the nature of the spectator's task."[62] Accordingly, he states that his own *Magellan* project "offers to the spectator the possibility of a posture that's so active in relation to the work that it borders on the utopian or it is utopian."[63] In Frampton's utopia, the manifestly schematic and permutational structures of his films signal to the viewer that his or her attention is being directed in a deliberate and purposive manner. Thus, the challenge to conventional viewing practices offered by each of his films is met by viewers who assume a reflective stance. From within that stance, Frampton's viewers consider a range of issues, including the nature of temporal experience and the ways in which meaning can be ascribed to the sounds, words, and images encountered in a particular film.[64] These considerations revolve

61.   Hollis Frampton, n.d., Files of Anthology Film Archives, New York. Bershen's draft is titled "On Film, or the Ingression of Hollis Frampton." For the published version, see Wanda Bershen, "'Zorns Lemma,'" *Artforum* 10, no. 1 (September 1971), pp. 41–45.
62.   Simon, "Talking About *Magellan*," p. 22.
63.   Ibid., p. 9.
64.   In a revealing statement addressed to Jonas Mekas, Frampton explains that he is exploring how "the contents of the film frame may now resolve itself, and come to equilibrium, not only in space but in time as well—as, indeed, a whole work of film art may only come to equipoise in time. Or, if you will, in the mind, in our affections, since time would seem to be one of our supreme artifacts." Jonas Mekas, "Movie Journal," *Village Voice* (March 3, 1975), p. 75.

around the power of new montage structures, new ways of ordering the set or field, and around the thoroughly *constructed* nature of those structures.[65]

There is a concept that encapsulates a primary goal of Frampton's version of epistemological inquiry, one that appears in a discussion of organizational methodology as it pertains to *Surface Tension*, the 1968 film he describes as his first venture into the complexities of both horizontal and vertical montage. The "control structure" for a film, like Kenner's field analogy, is used to "hold it together," without resorting to "direct or obvious narrative."[66] According to Frampton's explanation of the term, the control structure becomes an instrument for the reduction or expansion of possibilities, depending upon the practitioner's inclinations. In the examples of Symbolism and Surrealism, traditions that attempt to release words or images "from the constraint of 'making sense,'" the aesthetic that attempts to liberate language from conventional structures of meaning explores the idea that "words actually construct or manufacture sense before our eyes."[67] Groupings of words, and of images, seem to produce their own "inherent" control structures, appearing to hold themselves together meaningfully, even within deliberately nonsensical constructions. Given the human tendency to look for meaning in the discernible elements of a human artifact, the communicating word or image often appears to be making meaning independently, "before our eyes." The reactionary response to the "rich, massive, and powerful" nature of the syntactic relations among the words and/or images of a particular artifact is reductive; it seeks to "limit the choice among those control structures and their actions," as in the essentialist attempt "to whittle painting down to intelligibility or a small set of intelligibilities." In contrast, by "mak[ing] possible a kind of naive 'use' of an enormous structure" such as language itself, Frampton's project composes control structures in order to ask the viewer to take up, within the practice of spectatorship, an expansive attitude toward the creation of meaning.

Yet the control structure is a very general concept, and in practice it cannot guarantee a realization of Frampton's utopian vision. In an unpublished letter from 1971, he praises *Tom Tom the Piper's Son* because it

> sorts the sheep from the goats. You gotta *love* FILM to dig it. In that sense, ZL [*Zorns Lemma*] may pull the punch—its [*sic*] possible to dig ZL (I think) through mere enjoyment of being in touch with your own head (rare enough, but perhaps not precisely the same thing).[68]

65.   Frampton's use of montage to solicit spectatorial participation has been addressed insightfully by a few scholars. The major study is Bruce Jenkins, "The Films of Hollis Frampton: A Critical Study," Ph.D. diss., Northwestern University, 1984; see also James Peterson, *Dreams of Chaos, Visions of Order: Understanding the American Avant-garde Cinema*; and Jim Hillier, "(nostalgia) (1971)," *Movie* 34/35 (Winter 1990), pp. 98–102.
66.   MacDonald, "Hollis Frampton," *Critical Cinema*, p. 43.
67.   Ibid., p. 44.
68.   Hollis Frampton, letter to Sally Dixon, May 25, 1971, Files of Anthology Film Archives, New York.

In Frampton's view, the viewer cannot bend *Tom Tom* to his or her own will. The manner in which Jacobs's film directs the viewer, through close-ups, for example, to various material or illusionistic details in the original footage, is, as the film-maker and numerous critics have pointed out, deeply didactic. To some significant degree, the viewer must share Jacobs's epistemological concerns or reject the film altogether. In contrast, the viewer of *Zorns Lemma* may construct a pleasurable aesthetic experience by following the matches between letters, words, and images in the alphabetical middle section of the film, or, more simply, by watching a montage of interesting images that unfolds without the added complica-tion of sound. Elsewhere, Frampton declares that "I've always thought of that game-playing aspect of *Zorns Lemma* as the fool's gold of the film" and that, in both *Zorns Lemma* and *nostalgia* (1971), this aspect "is a kind of bait, a lure, rather than the whole substance of the film."[69] Since the manifest structure of either film can be reordered as a simple, linear schema, Frampton wonders, in moments of doubt, whether the participatory viewer will neglect those knottier, more intricate tasks that call for a variety of interpretive approaches—formal, conceptual, inter-textual, historical, even autobiographical. Thus, Frampton's utopian position appears to have been tempered by an awareness of the risks he had undertaken, or at least of the possibility that the dynamically responsive spectator he seeks, the agent willing to "move his consciousness out of the pathetic and into the operational view of art," might not be there at all.

In Frampton's last direct citation of Kenner in print, a brief discussion of "the task of criticism" is followed by a quotation from *The Pound Era* that begins, "There is no substitute for critical tradition: a continuum of understanding, early commenced."[70] According to Kenner, contemporary readers have a better sense of "what to make of" a literary work when it is enriched by a significant corpus of critical response, initiated upon (and continued after) the work's publication. This is an issue addressed implicitly in Frampton's 1976 criticism of Sitney's text, to which we can return once more. Having surveyed Frampton's engagement with a major critical tradition, we can see that Sitney is at least partially correct when he discusses poetic tradition in the final pages of his Structural film chapter. After all, Sitney mentions Pound in his analysis of *Zorns Lemma*, and Symbolism appears in the final paragraph, as the aesthetic to which the Structural filmmakers return, since it allows "a new imagery" to arise "from the dictates of the form."[71] Despite his protestations, Frampton would seem to be in partial agreement with Sitney. But the critic's claim that the viewer's "perception of the film [*Zorns Lemma*] is a partici-pation in the discovery of the ordering," a claim with which the filmmaker would also likely find himself in accord, is not accompanied by any reference to Kenner's ideas (such as his notion that Pound's *Cantos* are comedies of discovery). Given

69.   MacDonald, "Hollis Frampton," *Critical Cinema*, p. 63.
70.   Frampton, "Digressions on the Photographic Agony," *Circles of Confusion*, p. 185.
71.   P. Adams Sitney, *Visionary Film*, p. 397.

the depth of his debt to Kenner's version of modernism, Frampton appears to be criticizing Sitney for attaching a label to a contemporary development too readily, before providing a more extensive genealogy of the ideas, attitudes, and beliefs of the filmmakers he analyzes in his book. In Frampton's reading, Bloom's version of the Romantic visionaries casts a long shadow over *Visionary Film*, obscuring a modern conceptual history of epistemological inquiry.

Thus, the crucial task for the revisionist is a matter of constructing different points of connection. Frampton's own words can take us only so far. While his writings and interviews do much to illuminate obscured lines of development, his highly playful approach, which embraces wit and irony, as well as indirect allusion and intertextual intricacy, seems designed to address an impossibly learned reader. This study comprises one contemporary reply to the practitioner's call for a continuum of critical response, and it is submitted in anticipation of a return to serious scholarship on his work.

Hollis Frampton filming sections of Magellan *at U.S. Steel Company, Pittsburgh, 1974. Photo: Mike Chikiris. Courtesy Anthology Film Archives.*

Hidden Noise: Strategies of Sound Montage in the Films of Hollis Frampton*

MELISSA RAGONA

The seductive equation made between silence and the sublime in avant-garde art practices reaches back as far as Ferruccio Busoni's *Sketch of a New Esthetic of Music* (1911), in which the Italian composer pointed to the moment of holds and rests in music as constituting the most profound and "essential nature of art." In a sense, silence for the historical avant-garde was something that could reveal that which was hidden or—to borrow from Heidegger—yet to be unconcealed. In keeping with this model, Marcel Duchamp's "assisted ready-made" *With Hidden Noise* (1916)—a ball of twine, bolted between two metal plates, containing an unknown object added by Walter Arensberg—was one of the first turns toward what Douglas Kahn has called the shift from the site of "utterance to that of audition."[1] This shift would mark language's entrance into Conceptual art practices.

By concealing both the sound source and the preparatory notes that culminated in a particular kind of "noise," Duchamp's enigmatic sculpture already pointed to crucial questions—of "signature," "composition," and "performance"—that informed the historical avant-garde's turning away from purely object-based works toward eventlike forms. In the postwar era, John Cage's *4'33"* (1952) made "hidden" silence the explicit content of the work. Cage's replacement of pitch with duration as a structuring principle shifted the emphasis from musical composition onto sound space. Silence was no longer a "rest" or "pause" or "gap" but unintentional sound, all that entered the space of duration.[2]

*   This essay is drawn from a larger, forthcoming book project on experimental film sound, *From Radio-Ear to Granular Voice: The Sound of Experimental Film*. The School of Art and the Center for the Arts in Society at Carnegie Mellon University gave research support and a critical forum in which to discuss some of the ideas presented here; my thanks to Liz Kotz, Marie Lovrod, Ernest Schimmerling, Tony Conrad, Abigail Child, and Malcolm Turvey for their readings and comments. Elizabeth Thomas, Assistant Curator of Contemporary Art, Bill Judson, former Curator of Film and Video at the Carnegie Museum in Pittsburgh, MM Serra at the Film-Makers' Cooperative in New York, and Robert Haller at Anthology Film Archives provided me with invaluable access to Frampton's films, files, and photographs.
1.   Douglas Kahn, *Noise Water Meat: A History of Sound in the Arts* (Cambridge, Mass.: MIT Press, 1999), p. 158. For a reading of event-based work with language that emerges in the wake of Duchamp and Cage, see Liz Kotz, "Post-Cagean Aesthetics and the 'Event' Score," *October* 95 (Spring 2001), pp. 55–90.
2.   F. T. Marinetti's *I Silenzi Parlano fra di Loro* (Silences Speak Among Themselves) of the early 1930s arguably set a precedent for Cage's work in its focus on silence as a kind of presence—an epistemological category as important, if not more profound, than sound.

In the world of avant-garde film, however, this radical Cagean silence often became all too easily assimilated into a more conventionally modernist poetics of silence that stressed the phenomenal purity of visual experience over the radical contingency of chance interpenetrations and juxtapositions. For example, for filmmakers such as Stan Brakhage and Andrew Noren, film sound tends to disrupt or taint a purely visual focus or image-based knowledge system.[3] In revisiting the work of Hollis Frampton—especially his sound films *Surface Tension* (1968), *Zorns Lemma* (1970), *Critical Mass* (1971), and *Mindfall* (1977–80)—we are brought back to a moment in avant-garde film history in which the status of the sound film was in question, both in terms of its political valence and its epistemological quest. In fact, Frampton's early (pre-1968) work is primarily silent, as he initially allied himself with the avant-garde position that the "talkies ossified cinema into a standard saleable product."[4] Other antirealist critiques argued that sync sound returned "the film image to the status of an object in nature."[5] For Frampton at this time, to renovate vision outside the straitjacket of Hollywood filmmaking and realist conventions of sync sound required purging film of both sound and language as bearers of overdetermined meaning and syntactic weight.

Yet, by the time he starts work on *Surface Tension*, Frampton is beginning to investigate sound precisely as a means of divesting film of its syntactical burden. Drawing from Sergei Eisenstein's concept of "vertical montage," which proposes that sound can offer a crucial "contrapuntal" or "overtonal" relation to visual montage, Frampton's cinema generates a series of procedures that systematically confound the relations between image and sound, as well as between sound and language. By breaking with a purist impulse to cleanse the filmic image of the corrupting influences of sound and language, Frampton would reinvent film sound not as a tool for a naturalized filmic realism or straightforward narration, but instead as a crucial vehicle for disrupting what he termed the "horizontal axis" of conventional film narrative. Rather than reinforcing the linear, syntactic, meaning-producing properties of narrative film, sound—and indeed, verbal language itself, divested from its subordinate position as sync-sound dialogue and explanatory

3.   Annette Michelson describes this moment: "For the history of independently made film of the postwar period is that of a transvaluation of values through which an enforced reversion to an artisanal mode of production (that of the silent, 16mm format) enables the conversion of necessity to virtue"; see her "Frampton's Sieve," *October* 32 (Spring 1985), p. 153. Brakhage's approach to sound (and silence) is far too complex and varied to be accounted for here. Though the major part of his film and theoretical work was indeed concerned with what the "eye" could perceive, he nonetheless thought deeply about sound through his relation to modernist music, paying close attention to works of Olivier Messiaen, Pierre Boulez, Henri Pousseur, and Karlheinz Stockhausen, among others. In "Film and Music" (1966), Brakhage recounts that he "studied informally with Cage and Varese" in order to find a "new relationship between image and sound" and a "new dimension for the sound track." In *Essential Brakhage* (Kingston, N.Y.: McPherson and Co., 2001), p. 78.
4.   "Hollis Frampton: An Interview by Michael Snow," in *New Forms in Film*, ed. Annette Michelson (Montreux: Dorbax, 1974), p. 61.
5.   Fred Camper, "Sound and Silence in Narrative and Nonnarrative Cinema," in Elizabeth Weis and John Belton, eds., *Film Sound: Theory and Practice* (New York: Columbia University Press, 1985), p. 371.

caption—would give Frampton entirely new models for investigating film structure and montage. In order to rethink the possibilities for vertical montage in the postwar era, Frampton turned to the permutational and operational forms used in experimental music, Minimalist sculpture, and set theory. These heterogeneous models allowed Frampton to envision a filmmaking practice that could resolve or at least complicate the oppositions set up between narrative and nonnarrative filmmaking, synchronous and asynchronous sound, and, ultimately, silent versus sound films.

To understand Frampton's unorthodox use of sound, which perhaps owes more to 1920s Soviet experiments in sound montage than to the 1950s poetics of silence propagated by the critical literature surrounding Brakhage, we need to take seriously Frampton's use of paradoxical systems, drawn from his idiosyncratic reading of that branch of mathematics known as set theory.[6] While Frampton's gnomic pronouncements about systems theory, topos theory, and a host of other mathematical and scientific discourses risk becoming unintelligible (or marginalized) to a generation of film theorists raised on semiotic and psychoanalytic models, a series of quasi-scientific and quantitative models nonetheless allowed him to open up operations of meaning-production beyond what he saw as more normative, "closed" systems like semiotics.

One of the most compelling aspects that set theory offers film theory is that it provides a mode of analysis that uses its own object to study itself: "set theory is not a branch of mathematics but the very root of mathematics from which all branches of mathematics rise."[7] For Frampton, set theory permits the abstract representation of film's capacity to catalog intersecting planes of perception in infinite combinations, allowing him to perceive and articulate the expansive range of film in a way that semiotics could not. Of course, the Saussurean model of semiotics that Frampton had encountered in film criticism of the 1970s also included a metalinguistic function that reflected upon its own language and processes. However, set theory spoke more directly to his ideas about montage, since its principles describe unbounded ways of dividing and ordering materials. In contrast, the communicative paradigm formalized by Roman Jakobson (drawn from the information theory of Claude E. Shannon) proposed a kind of "verbal loop" or circuit that depended on six components in any speech event: sender, receiver, message, code, contact, and context.[8] This relatively "closed" system presented communication as its ultimate object,

6.   In their readings of Frampton's project in the 1985 *October* special issue on his work, Allen S. Weiss and Annette Michelson come closest to recognizing the importance of his explorations in set theory for his filmmaking practices. In her essay "Frampton's Sieve," Michelson points to the relationship between Frampton's interest in mathematics and comparative grammar, and the retrograde inversions employed by Arnold Schoenberg and Anton Webern. In her reading of *Critical Mass* (1971), Michelson puts her finger on the pulse of Frampton's systemic method, especially when she implies that "gesture and sound" seem to be what reinforce the semantic engine of much of his work during 1968–73—the critical period of *Palindrome* (1969), *Surface Tension, Zorns Lemma*, and the *Hapax Legomena* series (1971–72). Michelson, pp. 160–62.

7.   Robert L. Vaught, *Set Theory: An Introduction* (New York: Springer-Verlag, 2001), p. 1.

8.   See Roman Jakobson, "Linguistics and Poetics" (1958), in *Language and Literature* (Cambridge, Mass.: Harvard University Press, 1987), pp. 62–94.

whereas set theory offered a world free of intended speech, a world that could account for infinite sets of relations unhinged from a unidirectional matrix.

While Frampton—like his contemporaries Tony Conrad, Paul Sharits, Michael Snow, and Joyce Wieland—was interested in film as a form that could expand as well as reflect consciousness, one of the main thrusts of his work was to pose an epistemology unique to film. In "Notes on Composing in Film" (1975), he calls for this: "We must invent a terminology, and a descriptive mode, appropriate to our object: a unique sign that shall have as its referent the creative assumptions proper to film and to film alone."[9] While he continues to use the language of semiotics as a way of describing his epistemological approach to film, he is also struggling with its limitations: "The compound sign and referent is, of course, a closed system; and all closed systems, as we know, tend to break down and to generate discrepancies and contradictions at their highest levels."[10]

My contention here is that Frampton uses elements of conceptual mathematics in order to open up what he believed was the "closed system" that film semiotics had begun to develop in the late 1960s. Borrowing its title and form from aspects of set theory, *Zorns Lemma* of course became the flagship example of Frampton's use of mathematical procedures in film. However, the underlying principles of this approach to filmic materials structure all of his post-1968 production. Even before beginning work on *Zorns Lemma*, Frampton was thinking of set theory in relation to film, especially in reference to his growing *Magellan* project. In a 1964 letter to his friend Reno Odlin, Frampton explains in somewhat hermetic terms:

> *Zorns Lemma* states that within every partially ordered set there is a maximal fully ordered set. The excernment of the fully ordered set constitutes a cut. Where there are several possible cuts, the set of all cuts constitutes the maximal ordered set. All cuts, the operations whereby they are made, the elements that constitute each of them, the intelligible species of their distinctness one from another, AND the residue of totally unordered elements left outside defined and applied, and all elements identified, the field is not closed.[11]

This passage comes out of a rich exchange from 1958 to 1968 between Frampton and Odlin about what would become *Clouds of Magellan*; the passage begins to suggest some of the profound discoveries or "openings" set theory made possible for film, allowing Frampton to isolate, identify, and exploit film's medium-specific systems, as well as locate the excess of film's own systemic behavior. Frampton's unorthodox reading of set theory may have been inspired by his discussions with Carl Andre. In one of the published dialogues between Frampton and Andre (1962–63), "On the Movies and Consecutive Matters," Frampton

9.   Hollis Frampton, "Notes on Composing in Film," in *Circles of Confusion: Film, Photography, Video, Texts 1968–1980* (Rochester, N.Y.: Visual Studies Workshop Press, 1983), p. 123.
10.   Ibid.
11.   Reno Odlin, "Letters from Framp 1958–1968," *October* 32 (Spring 1985), p. 47.

implies that Andre first introduced him to thinking about the "cut" in film in terms of Dedekind's "cut," a mathematical theorem that characterizes real numbers as "the system of cuts of rational numbers."[12]

> *Frampton:* It seems to me it is a kind of cut, in a sense you have used recently.

> *Andre:* Ah, Dedekind. A number is represented as the partition of a line segment. "N" can then be the highest value to the left of the cut or the lowest value to the right of it. An irrational number may even be assigned to the cut itself, which is empty, in the sense that the cut a pair of scissors makes across a piece of paper is empty, but present and evident. By extension one might say that any single perception is a cut across the spectrum of stimuli available to us. The cut itself then is not perceived; it is an operation, not a quantity.[13]

This simple maxim fired Frampton's imagination, especially in terms of his interest in analyzing the "cut" in film as the "cut" in the order of film. For Frampton, Dedekind's construction of real numbers in terms of cuts in the rationals enabled him to think of film editing as a method of passage from discrete to continuous time. Via Andre's radical understanding of sculpture as a kind of cut in space ("A thing is a hole in a thing it is not"), Frampton was able to bring this sense of the cut as a perceptual operation to a complex rethinking of filmic montage. In Frampton's project, words, images, and sound would all be subjected to ordering schemas drawn from an array of conceptual mathematical systems; yet rather than repressing the referential dimension of these materials, Frampton's antilinear, interpenetrating montage would instead propose to use film to record, catalog, and reorder the perceptual world.

Surface Tensions: Membership, Translation, Duration

Made during Frampton's exploration of the possible relationships between set theory and Structural film, *Surface Tension* acts, I will argue, as an early blueprint for his works that explore the formal ordering of film through what he understood as its "membership attributes." During this period, Frampton's experiments in sound, voice, and text helped him isolate and identify subsets of this "membership" by using the complex ordering properties of language as an analogue and counter-system to film's metered form.[14]

12.   Shaughan Lavine, *Understanding the Infinite* (Cambridge, Mass.: Harvard University Press, 1994), pp. 10–11.
13.   *Carl Andre, Hollis Frampton: 12 Dialogues 1962–1963*, ed. Benjamin H. D. Buchloh (Halifax: Nova Scotia College of Art and Design, 1981), p. 55.
14.   Peter Kubelka, beginning in 1956 when he began work on *Adebar*, developed what he called the metric film, whereby "every part of the film is precisely measured and set into relation to the film as a

Surface Tension—a title, like *Zorns Lemma*, that refers to a formal process—is literally the cohesive forces between liquid molecules that form a "film," which, in turn, make it difficult to move an object through a surface. *Surface Tension* evidences Frampton's fascination with Duchamp's and Joseph Cornell's boxes: the film is structured as a triptych, containing three discrete segments; the final sequence is literally a box, a fish tank submerged in ocean water. Each section serves as a kind of "box," collecting a (silent) image track, an unseen sound, a text, and a counting device. Not only does the viewer struggle to establish correlations and relations among these disjunctive tracks, but, in Frampton's boxlike structure, these assembled materials somehow come to substitute for one another—as if image, sound, language, and number could comprise open systems of interchangeable sets. Most notably, by repeatedly measuring the duration of human speech against a quantitative counting device, *Surface Tension* insistently attempts both to correlate and unravel the incommensurable infrastructures of language and mathematics.

The first sequence juxtaposes a moving body with a grid of an electrical clock face—a knowing nod to Eadweard Muybridge's early photographic documentations of human and animal movement measured against gridlike backdrops.[15] An actor, appearing to talk very expressively (we do not hear his words), seems to mimic the changing second-hand numbers on the clock as they fly past him on the left. In a sense, the actor is timing his own performance—he adjusts the clock at the end of each sequence. His muted speech runs alongside the looping numbers, effectively turning his speech into a counting system. Similar to Paul Sharits's *Word Movie/ Fluxfilm 29* (1966), in which letters, speeding by in vertical streams, form words in slot machine-like chance combinations, *Surface Tension* here equates the temporality of "talk" with the quantitative measure of clocked time.

Frampton, however, pushes a mathematical reading of film even further than Sharits or Tony Conrad.[16] In a sense, he performs rather than represents film as a mathematical operation. Already in *Surface Tension*, Frampton was experimenting with Zorn's Lemma as a way of thinking about film editing/ordering: every set can be well-ordered, and within each partial set there exists a maximally ordered set. The entire opening section consists of five sets of timed speech acts; two are eleven minutes, two are nine minutes in duration, and the fifth begins at twenty-three

---

whole, and that every part of the film communicates with all the other parts." Thomas Korchil: http://www.kortfilmfestivalen.no/arkiv/english/articles/99_PeterKub.html.

15.   Frampton's interest in Muybridge was spurred by his own fascination with photography as a proto-cinematic language. Muybridge's interest in mapping sequential movement through photographic time reflected Frampton's own aesthetic inquiries from his black-and-white photography series *Word Pictures* (1962–63) to their transposition into "moving pictures" in *Zorns Lemma*; see Christopher Phillips, "Word Pictures: Frampton and Photography," *October* 32 (Spring 1985), p. 65. Frampton, with Marion Faller, also spoofed Muybridge's *Motion Studies* in his *Sixteen Studies from Vegetable Locomotion* (1975), replacing humans and animals with vegetables.

16.   Tony Conrad studied mathematics at Harvard and was a colleague of Frampton and Paul Sharits in Media Studies at SUNY Buffalo during the '70s and early '80s. In Conrad's video, *Cycles of 3's and 7's* (1976), harmonic intervals that would ordinarily be played by musical instruments are represented through the computation of their arithmetic relationships or frequency ratios on a calculator.

minutes and eleven seconds. These five "sets" of timed sequences—all partial sets of incomplete speech acts—become fully ordered sets as they are divided into the logic of their "cuts" according to an underlying numerical schema.

In Frampton's search for an "open system" of selection and combination in and beyond language, sound becomes crucial. For example, the persistent ringing of the telephone in *Surface Tension*—beginning with black leader and continuing throughout the first segment of the film—emphasizes the actor's muted speech. This intrusive nagging ring reminds the viewer that the speech is neither intelligible or accessible: we only hear the ringing phone. Nor is the actor himself cognizant of the sound around him: he never picks up. Nevertheless, we are lulled into the correlation between counting (numbers) and reading (gestures). The repetition of the ring (thirty-seven times) also reiterates the stopping and starting of each sequence—its recurrence, insistence, and eventual end as the film fades to black.

The rest of the film mirrors this structure of repeating sets and, at the same time, implicitly reflects on the metalanguage of "membership" through systems of translation and, as Frampton stressed in his "Notes on Composing in Film," mistranslation or misreading. A voice-over in German by Kasper König describes an unseen film in three parts. The first section recounts the story of a woman from Philadelphia who is invited to go to the south of France for the weekend. König comments on the scene as if recounting his viewing of it on film: "What's so strange is that the color of this first section is the color of an American cigarette advertisement. And I don't think this could have been achieved without the help of professional film/lighting technicians." He continues by describing two other sections of this unseen film: a twelve-minute black-and-white documentary, and a twenty-minute-long sequence shot on water that has a brownish sheen like the color of "chocolate sauce."

The entire voice-over occurs over a relentless montage of single-frame shots of city streets. This montage gives the section a breathless speed, a velocity that is heightened in contrast to the halting, slow-paced rhythm of the German voice-over. König's commentary is cut off by a lengthy, piercingly loud beep that segues us into the "real" third section of *Surface Tension*. The untranslated German speech is used here as another way of staging the "open systems" of interchangeable sets. The stories told in German act as a MacGuffin: the real tension exists between the single-framed frenetic images of an American city and the languidly paced *voice* unfolding against them. Image bytes are measured against sound bytes, and the axiomatic structures of translation and conversion are referred to, but not enacted.

The flashing single-word texts that comprise the third section of *Surface Tension* make it appear as though translation is occurring, but instead the system is cut again: individual words stand in for a missing narrative, some flashing like a marquee over a macabre seascape in which a trapped, mocking goldfish floats midscreen. The triptych structure is again emphasized, as an intertitle announces "Part 1: 20 minutes; Part 2: 5 minutes; Part 3: 5 minutes"—repeating the metastructure of *Surface Tension* through the faux dimensions of a film within a film. Through this series of mismatched sets, *Surface Tension* inaugurates the paradigm for Frampton's experiments in sound-image configurations. Its puzzle-like structure plays with Duchampian hidden noise: we never see the phone that rings, the German man whose voice we hear, or the obscure industrial machine that buzzes throughout the final section. The film's three "boxed sets" of image, language, sound, and number give the viewer a selection of potentially mutually exclusive nonempty sets, but in each we are given markers of what Frampton terms "a characteristic sensible shape in space and time."[17]

The Perceptual Events of Ordered and Open Systems

Enclosed is my standard blah. It's not quite up-to-date. You can add, prestigiously, that *Zorns Lemma* was the first really hardnosed badassed feature to be shown in the "regular" screenings in the New York Film Festival. I mean in Philharmonic Hall, not the Alice Tully Freak show. (THAT was funny as hell. I'll tell you all about it in January.) Also, three bits of P. Adams's. The two unpublished are ad copy from the forthcoming new Coop catalog. There are three more articles due out momentarily whatever that means, & Im starting to resent *Zorns Lemma* SLIGHTLY, telling people that I have in fact made 14 other films etcetera.

—Hollis Frampton, letter to Sally Dixon, 1970[18]

Whereas *Surface Noise* plays with the idea of sets as boxes, *Zorns Lemma* synthesizes two closely related concepts from set theory: the principle of the Axiom of Choice and, as the title suggests, Zorn's Lemma.[19] For Frampton, the two most important ideas that stem from these mathematical assertions include: "partial ordering" (as in the Zorn Lemma) and "well ordering" (a consequence of the Axiom of Choice).[20] In Frampton's cinematic version of the Zorn Lemma, he loosely reproduces the operations of partial ordering through his use of the alphabet. The twenty-six letters provide a "maximal chain" or partial ordering of the larger structure of the film. In mathematics, a maximal chain is partially ordered through some kind of rule, and this rule, in turn, establishes a particular transitive relation between set members, i.e., if $x < y$ and $y < z$, then $x < z$. Frampton plays with this transitivity when he substitutes certain letters and often pairs of letters with images of everyday human activities: a woman talking, someone washing her hands, a child swinging, a

17.   Frampton, "A Pentagram for Conjuring the Narrative," *Circles of Confusion*, p. 62.
18.   Letter to Sally Dixon, curator of Film and Video at the Carnegie Museum, October 26, 1970. Frampton files at Carnegie Museum, Pittsburgh.
19.   The formal statement of the Zorn Lemma in mathematics is: "Let P be a partial ordering. Suppose that whenever C is a chain of P, there exists an upper bound for C in P. Then P has a maximal element." The proof of the Zorn Lemma uses Axiom of Choice. There is also a proof of the Axiom of Choice that uses the Zorn Lemma. Mathematicians often see Zorn's Lemma, the Axiom of Choice, as well as Kuratowski's Lemma (which Frampton actually quotes as Zorn's Lemma) as equivalent.
20.   Zorn's Lemma is most easily understood through the Axiom of Choice, which states: "Let C be a collection of nonempty sets. Then we can choose a member from each set in that collection. In other

Hollis Frampton. Zorns Lemma. *1970.*
Bottom photo: Biff Henrich.
Courtesy Anthology Film Archives.

man dribbling a basketball, hands peeling an orange, someone driving a car. By establishing "limits" within the alphabet through substitution—i.e., *E* is replaced by a woman talking (in double exposure), *G* is substituted with someone washing her hands, *H* is taken over by an image of an anonymous man walking down a Manhattan street—Frampton establishes a "higher order substitution," wherein an image represents a letter, setting both its upper limits (in terms of a partial ordering), as well as revealing the arbitrary relations implied in alphabetic signification. Yet the effect of the substitutions is ultimately to emphasize the structural incompatibility of letters and numbers. The intelligibility of language presupposes a prior cut, just as the arbitrary phoneme cuts into the quantitative image continuum of the film.

While *Zorns Lemma* began with a stilted read of the nineteenth-century Massachusetts Bay State Primer, here Frampton pokes fun at such intended correlations of sound, order, and sense. Narrative, Frampton implies, has been hoodwinked by a deadly, predictable, finite order. The randomized image sequences suggest parallel problems in the way we think about ordering in mathematics and in language. The cardinal numbers with which we count (one, two, three) and the ordinal numbers through which we order events (first, second, third) help us in the way a good, Aristotelian narrative does: they point to location, position, and order of events. They offer a palatable approach to the seeming finite world: a beginning, a middle, an end. In contrast to narrative or even Eisenstein's "metric" montage, set theory offered Frampton a way to think about infinite sets in a "well-ordered" but nonsequential way.[21] Exposing the pitfalls of measuring cinematic time through finite measures (narrative, number of frames per second), Frampton was able to point to the vertical structures of film montage through both the desecration of the ordinal power of the alphabet as well as to his reflexive play with the "consecutive" frames of film.

Mathematics and Language

Writing—the visual cue of words themselves on the screen—became a central analogue for the "finite series of shots," which, like their counterpart in narrative, exist in "real time."[22] In conversation with Frampton in the early 1970s, Brakhage proposed: "For any finite series of shots ['film'] whatsoever there exists in real time a rational narrative, such that every term in the series, together with its position, duration, partition and reference, shall be perfectly and entirely accounted for."[23] Frampton then transposes Brakhage's "axiomatic theorem for narrative" into a series of mathematical equations:

P = 30 can also mean:
$$P = \frac{P}{3} + \frac{P}{5} + \frac{P}{6} + \frac{P}{10} + 6 \quad [24]$$

By stripping language of its syntactical meaning and position through the use of numbers (and their membership sets), Frampton achieves a measured indifference to linguistic affect and, in turn, dramatic effect. P = 30 can be expanded, as any one narrative can, into any number of divisible representations (such as above). Duchamp had described a similar process in his marginal notes, "algebraic comparisons," for *The Green Box* (1912), in which the ratio *a/b* stands in for the narrative history describing the reception/rejection of his works: *a* representing the work(s), *b* standing in for its (or their) exhibition possibilities/conditions.[25] Duchamp was interested in the notion of ratio to investigate the extended durations

---

words, there exists a function f defined on C with the property that, for each set S in the collection, f(S) is a member of S." Let me illustrate the Axiom of Choice with a simple but vivid example: suppose that on the floor in front of you are some buckets. Somehow you know that each of the buckets has at least one object inside it. You could then order it: you could go through and pick one object out of each bucket. (This would constitute a set.) This is easy: the choices are finite. However, the Axiom of Choice says that when there are an infinite number of buckets—a seemingly overwhelming and impossible task—there is still a way to choose (a way to order sets).

21.   In "A Dialectic Approach to Film Form," in *Film Form: Essays in Film Theory* (Harvest Books: 1969), Eisenstein defines metric montage as a technique of film editing in which shots are joined together according to their length, in a formula/scheme corresponding to a measure of music. Eisenstein's *October* (1927) is a classic example of the use of metric montage.

22.   Frampton, "A Pentagram for Conjuring the Narrative," *Circles of Confusion*, p. 63.

23.   Ibid.

24.   Ibid.

25.   Marcel Duchamp, "*The Green Box*" [marginal notes, 1912], in *The Writings of Marcel Duchamp*, ed.

Frampton. Zorns Lemma. *1970. Clockwise from upper left: For the letter* X; *for the letter* Y; *for the letter* Q; *for the letter* Z. *Courtesy Anthology Film Archives.*

of reception and display. By using the alphabet as a colossal set, Frampton offers a similar idea of ratio by juxtaposing "found word sets" with two other particular image sets: elemental images, implying recurring structures from nature (fire, water, earth) ,and routine images, pointing to repetitive everyday durational activities (talking, walking, eating).

The different kinds of filmed durations represented here emerge from Frampton's keen awareness of the relationships between language and iconicity and, ultimately, their embodied forms (talking, listening, reading, writing). The kind of time that counting or listing represents (what Allen Weiss calls the "enumerative") is quite different from the kind of time the referentiality of language represents. Filmic time that can both use and disrupt such durational structures functions, Frampton argues, more algebraically like a "polyhedron": "The existence

Michel Sanouillet and Elmer Peterson (New York: Da Capo Press, Inc., 1973), p. 28. In *Kant After Duchamp* (Cambridge, Mass.: MIT Press: 1999), Thierry de Duve elaborates upon this ratio in terms of its illustration of the exhibition histories connected to Duchamp's *Nude Descending a Staircase* and *Fountain* (pp. 131–43).

of the whole body [suspended, weightless, in a void, with each of its vertices touching . . . the surface of an iridescent imaginary sphere] is utterly dependent upon the integrity of all its facets: every facet represents a story."[26] Thus, Frampton's method of traversing the enumerative with embodied activities creates a chordlike effect: vertical and horizontal axes of language and image intersect and begin to "play" each other in dissonant but contiguous ways. This is a kind of vertical image montage that Frampton will continue to experiment with and fully utilize in his sound work by the time he begins *Mindfall* (Part I of *Magellan*).

In its desire to express an overtonality that is more about temporal simultaneity than language play, *Zorns Lemma* is not unlike Sharits's *S:TREAM:S:S:ECTION:S:ECTION:S:S:ECTIONED* (1968–71). As Sharits would say about *S:TREAM*, the relationship in "simultaneous occurrence and in overlapping structural (or waveform) congruencies" occurs "not in the work but in perception itself"—in an almost indiscernible, continuous passage of both auditory and visual events.[27] Both films register a series of perceptual events, or as Frampton had imagined for *Magellan*, "an inventory of modes of perception and [the] classification that's involved."[28]

Paradoxically, the veritable flood of words that take over Frampton's work during this period (reaching its apex in the filmed script for *Poetic Justice* [1972]) represents Frampton's impulse to drain both the image and speech of their affective, prescriptive relationships to representation. Frampton's "open allusion" to alphabetization in *Zorns Lemma* stresses his use of letters as a system of random ordering, so that he could "avoid imposing [his] own taste and making them into little puns."[29] Writing, and the "lifting" of found words off signs, billboards, and graffiti (in *Zorns Lemma*) unhinge words from their subordinate position as synchronous accompaniment to image, while disrupting their static position as signs of articulated speech.

Instead of scratching directly on the surface of the film as Sharits does in *S:TREAM*, Frampton uses the momentum of editing, producing a series of interference patterns that produce a vertical structure on the horizontal sequencing of the alphabet. However, this systematic interruption is not necessarily about disruption, but instead sharpens the focus on perception as a nonlinear process. In this way, *Zorns Lemma* was a training ground for *Magellan*, in which "the parts of the whole thing, instead of following one another linearly, are constantly interpenetrating."[30]

26.   Frampton, "A Pentagram for Conjuring the Narrative," *Circles of Confusion*, p. 67.
27.   Paul Sharits, "—UR(i)N(ul)LS: TREAM: S: S: ECTION: S: ECTION: S: S: ECTIONED (A)(lysis)JO: 1968–70," *Film Culture* 65–66 (1978), p. 16.
28.   Frampton in Mitch Tuchman, "Frampton at the Gates" [interview], *Film Comment* 13, no. 5 (1977), p. 58.
29.   Frampton in Peter Gidal, "Interview with Hollis Frampton" [1972], *October* 32 (Spring 1985), p. 94. In 1970, the same year as Frampton's *Zorns Lemma*, Carl Andre used an alphabetical ordering of chemical symbols: Al, Cu, Fe, Mg, Pb, and Zn for his floor installation of *37 Pieces of Work* (Guggenheim Museum), which consisted of an array of foot-square plates of aluminum, copper, steel, magnesium, lead, and zinc. "Each metal was used alone to constitute one 36 unit square, then alternated checkerboard fashion, with each of the other metals, thus demonstrating the possible permutations." David Bourdon, *Carl Andre Sculpture 1959–77* (New York: Jaap Rietman Inc., 1978), p. 32.
30.   Frampton in Tuchman, "Frampton at the Gates," p. 58.

A kind of ludic volley between images is echoed in the random play between words. Similar to other artists during this period, like Vito Acconci, Dan Graham, and Bruce Nauman, Frampton uses the performativity of writing, speech, and gesture in what Benjamin H. D. Buchloh elsewhere describes as "total opposition to traditional definitions of theatricality."[31] Thus, Frampton rethinks the phenomenological project in terms of a theatrical position that dissolves conventions of dramatic narrative by reducing speech to noise and plot to structural repetition as he does in *Critical Mass*. At the end of *Zorns Lemma*, Frampton employs the voices of six women reading a text by medieval theologian Robert Grosseteste punctuated, or made rhythmic, by the constant click of a metronome in one-second takes. Here the mathematical ordering principle turns performance into operation without losing the performativity of its parts. The numerical performs the linguistic and the imagistic quietly, sparingly, and not unironically: "When the number one of form and the number two of matter and the number three of composition and the number four of entirety are added together, they make up the number ten which is the full number of the universe."[32] The mechanical, almost computer-generated sounding voices that accompany two figures walking out toward the snowy horizon signal a strangely re-embodied, mathematical analysis of the film's construction.

While Frampton is building a case for the metahistory of film as a catalog of phenomenological, sensory perceptions, "the total historical function of film, not as an art medium, but as this great kind of time capsule," he is also occupied with its ability to perform language beyond what he describes as the "puritanical, authority-ridden, death-saturated" ideologies of American Midwestern culture, another kind of linguistic metahistory of which he and his contemporaries were products.[33]

Streams of Utterance in Critical Mass

Writing, for Frampton, is "a kind of talking."[34] In *Critical Mass*, he uses audio design to write his sound track in a circuitous form so that sound and film function

31.   Benjamin H. D. Buchloh, "James Coleman's Archeology of Spectacle," in his *Neo-Avantgarde and Culture Industry: Essays on European and American Art from 1955 to 1975* (Cambridge, Mass.: MIT Press, 2000), p. 153.

32.   Text loosely adapted from Robert Grosseteste's *On Light or the Ingression of Forms* (thirteenth-century manuscript) by Frampton for *Zorns Lemma*. In "Frampton's Lemma, Zorn's Dilemma," Allen S. Weiss focuses on Grosseteste's "theology, ontology, and cosmology of light," but Grosseteste was also a mathematician, writing on geometry and optics as well as astronomy. Brakhage, however, was more interested in Grosseteste's focus on light than Frampton. At the 1974 Canegie Institute premiere of *Text of Light*, he paraphrased Grosseteste's *On Light or the Ingression of Forms*: "All that sense can comprehend, is Light: because it partakes of that which it is." Arthur Cantrill, "The Text of Light," *Cantrills Filmnotes* 21/22 (April 1975), pp. 32–53.

33.   Gidal, "Interview with Hollis Frampton," p. 98.

34.   Ibid., p. 99.

in "symmetrical orbit around one another."[35] While many of his other works pay homage to early cinema or proto-cinematic phenomena, *Critical Mass* serves as Frampton's most sustained critique of the advent of the Hollywood "talkie": "It was not simply sound, then, that threatened to destroy all the 'present formal achievements' of montage, but the dubious gift of speech, the Prime Instance of language, the linear decoding of the terrain of thought into a stream of utterance."[36]

Avant-garde directors from Eisenstein to Brakhage, Frampton argues, manifest a propensity for logophobia: the word threatened to sully the ideal form of the image. Embracing the "corrupting" capacities of language, Frampton uses the spoken word in *Critical Mass* as he did the written script in *Poetic Justice*: it functions as a virus, transmutating, morphing, paralleling, and infiltrating the graphic rhythms and dimensions of the image. As Michelson notes, "Frampton saw his task as the devising of a rigorous scheme for the organization of the material such that it would still 'rhyme' in various ways with the enacted incidents."[37] Though Frampton is influenced by Eisenstein's dictum that sound should be in "distinct nonsynchronization" with images, he is also critical of Eisenstein's fear that language would somehow corrupt the image, or as Eisenstein charged, "retard its tempo."[38]

According to Frampton, the only kinds of systems that would deter language's inertia-ridden influence on the moving image would have to be "a universal natural language," or a "perfect machine."[39] The former he saw in mathematics or science, the latter in the apparatus of film. *Critical Mass* addresses the problem of language in terms of its potential to stagnate the cinematic soundtrack into what he derides as an "information channel" for montaged images.[40]

By staggering successive shots of male and female speakers so that they collide (one hitting right before the other has finished), Frampton achieves through analog editing techniques what would come to be known as digital delay. The overlapping words cause a dislocation between the action and the sound of speaking. As in the opening of *Zorns Lemma*, Frampton begins *Critical Mass* in black with voice-over, but a tripping, doubling effect is already in action:

> just fine, just fine/where the hell were you?/I was just away/away where?/away where?/you know, ha/you know, ha.

While in the first section of the film, relationships between the speaking subjects and language remain somewhat intact, by the end of the film gendered as well as syntactical arrangements of speaking dissolve: the female speaker's voice seems to come from the male speaker (and vice versa) and often, especially during the sections where the image goes to black, their voices merge into a glossolalia of phonemic utterances.

35.   Hollis Frampton, "Film in the House of the Word" [1981], *Circles of Confusion*, p. 85.
36.   Ibid., p. 82.
37.   Michelson, "Frampton's Sieve," p. 163.
38.   Frampton, "Film in the House of the Word," p. 84.
39.   Ibid.
40.   Ibid., p. 85.

Frampton. Critical Mass. *1971. Courtesy Anthology Film Archives.*

Thus the enacted "script" in *Critical Mass* (like the written script in *Poetic Justice*) acts as an extension of the recording device of film: its narrative meaning has universal significance, a discursiveness that functions regardless of its distinctive detail or context. Brakhage confirms this, when he notes that *Critical Mass* "is quite universal, it deals with all quarrels (those between men and women, or men and men, or women and women, or children, or war)."[41] This kind of script acts, for Frampton, almost like an optical sound track, its visual cues marking variations in, rather than illustrations of, sound.

Recording Machines: Writing, Photography, Film

The dialectical relationships between writing and image initiated in *Zorns Lemma* (which was first imagined as a photographic project) are taken up even more explicitly in *Nostalgia* (1971) and *Poetic Justice*.[42] The possible relations between the recording devices of photography, film, and writing were already being theorized by Frampton in terms of image-sound relations in 1964 when he wrote to Odlin about his thoughts for *Clouds of Magellan*:

41.   Stan Brakhage, *Film-Makers' Cooperative Catalogue No. 7* (New York: Film-Makers' Cooperative, 1989), p. 171.
42.   As Phillips notes, "His series of black-and-white photographs of environmental words, *Word Pictures* (1963–63), served as the germinal idea for *Zorns Lemma*; *Nostalgia*, which features the burning of twelve of Frampton's early photographs to the accompaniment of an asynchronous, mock-confessional, spoken narrative, can be seen as the filmmaker's interim judgment on his prior incarnation as a still photographer." Phillips, "Word Pictures: Frampton and Photography," p. 65.

A constellation is an "image." The image may be nothing more than a roughly isosceles triangle, but there it is. But that image is not a whole and literal DRAWING, it is a group of elements that we construe meaningfully, as we construe the letters b-i-r-d, a constellation of unrelated sounds, as the general name of feathered flying warmblooded egglayers. Or, a-b-c-d-&c as the alphabet, our name for an arbitrary grouping of a small number of symbols standing for a rather larger number of the sounds a human throat can make.[43]

Language (and its substructures of alphabet, phonetics, syntax) helped Frampton figure film's relationship to legibility, while photography and its historical concerns with "selection, collection, and classification" propelled Frampton's desire to empty film of its diegetic affect.[44] In photographing a "shooting script" for *Poetic Justice*, Frampton achieves a parody of narrative filmmaking, as well as a complex rendering of the relationship of word to image. An inversion takes place: words act as instructional images that we only "see" through reading the text that appears, as written shot directions, on the screen. "You," the spectator/reader, become interpolated, at once, as director, camera operator, and actor: "you lower a camera from your eye," "your face in profile, squinting through camera."

Inspired by Edward Weston's approach to the photograph as that which, like language, is "doubly identified—once with itself, and once again with its referent," Frampton calls for a stripping of film, the visual image or the linguistic artifact to their own "proper set of specifications."[45] What the works of Samuel Beckett, Jorge Luis Borges, or Alain Robbe-Grillet have in common with photography, implies Frampton, is their ability to "strip the Thing that is being said, the referent of the discourse" so that their objects (words, images) refer only to the materiality of their operations.[46] Similarly, in *Poetic Justice*, causality and temporality have been dispossessed from the text (as we read it) and our viewing takes place in a time that is "explicitly and entirely disjunct from the atemporality of the text."[47]

As the hand holding a still photograph would interrupt the filmic space in *Poetic Justice*, the photographs burning over the stove (accompanied by the synchronous voice-over out of chronology, etc.) in *Nostalgia* signaled a collapse of spatiotemporal relations in the world of 2-D forms. Frampton's use of voice-over for *Nostalgia* begins the project of inscription that would continue in *Poetic Justice* and other photographic/text projects of this period that explore the disjuncture of word-image relations. Bill Simon, writing in 1975, claims that in *Nostalgia*

there is always a gap between what we imagined from the spoken commentary and the actual photograph. Frampton induces an imaginative

43.   Odlin, "Letters from Framp," p. 46.
44.   Phillips, "Word Pictures," p. 64.
45.   Frampton, "Impromptus on Edward Weston: Everything in Its Place," *Circles of Confusion*, p. 142.
46.   Ibid.
47.   Ibid., p. 143.

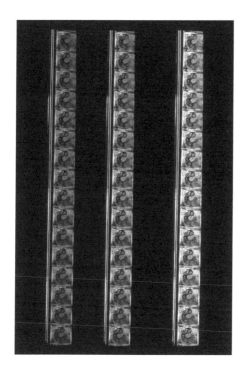

Frampton. Nostalgia. *1971.*
Courtesy Carnegie Museum, Pittsburgh.

visualization on our part and then jolts our imagination by showing us the real image. That jolt amply demonstrates the inadequacy of words to deal with images and the privileged status of an image.[48]

However, rather than privileging the "status of the image" over words, Frampton strives throughout his work to reveal how image-based knowledge is intimately, often brutally tied to systems of language.[49] The interpenetration of these meaning-producing systems is what he strives to reveal; thus he moves from examining the relations between text and image to a study of vertical sound-image arrangements.

Toward Vertical Sound Montage

Montage is not something I invented but something I inherited. I am pursuing suggestions latent in montage culture for 50 years. In these

48.   Bill Simon, "The Films of Hollis Frampton," *New Forms in Film*, p. 56.
49.   Michelson underlines how Frampton achieves a kind of "suspended violence" through his sound editing practices in *Critical Mass*: "The complex polyphony of the dissociative cutting projects the uncontrollable chain of recrimination, of violence suspended, rather than arrested, unresolved, irresolvable" ("Frampton's Sieve," p. 163). A similar project is taken up by Martin Arnold in *Passage à l'Acte* (1993), in which "noise and language become sound events of equal value and importance"—an aggressive, stuttering sound track that underlines the hegemonic narratives of white masculinity in Hollywood films of the 1950s and early 1960s. See Scott MacDonald, "Martin Arnold" [interview], *A Critical Cinema 3: Interviews with Independent Filmmakers* (Berkeley: University of California Press, 1998), p. 360.

sections, I am tilting at the windmill of linearity. I am concerned with
vertical montage.

—Hollis Frampton, 1980[50]

In the unfinished *Magellan*, begun in 1972, Frampton had hoped to construct
360 one-minute films with sound. However, only *Cadenzas* (1977–80), *Mindfall*
(1977–80), and *Gloria!* (1979) have sound, and a large part of the project remains
unfinished, due to Frampton's untimely death in 1984.[51] In this never-to-be
completed masterwork, vertical montage was to be the main strategy for achieving
the incessant movement of "interpenetrating" structures of the metahistory of
film, replete with all four solstices and equinoxes, as well as the metaphoric
adventures of Ferdinand Magellan's circumnavigation of the globe.

Sound—especially Frampton's goal of achieving a vertical sound montage—
was to be of central importance in his pursuit of what he saw as the "largest
possible inventory of modes of classifying and perceiving experience" (a project
begun in *Zorns Lemma*).[52] In a sense, Frampton approached sound as an incomplete
project in cinema history, which was lost after the advent of the "Talkies." The
complexity of this project, Frampton believed, was lost again after Eisenstein's and
Vertov's studies in film sound were curtailed by "the extreme pressure of Stalinist
'restoration.'"[53] Especially compelling for Frampton was Eisenstein's focus on the
simultaneity of radically disparate elements of sound and image:

> From the viewpoint of montage structure, we no longer have a simple
> horizontal succession of pictures, but now a new "superstructure" is
> erected vertically over the horizontal picture structure. Piece for piece
> these new strips in the "super-structure" differ in length from those in
> the picture structure, but needless to say, they are equal in total length.
> Pieces of sound do not fit into the picture pieces in sequential order,
> but in simultaneous order.[54]

In *Birth of Magellan: Mindfall* (Parts I and VII), the sounds that accompany
shots of "lush rainforest flora and fauna, oceanscapes" in Puerto Rico are
"mechanical"; they tend to be associated with communication—teletypes, printing
presses, and telephones.[55] Frampton, in a sense, revisits the mechanical nature of
sound invention and interfaces it in an ironic relationship with the primeval land
of the "new world" as "discovered" by Columbus on his second voyage.

50.   Frampton in Amy Taubin, "Tilting at Linearity," *SoHo Weekly News* (1980), p. 58.
51.   Brian Henderson, "Propositions for the Exploration of Frampton's *Magellan*," *October* 32 (Spring
1985), p. 133.
52.   Tuchman, "Frampton at the Gates," p. 58.
53.   Frampton, "Film in the House of the Word," p. 81.
54.   Sergei M. Eisenstein, *The Film Sense*, trans. and ed. Jay Leyda (New York: Harcourt Brace
Jovanovich, 1974) p. 78.
55.   Bill Simon, "Talking about *Magellan*: An Interview with Hollis Frampton," *Millennium Film
Journal* 7/8/9 (Fall–Winter 1980–1981), p. 16.

Reminiscent of his montage method in *Zorns Lemma*, Frampton builds a catalog of sound-image relationships and then begins repeating them in syncopated, hurried rhythms—suggesting their interchangeability (sound for image and vice versa), as well as their collision. Noticeably absent is the stark, Minimalist sensibility of his earlier films, which contributed to his aesthetic experiments with set theory and drew crisp lines around images (which were often words), using sound to repeat the systemic quality of sharply metered cuts of footage. Instead, with the agility of a Marie Menken-like roving camera eye on foliage, Frampton creates an almost lyrical sense of an Edenic landscape: violets, lilies, water, rocks, animals, succulents, trees, sky. This arcadian world, however, is intermittently interrupted with television or even computer-like commercial wipes: bright, graphic diagonals and dizzying iris shots that separate many of the images in both parts of *Mindfall.* Matching the rude, funny, graphic wipes, Frampton's sound track bursts with unpredictable segments of cartoon sounds, often blasphemously juxtaposed against churches or temples.

Missing, often, from analyses of *Magellan* is Frampton's charge that this metahistory is also intended to be a comedy.

> In an interview with James Joyce that took place in the '30s, after *Ulysses* had been in print for several years, Joyce remarked that after all this time, no one has yet noted that the book was funny. I consider the *Magellan* cycle a comedy.[56]

And yet, Frampton had somber, grandiose aspirations for *Magellan.* His goals included the rationalization of the history of art, resynthesis of the film tradition, making malleable the sense and notion of time in film, examining the function of the written and spoken word in film, rethinking the synesthesic "problem of sound in film," making "rhetorical" or technological options available to film (digital processing, video synthesizers), and revealing how film is "an epistemological model for human consciousness."[57]

The tension between the comic and the systemic in Frampton's later films is part of the larger project of attempting to create a vertical montage structure. Sound functions as a central part of this project, insisting upon the "moveability, the portability, the malleability of the montage piece."[58] In *Magellan*, sound functions much as image had functioned in *Palindrome* (1969). We hear locomotives, water, cars, bowling. Then we hear the same in reverse: bowling, cars, water, locomotives. As Brian Henderson notes: "*Palindrome* would maintain its identity shown backwards—not only in reverse order but upside down."[59] It is this kind of palindromic sound montage that Frampton is exploring in terms of how it can create vertical as well as horizontal relationships with cinematic images and other audio constructions.

56.   Taubin, "Tilting at Liberty," p. 58.
57.   Hollis Frampton, "Statement of Plans," *Magellan* grant proposal, ca. 1971, Frampton files at the Carnegie Museum, Pittsburgh.
58.   Bill Simon, "Talking about *Magellan*," p. 17.
59.   Henderson, "Propositions for the Exploration," p. 137.

As Michelson suggested, the palindromic not only stems from literary models, "but just as surely from Frampton's experience of serial composition, employed by Schoenberg and Webern."[60] Frampton was most likely aware of Morton Feldman's post-serial composition of the same name, *The Straits of Magellan*, from 1961, in which Feldman creates a similar tension between what he calls "simultaneous sounds" and "successively played single notes."[61]

Although Frampton is constructing sound within the frame of Eisenstein's and Vertov's calls for an asynchronous relationship between sound and image, he is also reexamining the complexity of synchronous sound, or as he put it: "simultaneous availability of essentially covalent chains of causal linkage."[62] As he explains in a 1980 interview with Bill Simon, "The most unsettling [issue about film sound] concerns the notion of sync-sound itself. Because sync-sound, as we have it in the movies, is an absolute artifice that is concerned not with generating but with excluding synchronous sound."[63] The routine of comedy, with its expected laugh lines, gag effects, or subtle, ironic twists, makes a travesty of the purported technical agility of synchronous sound technology. Canned laughter can be turned on or off with ease, a line can by synched with a laugh, or a shot–reaction shot can serve the gag-laugh sequence. As Frampton would put it, "synchronicity is a lot more obscure, a lot less clear" than the movie industry's plastic use of it suggests.[64] In *Magellan*, Frampton camps the industry of sync sound: cactus prickers purr with the sound of a pneumatic hammer, rivers honk as if they're busy urban streets, phallic towers topped with flaming torches are accompanied by five minutes of canned laughter.[65]

Found Noise

If Ezra is my father, then Rrose Selavy is my mother.

—Hollis Frampton, 1971[66]

From his earliest micro-experiments in *Surface Tension* to his grand project, *Magellan*, Frampton's studies in sound montage were permeated with a sense that sound—if done right—could transform the cinematic project even more profoundly

60.   Michelson, "Frampton's Sieve," p. 160.
61.   Feldman, http://swipenet.se/sonoloco9/mode/feldman4.html.
62.   Simon, "Talking about *Magellan*," p. 16.
63.   Ibid., p. 17.
64.   Ibid.
65.   Even earlier, in *Special Effects* (1972), Frampton is experimenting with *Magellan*'s ironic, humorous relationship to synchronous sound. The sound track, which was generated entirely on a Buchla synthesizer, screams like a sci-fi thriller over a cartoonlike square made of dotted lines, threatening to float off the screen (and acts as its nemesis, mirroring the limits and possibilities of both the cinematic "frame" as well as the projection screen). It also demonstrates the tenuous relationship sound has to the visual, making a vaudeville out of what Michel Chion has called the acousmetre (disembodied voice) and sound's ability to float on and off the screen or to be everywhere at once.
66.   Letter to Sally Dixon, August 22, 1971. Frampton files at Carnegie Museum, Pittsburgh, n.p.

than phenomenological silence. *Palindrome* is Frampton's *Hidden Noise*. As Michelson has suggested, Frampton's systemic montage projects were as deeply related to his lifelong literary interests in the great open systems of Pound, Joyce, and Stein as they were to the serialists and post-serialist composers, or, most importantly, to the experimental music of John Cage.

Finally, Frampton saw *Magellan*, especially *Mindfall*, as having an intimate relationship to Duchamp's layered projects, especially *The Bride Stripped Bare by Her Bachelors, Even (The Large Glass)* (1915–23) and its written component, *The Green Box* (1912–34). Frampton invokes Duchamp's *Large Glass* as early as 1964 in a letter to Odlin in order to explain how he imagines his master project, *Magellan*: "Both MAGELLANS to be rather kits along the lines of BRIDE/BOXES, etc., that is, the pieces to be accompanied by their working-drawings, macquettes, etc. CLOUDS in particular will need a substantial atlas or installation manual."[67]

In an informal note, almost a doodle, found at the Carnegie Museum Archive, Frampton draws a rectangle around the word *Magellan* and, next to it, writes: "green box." Then, he writes "Mindfall," underlines it, and next to it writes "Sound," and circles the latter several times.[68] In a sense, Frampton sees the sound in *Mindfall*, and eventually the larger *Magellan* project, as enacting a similar turn that Duchamp's written notes in the *Green Box* would do for *The Bride Stripped Bare* (Duchamp's writing on *Hidden Noise* would serve similar purposes): it would translate

67.   Odlin, "Letters from Framp," p. 45.
68.   Bill Judson, former film and video curator from the Carnegie Museum, believes that if this doodle is not from Frampton directly, it was made by him during a phone conversation with Frampton (in October of 1978), as per Frampton's description of his plans for further development of *Mindfall* and the larger *Magellan* project.

Frampton. Special Effects. 1972. Courtesy Anthology Film Archives.

and extend the visual into a system of linguistic and mathematical terms. This
system, like Frampton's film projects, contained horizontal and vertical axes,
which Duchamp described in the *Green Box* as slowly losing their positions to one
another: "there is gradually less differentiation from axis to axis, all the axes
gradually disappear in a fading verticality."[69] For Frampton, Duchamp takes
Eisenstein's notion of vertical montage and turns it on its head: the inscriptive of
the visual performs itself underneath an open system. Through his experiments
in sound montage, Frampton discovers the horizontal axis slowly turning into the
vertical—always already there in audible rotation.

69.   Marcel Duchamp, "*The Green Box*," p. 29.

History and Ambivalence in Hollis Frampton's *Magellan**

MICHAEL ZRYD

Magellan is the film project that consumed the last decade of Hollis Frampton's career, yet it remains largely unexamined. Frampton once declared that "the whole history of art is no more than a massive footnote to the history of film,"[1] and *Magellan* is a hugely ambitious attempt to construct that history. It is a *meta*history of film and the art historical tradition, which incorporates multiple media (film, photography, painting, sculpture, animation, sound, video, spoken and written language) and anticipates developments in computer-generated new media.[2] In part due to its scope and ambition, Frampton conceived of *Magellan* as a utopian art work in the tradition of Joyce, Pound, Tatlin, and Eisenstein, all artists, in Frampton's words, "of the modernist persuasion."[3] And like many utopian modernist art works, it is unfinished and massive. (In its last draft, it was to span 36 hours of film.)[4] By examining shifts in the project from 1971–80, as Frampton grapples with *Magellan*'s metahistorical aspiration, we observe substantial changes in his view of modernism.

After an initial expansive phase in the early 1970s influenced by what he called "the legacy of the Lumières," Frampton wrestles with ordering strategies that will be able to give "some sense of a coherence" to *Magellan*, finally developing the *Magellan* Calendar between 1974–78, which provided a temporal map for each individual film in the cycle.[5] But during 1978–80, an extraordinarily fertile

*   I am grateful to the following colleagues who supported the writing and revision of this essay: Kenneth Eisenstein, Tom Gunning, Annette Michelson, Keith Sanborn, Tess Takahashi, Bart Testa, and Malcolm Turvey. Invaluable research access to Anthology Film Archives' resources was provided by Robert Haller.
1.   Hollis Frampton, "Notes on Composing in Film" (1976), *Circles of Confusion: Film, Photography, Video, Texts 1968–1980* (Rochester, N.Y.: Visual Studies Workshop Press, 1983), p. 123.
2.   Peter Lunenfeld's chapter on Frampton, "The Perfect Machine," in *Snap to Grid* (Cambridge, Mass.: MIT Press, 2000), notes resonances between *Magellan* and new media.
3.   Frampton, "Notes on Composing," p. 119.
4.   *Magellan*'s incompletion is all the more poignant given Frampton's early death from cancer at age 49 in 1984.
5.   See Hollis Frampton, "<CLNDR>: AN ANNOTATED CALENDAR FOR MAGELLAN / VERSION 1.2.0=DEC 1978," unpublished production notes, Anthology Film Archive (AFA) files. A disclaimer was added to the title: "(SUBJECT TO CHANGE WITHOUT NOTICE)."

OCTOBER 109, Summer 2004, pp. 119–42. © 2004 October Magazine, Ltd. and Massachusetts Institute of Technology.

period of production for Frampton, the filmmaker turns toward a more ludic modernism to rescue *Magellan* from the reductive logic and arid systematicity, which he comes to think of as one of "modernism's defects." In 1977–78, Frampton's essay "Impromptus on Edward Weston" criticizes the "frowning" modernist masters (Pound, Weston); and in an essay published in 1980, "Inconclusions for Patrick Clancy," Frampton joins the side of those he called modernist "heresiarchs" (among whose ranks he includes Joyce, Duchamp, and Cage), and the "special heritage" they impart:

> impossibly, in the midst of a double effort (repair modernism's defects, reassume the burden of its emblem) one is required to be efficacious, and to sustain that thing, dogmatically abjured by visual modernism during its last days, which goes by the ancient name of wit.[6]

Frampton seeks to rescue modernism from its defects by combating what he perceives to be its dogmatic flight from "wit," understood here in its most capacious sense.[7] Frampton's embrace of wit is evident throughout his career. But, I argue, his critique of *system* becomes more and more pointed through the course of the *Magellan* project, and more discernible in the late 1970s as he encounters Michel Foucault (and his critique of Jeremy Bentham) and confronts the totalizing logic implicit in *Magellan*'s original "rationalized" and "totally inclusive" ambition, embracing instead a self-ironizing form of modernism.[8]

In what follows, I show how Frampton's conception of metahistory initially burdens and then finally enables the *Magellan* project. His late-1970s self-critique of *Magellan*'s totalizing modernist aims leads Frampton to turn to a ludic modernism informed by irony, facilitating a conceptualization of *Magellan* in which aleatory and structuring principles are balanced through an engagement with early film history. I conclude the essay with analyses of the two late-1970s films that use early film footage, *Gloria!* (1979) and *Cadenza I* (1977–80), which bookend the *Magellan* Calendar, and which point back into film history as concrete metaphors for modernist masterworks in the arcana of early story films. In *Gloria!*, two short films depicting the myth of Tim Finnegan stand for Joyce's *Finnegans Wake* (1939). In *Cadenza I*, a Biograph short, *A Little Piece of String* doubles for Duchamp's *The Bride Stripped Bare by Her Bachelors, Even (The Large Glass)* (1915–23). These framing films signal an ironic relation to art historical tradition as early films are integrated into *Magellan* as naive precursors to modernist classics.

6.   Hollis Frampton, "Inconclusions for Patrick Clancy," *Marginal Works: Atopia—No Man's Land* (Utica, N.Y.: Utica College of Syracuse University, 1980), n.p. [Catalog for an exhibition of photographs by Patrick Clancy, March 27–April 11, 1980.] Frampton only used the word "postmodernism" once in his published writings, in "Inconclusions," and understood it to involve an internal critique of modernism.
7.   According to the *Oxford English Dictionary*, "wit" refers first to the faculty of "consciousness or thought," encompassing reason, experience, perception, and knowledge, and later acquired its colloquial meaning of "cleverness" seated in "intellectual ability; genius, talent, cleverness; mental quickness or sharpness."
8.   Terms used in Frampton's *Magellan* grant proposal (to unspecified foundation), ca. 1971.

In an early grant proposal for *Magellan*, Frampton saw the new project continuing the concerns of his earlier work (time, structure, language), while engaging new aesthetic parameters (animation, sound), all "subsumed within the synoptic working out of a single metaphor . . . the voyage of Ferdinand Magellan, the first circumnavigator of the world." The two major conceptual goals are, first, the "rationalization of the history of the art. 'Making film over as it should have been,'" and second, articulating "the notion of an hypothetically totally inclusive work of film art as epistemological model for the conscious human universe."[9] Frampton recognized the "hopelessly ambitious" scope of *Magellan*: as a metahistory of film, it encompasses not only its past but its ideal form ("film as it should have been"), and models consciousness itself.

Frampton is faced with two central tensions in relation to the responsibilities that the metahistorical modernist artist in film takes on in a project of this scope: the first formal, balancing order and contingency; the second historical, balancing film's "immaturity" with tradition.[10] The first tension derives from what Frampton identifies as film's medium-specific "axiomatics." Many of these axiomatics are found in the powers of control and articulation that framing, narrative (for Frampton, something closer to the notion of sequencing than story), and montage afford the film artist.[11] Balancing these powers is photographic illusionism, an axiomatic that threatens to escape articulation altogether in the plenitude and contingency of the photographic image, and the "affective universes" it contains. Frampton, taken early on with the long-take Lumières *actualités*, finds himself overwhelmed by the sheer excess generated by their "primal" image, in which you simply "place the frame [and] see what will transpire."[12] In tension with this plenitude, Frampton attempts a series of ordering strategies, including mathematical, calendrical, and encyclopedic models mobilized for *Magellan* as a whole and for individual films in the cycle. In the end, both illusion and articulation threaten to be inadequate to the ambitiousness of the stated scope of the project, which means to account for both the axiomatic and historical richness of the art.

The second responsibility that the modernist artist in film faces is to film history, a history which, as Frampton understands it, is immature and undeveloped: "Of the whole corpus the likes of *Potemkin* make up a numbingly small fraction."[13] The prominence of early film in *Magellan* suggests that it applies a partial salve to

9.   Ibid., p. 5.
10.   Frampton, "For a Metahistory of Film: Commonplace Notes and Hypotheses," *Circles of Confusion*, p. 113.
11.   Frampton's turn toward animation, computer imaging, and sound in the latter years of the *Magellan* project suggest even further areas of articulation.
12.   Simon Field and Peter Sainsbury, "*Zorns Lemma* and *Hapax Legomena*: Interview with Hollis Frampton," *Afterimage* 4 (1972), p. 63.
13.   Frampton, "Metahistory," p. 113.

these anxieties, first in the promise that film might have a strong history to metahistoricize, and second, in providing raw material for ironic appropriations and reworkings of modernist masterworks.

Noël Carroll reminds us that Frampton's metahistory is first and foremost important for the fact that it is "artistically generative."[14] Carroll proposes that Frampton develops the notion of metahistory to reconcile productively two opposing approaches to film theory and art criticism of the '60s, '70s, and '80s that were central to Frampton's thought: "the essentialist approach and the historical approach."[15] We find the concatenation of these two approaches in Frampton's proclamation at the conclusion of "For a Metahistory of Film": "The metahistorian of film generates for himself the problem of deriving a complete tradition from nothing more than the most obvious material limits of the total film machine."[16] "Obvious material limits" conform to "essential," medium-specific qualities. "Tradition," however, introduces an historical dimension, situating the metahistorian's work in relation to a sequence of past artifacts.

Carroll notes one option for reconciling these two approaches: "Now the essentialist after Hegel has the wherewithal ready to hand to accommodate a commitment to essences with a commitment to history, [that is] the postulation that history unfolds . . . according to an essential plan."[17] The problem with this option, as Carroll says, is that it posits a teleology that threatens the artist's activity of art making; the new would be, by definition, impossible: "The teleological reconciliation of essence and history implies that once the essential destiny of an artform is reached, the form effectively dies . . . scarcely a viable *modus operandi* for the working avant-gardist."[18] Instead, Carroll proposes that Frampton turns to an inverted teleology that makes the artist an active metahistorian:

> The metahistorian of film, though open to the history of film, does not see film history as converging on the present. The actual history of film is mongrel; there is no destiny inscribed within it. Rather, now, in the present, the metahistorian takes stock of the mess of film history and targets certain conditions of the medium, which seem to him to represent its quintessence. For Frampton, these conditions appear to comprise: framing, photographic illusionism, and narrative.[19]

14.   Noël Carroll, "A Brief Comment on Frampton's Notion of Metahistory," *Millennium Film Journal* 16/17/18 (Fall–Winter 1986–87), p. 205.
15.   Ibid., p. 200.
16.   Frampton, "Metahistory," p. 115. Frampton himself later declared, "That article, which is nine years old, was, in my mind, quite openly a manifesto for a work that I was at that moment thinking quite seriously about undertaking, namely the *Magellan* project." Bill Simon, "Talking about *Magellan*: An Interview with Hollis Frampton," *Millennium Film Journal* 7/8/9 (Fall–Winter 1980–1981), p. 15.
17.   Carroll, "A Brief Comment," p. 203.
18.   Ibid., p. 204.
19.   Ibid.

As Carroll notes, these three conditions are enumerated in Frampton's 1972 essay, "A Pentagram for Conjuring the Narrative."[20] Carroll continues:

> Now in the actual history of film—the accumulation of footage since Edison—these conditions were not in fact rigorously and self-consciously explored. It becomes the task of the metahistorian to make up for this shortcoming, to, in effect, envision the history of film as it would have been had it been rigorously self-conscious, and to reconstruct it "axiomatically." The metahistorical filmmaker, that is, imagines what the history of film *should* have been (according to his criteria) and then goes on to make it.[21]

As Carroll concludes, "The crucial consequence of this maneuver is that it places our filmic tradition . . . in the future"; it "awaits invention."[22] The avant-garde artist is thus given agency in history.

Carroll's account elucidates the generative aspects of such a metahistorical move: the artist is freed to choose the criteria upon which the systematic "making film over as it should have been" will be based.[23] But Carroll's brief essay only offers two options, i.e., that history either conforms to a version of Hegelian destiny—which Carroll properly says Frampton rejects—or that history is "mongrel," a formulation of history that I would argue is unacceptable to Frampton's sense of tradition. Carroll admits he is less concerned with whether Frampton's notion of metahistory "is theoretically sound" than with recognizing "that this theoretical sleight-of-hand was artistically generative."[24] But it is clear to me that this "theoretical sleight-of-hand" was attended by anxieties and restraints, which stemmed precisely from the tensions that Frampton observed in the relation of art to tradition. For Carroll, "the metahistorian of film proposes to create a fictional tradition in the future, oxymoronic as it may sound."[25] But Frampton's tradition is not simply a freely invented fiction; it presumes a complex past to ground a rich future.

T. S. Eliot's essay "Tradition and the Individual Talent" (1920), an essay to which Frampton frequently refers, usefully recasts Carroll's terms. Eliot speaks of "the relation of the poet to his past": "he can neither take the past as a lump, an indiscriminate bolus, nor can he form himself wholly on one or two private admirations, nor can he form himself wholly upon one preferred period. . . . The poet must be very conscious of the main current."[26] For Eliot, history cannot be entirely mongrel. Nor can the artist arbitrarily or subjectively choose the criteria by which he or she will approach history; Frampton's axiomatics cannot merely be

20.   Frampton, "A Pentagram for Conjuring the Narrative" (1972), *Circles of Confusion*, pp. 59–68.
21.   Carroll, "A Brief Comment," p. 204. Emphasis in original.
22.   Ibid.
23.   Frampton, *Magellan* grant proposal, p. 5.
24.   Carroll, "A Brief Comment," pp. 204–5.
25.   Ibid.
26.   T. S. Eliot, "Tradition and the Individual Talent," in *20th Century Poetry and Poetics*, ed. Gary Geddes (Toronto: Oxford University Press, 1969), pp. 441–42.

"one or two private admirations." Rather the artist must bow to the demands of the main current, i.e., tradition, and tradition "compels" the artist to have historical consciousness:

> [Tradition] involves, in the first place, the historical sense [that] involves a perception, not only of the pastness of the past, but of its presence. The historical sense compels a man to write not merely with his own generation in his bones, but with the feeling that the whole of literature of Europe from Homer, and within it the whole literature of his own country, has a simultaneous existence and compels a simultaneous order. This historical sense, which is a sense of the timeless as well as of the temporal and of the timeless and the temporal together, is what makes a writer traditional. And it is at the same time what makes a writer most acutely conscious of his place in time, of his contemporaneity.[27]

Eliot, like Carroll, proposes a solution to the conflicting demands of essence (the timeless) and history (the temporal), a solution that also contains a paradox— and a cost:

> The existing monuments form an ideal order among themselves, which is modified by the introduction of the new (the really new) work of art among them. The existing order is complete before the new work arrives; for order to persist after the supervention of novelty, the whole existing order must be, if ever so slightly, altered; and so the relations, proportions, values of each work of art toward the *whole* are readjusted; and this is conformity between the old and the new. Whoever has approved this idea of order, of the form of European, of English litera-ture, will not find it preposterous that the past should be altered by the present as much as the present is directed by the past. And the poet who is aware of this will be aware of great difficulties and responsibilities.[28]

Eliot's formulation provides a neat synopsis of Frampton's metahistorical project. Tradition exists as an ideal but not inflexible set of patterns; it adapts to change, existing, as Carroll puts it, in the future, awaiting invention by "really new" works. But what are these "great difficulties and responsibilities"? They are not what Carroll sees as the threat of the Hegelian option, the abnegation of artistic invention and the new, both of which are given a place in history by Eliot. Rather, it is that the very agency granted to the artist of the really new to change the

---

27.   Ibid., p. 440.
28.   Ibid., p. 441. Emphasis in original. Frampton provides a typically compact and ironic summary of Eliot's point in a 1972 interview when he catalogs different conceptions of time: "Or: there's time as an elastic fluid. The frog Tennyson leaps into the elastic fluid and creates waves, which ultimately joggle the cork Eliot. Or, in Eliot's view, the elasticity travels in both directions; tradition and individual talent. Eliot, of course, says that Eliot has changed Tennyson, and that is clearly true." In Peter Gidal, "Interview with Hollis Frampton [1972]," *October* 32 (1985), p. 100.

tradition carries a burden of responsibility: the modernist artist attempting to remake his or her art must get it right.

Eliot provides terms that facilitate a combination of appropriation as an aesthetic strategy (i.e., the self-conscious reworking of material into art works) with an understanding of the material's historical nature. Eliot insists, at one level, on a nonevaluative or nonprogressive theory of art history, one that would reject dismissing early forms of art as primitive, yet values the artist's intentionality and self-consciousness in relation to the past:

> [The artist] must be aware of the obvious fact that art never improves, but that the material of art is never quite the same. He must be aware that the mind of Europe . . . is a mind that changes, and that this change is a development which abandons nothing en route, which does not superannuate either Shakespeare, or Homer, or the rock drawing of the Magdalenian draughtsmen. That this development, refinement perhaps, complication certainly, is not from the point of view of the artist, any improvement.
>
> Someone said: "The dead writers are remote from us because we *know* so much more than they did." Precisely, and they are that which we know.[29]

Frampton, via Eliot, escapes a teleological destiny of art—art does not "improve"—but he retains the notion of self-consciousness as a consequence of the accumulation of memory through history. Self-consciousness captures both a resolution of the demand for Carroll's essentialist and historical approaches and the ambivalence that comes with the paradox of understanding oneself as an historical subject. Self-consciousness allows the artist to make certain essential claims in relation to his investigation of the tradition of art by providing him with a subject position from which he can search for origins and attempt to discover what Frampton called "the really binding conditions of the art."[30] The method of that investigation, however, is one that requires a self-conscious understanding of the contingency of that search for origins. Historical origins exist but Frampton can only begin to explore them by considering himself as a contingent historical subject. Frampton *needs* history to ground his search *and* enforce its contingency.

But the artist must have a sufficiently "ordered" tradition to modify. Through the mid-1970s, Frampton often expressed anxiety about his need to complete *Magellan* given that it "needed to establish its own [historical] context." At a discussion in 1977 in San Francisco, he worries about the problem of making a large work like *Magellan*:

> OK, *Finnegans Wake*, a bulky work, assumes the existence of literature. I cannot in the same sense assume the existence of film. . . . film has not

---

29.   Eliot, "Tradition and the Individual Talent," p. 442. Emphasis in original.
30.   Field and Sainsbury, "Interview with Hollis Frampton," p. 73.

thus far achieved levels of organization that are in any means comparable with literature, and especially, I think it has not constituted itself as a mode of production on the one hand or a field of cultural potentialities on the other such that it can contain the large work. This is film outside of film, for the most part. So that I'm not interested nearly so much in performing a special task within film as I am of, not seeking, but redefining the boundaries of filmic discourse. So that my worries aren't the same as they would be if I were, for instance, writing a 1,000-page novel. I worry about other things, like, for instance, am I totally haywire? Seriously. Am I going to finish the goddam thing? You see, this is a serious problem. If you don't finish an epic poem it is a more or less magnificent ruin. *The Canterbury Tales . . . The Cantos. . . .* This I probably have got to finish or I have blown the whole thing, in my own mind, since it has the problem of establishing its own context.[31]

Frampton worries that film has insufficient history, as an art form allied to and commensurate with other modernist projects, to contain a metahistory like *Magellan*. The problem of establishing context, then, falls directly onto his shoulders.

Frampton looks to early film for this context. In his 1979 Whitney Museum lecture on early film, "An Invention Without a Future," Frampton, like Eliot in the beginning of "Tradition and the Individual Talent," addresses himself to those who would make claims to an art's novelty without grasping its history. He concludes his lecture with a plea for historical research:

So that finally, there is one thing we should stop doing. We should stop calling ourselves new. We are not. They were new. We are old, and we have not necessarily aged as well as we should. To cite Eliot again: he reports himself as answering to someone who objected to, I suppose, Shakespeare, Dante, and Homer on the grounds that we know more than they did by replying, "yes, we do, and they are precisely what we know." We also know more than that very early cinema did. Unfortunately, they are not precisely what we know. We are only beginning to penetrate the phantom, the fiction of the copious and the readily available, to poke around in dusty attics, into the sort of mausoleums guaranteed by a rapacious copyright system, for example, and to retrieve heaven knows what—probably not Shakespeare, Dante, and Homer—it would be nice to know who that Homer of film will ultimately be perceived as, by the way, let alone the Dante—but at least something of the context in which those texts, if they ultimately are exhumed, will be perceived.[32]

31.   Henry Hills and David Gerstein, "St. Hollis (part 2)," transcript of post-screening discussion, *Cinemanews* 3/4 (September 1978), p. 15.
32.   Hollis Frampton, "The Invention Without a Future," lecture delivered at the Whitney Museum of American Art, New York, November 17, 1979, as part of lecture series "Researches and Investigations into Film: Its Origins and the Avant-Garde." Transcript in AFA files, pp. 17–18. Reprinted in this issue, pp. 65–75.

The context provided by film history will form the grounds for its metahistory. And if history as context is formed ultimately by texts, then Frampton can formulate a concrete strategy for working out the paradox of a tradition in the future: early film texts are part of the same tradition that Frampton's metahistorical project is forming—but they do not enter that tradition until they are exhumed. In other words, the construction of Frampton's dynamic tradition through the investigation and recontextualization of historical texts is facilitated both by the work of the artist and the archivist, condensed in the figure of the metahistorian. Early film is simultaneously the scrap heap of history and the monuments of its tradition as found and reworked by the metahistorian. Thus Frampton articulates the rationale and method of appropriation of film texts:

> There is no evidence in the structural logic of the filmstrip that distinguishes "footage" from a "finished" work. Thus, any piece of film may be regarded as "footage" for use in any imaginable way to construct or reconstruct a new work. Therefore, it may be possible for a metahistorian to take old work as "footage," and construct from it identical new work necessary to a tradition.[33]

Film history facilitates and is facilitated by the work of the artist metahistorian. The value of this appropriation is generated by the artist through the scope and intensity of his or her devotion, here "duty," to tradition:

> [The metahistorian] is occupied with inventing a tradition, that is, a coherent wieldy set of discrete monuments, meant to inseminate resonant consistency into the growing body of his art.
>
> Such works may not exist, and then it is his duty to make them. Or they may exist already, somewhere outside the intentional precincts of the art (for instance, in the prehistory of cinematic art, before 1943). And then he must remake them.[34]

The burden of this duty is such that Frampton names "Insomnia," a figure of exhaustion and restlessness, as *Magellan*'s muse.

In the end, Frampton recasts Eliot's essay on tradition via the singularly appropriate figure of Louis Lumière, underlining the crucial role played by early film and the search for history in Frampton's project. Frampton refers to the title of his lecture, Lumière's famous aphorism, "Cinema is an invention without a future" (which also serves as the epigram of the "Metahistory" essay) and suggests that Lumière was

> touched for a moment with an insight, newly implied if not original, about history. From a certain point of view it was impossible at the

---

33.   Frampton, "Metahistory," p. 114.
34.   Ibid., p. 113.

Marion Faller. Hollis Frampton editing filmstrips,
ca. 1978. Courtesy Marion Faller.

beginning, as Lumière said "let there be light," for the cinematograph to have a future because it did not have a past. Now the future is, after all, something that we manufacture. We can be willful about it and perverse, if we wish, but nevertheless even our willfulness, even our perversity is ordinarily understood to be subsumed by a temporal machine containing and originated and guided by human beings called historical process. Until such time as there is a past of some sort, a history, furthermore, of some sort, that is, a past which has been examined, has been subjected to a critical, a theoretical analysis, there can be no future because there is no apparatus for prediction and for extrapolation. I do not mean, of course, that history in any exact sense is something that is guaranteed by the possession of a past. Only its possibility is guaranteed. . . . So that it is only now, I think, that it begins to be possible to imagine a future, to construct, to predict a future for film, or for what we may generically agree to call film and its successors, because it is only now that we can begin to construct a history and, within that history, a finite and ordered set of monuments, if we wish to use T. S. Eliot's terms, that is to constitute a tradition.[35]

All an artist's willfulness and perversity, his creative capacity for invention, is subsumed to historical process. That process requires historical subjects to uncover and analyze the past as a precondition to constructing a tradition in the future. This analysis, crucially, requires and values self-consciousness in the historical subject. Finally, the creation of a historical tradition is always contingent, not guaranteed—but it is at least possible. It is at this threshold of theoretical possibility that *Magellan* as a metahistorical project gets off the ground—and dives head first into the archive.

Foucault and Frampton

A useful figure to consider in relation to Frampton's shifting sense of history over the course of *Magellan*'s production is Michel Foucault, whom Frampton quotes in a 1978 essay:[36]

Order is, at one and the same time, that which is given in things as their inner law, the hidden network that determines the way they

35.   Frampton, "Invention," pp. 16–17.
36.   I am not certain when Frampton first encountered Foucault's work. Notably, Foucault lectured at SUNY Buffalo in 1970 and 1972 (where Frampton taught from fall 1973 through February 1984), and in New York in 1973. See Didier Eribon, *Michel Foucault*, trans. Betsy Wing (Cambridge, Mass.: Harvard University Press, 1991), p. 311. Both Frampton and Foucault published essays in the first issue of *October* in 1976. I am grateful to Bart Testa for pointing to early film and Foucault as research avenues for Frampton's late work. See Bart Testa, *Back and Forth: Early Film and the Avant-Garde* (Toronto: Art Gallery of Ontario, 1992).

confront one another, and also that which has no existence except in
the grid created by a glance, an examination, a language; and it is only
in the blank spaces of this grid that order manifests itself in depth as
though already there, waiting in silence for the moment of its
expression.[37]

This quotation can be read as a distillation of the *Magellan* project. The axiomatics of film that Frampton seeks systematically to chart comprise the "order," "the
inner law," of the network hidden within the scrap heap of cinematic history, that
mass of "things" to be expressed in language. That "hidden network" is less
exposed than brought into existence through the "grid" of Frampton's investigation
(most explicitly and schematically laid out in the *Magellan* Calendar), generated
through Frampton's "glance," his self-conscious labor that seeks to manifest a cinematic language, which until now has lain in "silence for the moment of its
expression"—film made over as it should have been.

Frampton's affinity with the Foucault of *The Order of Things* (1973)—another
metahistory of grand proportions—is evident in the striking resonance between
the playful critique of the Enlightenment outlined in the opening sections of
Frampton's "Metahistory" essay and Foucault's sketch of the classical episteme in
The Order of Things. Foucault describes the modifications in consciousness that
attend a shift to the classical episteme from the Renaissance episteme:

A complete enumeration will now be possible. . . . Comparison . . . can
attain to perfect certainty. . . . Complete enumeration, and the possibility
of arranging at each point the necessary connection with the next,
permit an absolutely certain knowledge of identities and differences:
"Enumeration alone, whatever the question to which we are applying
ourselves, will permit us always to deliver a true and certain judgment
upon it."[38]

Frampton too describes a historical shift to "a time of absolute certainty,"[39] a time
based on assumptions about the possibility of complete enumeration and seamless
comparison in "facts":

The world contained only a denumerable list of things. Anything could
be considered simply as the intersection of a finite number of facts.
Knowledge, then, was the sum of all discoverable facts.
    Very many factual daubs were required, of course, to paint a true
picture of the world; but the invention of the fact represented, from
the rising mechanistic point of view, a gratifying diminution of horse-

37.   Quoted in Frampton, "Impromptus on Edward Weston: Everything in Its Place" (1978), *Circles of Confusion*, p. 159.
38.   Michel Foucault, *The Order of Things: An Archaeology of the Human Sciences* (New York: Vintage Books, 1973), p. 55.
39.   Frampton, "Metahistory," p. 109.

power requirement from a time when knowledge had been the factorial of all conceivable contexts.[40]

Frampton locates the conceptual origins of the cinema in this time as a product of new defining terms of knowledge and consciousness based in a drive toward complete representation. Frampton asserts that before this time, representations of the world, i.e., histories, depended on "contexts" of understanding. Histories were acknowledged discursive constructions whose aim was not a mechanistic sum of facts but rather a conscious reflection "upon the qualities of experience in the times they expound": "These artifacts shared the assumption that events are numerous and replete beyond the comprehension of a single mind. They proposed no compact systematic substitute for their concatenated world; rather they made up an open set of rational fictions within that world."[41] Frampton calls these fictions "metahistories of event." This version of history calls claims to certainty into question and insists upon the importance of perspective, the "glance"— whose specificity and even humility understood the epistemological limitations that any acknowledgment of perspective imposes.

With *Magellan*, Frampton was attempting to "open" further the "set of rational fictions" that would provide "contexts of understanding" for art and film, and move beyond his earlier acclaimed work like *Zorns Lemma* (1970) and *Hapax Legomena* (1971–72), which he had come to see as schematic. But this move, again, creates a dilemma, one that he saw reflected in the relative lack of university film rentals for the *Magellan* films:

> What the hell are you going to do with *Magellan?* . . . I myself have the fondness that everybody has for things that are clear, for summary works, but it can't all be like that. Indeed, most of it cannot be like that. To use a favorite example of mine, the summary work is like the fictions of chemistry. Inorganic chemistry purports to study such things as "cobalt." Well, in a certain sense, yes, there is such a thing as cobalt, but it is a product of the laboratory. It's a fiction. There is no such thing in nature as the chemistry of cobalt. There is dirt, but nobody wants to have anything to do with the chemistry of dirt because dirt is in fact genuinely complex. So you can teach *Surface Tension* [1968] or *Zorns Lemma* because they are like the chemistry of cobalt, but if you're going to get involved with *Magellan*, then, of course, you're up to your eyeballs in the chemistry of dirt.[42]

This is the central problematic (and pleasure) of *Magellan*: Frampton's metaphorical voyage is in search of the "genuinely complex." But the problem is a double one. On the one hand, we have the chemistry of dirt, of reality, which exceeds the

40.   Ibid., p. 108.
41.   Ibid., p. 107.
42.   Scott MacDonald, "Interview with Hollis Frampton," *Film Culture* 67/68/69 (1979), p. 175.

complexity of our laboratory (or artistic) fictions. On the other hand, as Frampton said on another occasion, "We have this awful problem, of course, and that is that the universe is far simpler—infinitely complex as it is—than any of our explanations of it."[43] *Magellan* is Frampton's attempt to confront this paradox: how to chart the already infinitely complex—the world—with the even more cumbersome aesthetic forms and languages at our disposal.

Panopticon

In his Whitney Museum lecture on early film, Frampton conjectures

that the photograph and then film and now, heaven help us, that thing that begins with "v," may eventually be seen . . . tentative attempts, at once complete and approximate, to construct something that will amount to an arena for thought, and presumably, as well, an arena of power, commensurate with that of language.[44]

Frampton's understanding of visual forms as an arena of power is most explicitly signaled by his allusions to Jeremy Bentham's Panopticon (and Foucault's reading of Bentham's device in his essay "Panopticism").[45] From 1972 on, Frampton shot numerous one-minute films in imitation of Lumières' *actualités*; in the 1978 *Magellan* Calendar, they are labeled "Pans," short for Panopticon.[46] This renaming takes place concurrently with a number of shifts in the project: the earnest and then ironic working through and appropriation of modernist masterworks through the mid- to late-1970s films; a conceptual shift from the "chemistry of cobalt" (system) to the "chemistry of dirt" (the world); and Frampton's increasing anxiety about the prospect of finishing *Magellan* even as the project expanded in length and complexity. The character of these shifts and the ambivalence they express are caught in a short fabula that Frampton published in 1978, "Mind over Matter," which contains an invocation of Bentham's Panopticon within a dark metaphor for *Magellan*.[47]

The seventh and concluding section of "Mind over Matter" describes a "becalmed . . . barge" on whose decks a surreal, Beckettian tableaux of modern horrors is depicted. The barge is a prison ship, a figural condensation of *Magellan*'s fleet with Bentham's prison. It is escorted by battle cruisers and guarded by a nuclear bomb: "Somewhere beneath us, a thermonuclear device that

43.   Lecture at Carpenter Center for the Visual Arts, Harvard University, December 1977. Transcript in AFA files.
44.   Frampton, "Invention," p. 15.
45.   Michel Foucault, *Discipline and Punish: The Birth of the Prison* (New York: Vintage Books, 1979).
46.   Seven-hundred-and-twenty "Pans" were planned for inclusion in the final version of *Magellan*; forty-nine extant films are collected in *Straits of Magellan: Drafts and Fragments* (1974).
47.   Hollis Frampton, "Mind over Matter," *October* 6 (Fall 1978), pp. 81–92.

may be armed and exploded by remote control is our only warden."[48] The Panopticon is named as a means of avoiding punishment: "THE COLONY SEEMS more distant, now, than the panopticon we were offered as an alternative."[49] This complex concatenation seems to replace the fear of visual policing that was meant to invite the submission to order in Bentham's Panopticon with the contemporary, but equally indiscernible and ominous, threat of nuclear obliteration. The architecture of the Panopticon as a figure of containment, meanwhile, is replaced by the colony, here presented as an invisible point at the edge of an ever-receding horizon of expansion. In the same way, the cyclical temporal structure of *Magellan*, what Frampton likened to an architectural sculpture in time, allows for a simultaneous containment and expansion of Frampton's aspirations for his project.[50] *Magellan*'s voyage in 1519–22 was similarly a figure of both the powerful drive behind the aspiration to expansionism and of the ultimate global limits of Western exploration.[51]

The narrator describes the contents of the ship and the purpose of the voyage:

> I HAVE NOT MENTIONED OUR cargo: a small box, or casket, bolted or welded amidships, made of quartz and bronze. By night it is lit, blindingly, from underneath. Inside, there is nothing more than a double handful of greyish pellets. They are all that is left of the brain of René Descartes, exhumed on the suspicion that it might still contain the germ of a truly complex thought. The outcome of the inquisition is still to be revealed; but the transportation of that relic is the secret motive of our voyage.[52]

If we read the becalmed ship as the *Magellan* project, this description of its cargo points to the heart of Frampton's anxiety and ambivalence about the project. The more complexity Frampton seeks for *Magellan*, the more expansive and ambitious the project becomes. But despite the critique of certainty and system articulated in "Metahistory" and elsewhere—echoed here in Frampton's disparaging invocation of Descartes—*Magellan* remains an Enlightenment project attempting to redefine essential limits. However much subjectivity is problematized, *Magellan* relies on a claim to self-consciousness perpetually attempting to end around its own foundations.

One way of thinking about how Frampton evades this contradiction is to observe the increasing self-consciousness of his critique of authority and power over the course of the 1970s. Frampton does not abandon the metahistorical project but he is more and more skeptical of master narratives of cultural and artistic history.

---

48. Ibid., p. 91.
49. Ibid., p. 92. Emphasis in original.
50. Lecture at Carpenter Center.
51. Frampton's consciousness of the colonial aspect of his *Magellan* metaphor is signaled in his use of imagery filmed in San Juan, Puerto Rico, in *Cadenza I*, the first film in the *Magellan* cycle.
52. Frampton, "Mind over Matter," p. 92.

In "Tradition and the Individual Talent," one of the "difficulties and responsibilities" that Eliot projects for the artist is a responsibility to "the mind of Europe"—"the whole of literature of Europe from Homer." Frampton understands that he is constructed by and subject to the cultural "mind of Europe," as is the cinema whose metahistory he will (re)make in *Magellan*. Frampton also acknowledges what Eliot calls a second "difficulty" of "the historical sense," i.e., remaining limited by the consciousness of one's own contemporaneity, a mere "factorial of conceivable contexts," subject to the demands and limitations of historical process. The success of Frampton's mediation of these two difficulties is directly proportional to his ability self-consciously to understand and contain tradition as historical but not masterful. Frampton will reject submission to the "mind of Europe" and its universalizing cultural claims.

This rejection is grounded in the ambivalent and ultimately ironic relation Frampton develops to art historical tradition. The quality of this ironic relation echoes Schlegel's conception of a nonreductive form of ironic skepticism that nonetheless remains generative for the artist. In "The Paradigm of Romantic Irony," Anne Mellor summarizes this impulse:

> The romantic ironist must begin skeptically. He must acknowledge the inevitable limitations of his own finite consciousness and of all man-made structures or myths. But even as he denies the absolute validity of his own perceptions and structuring conceptions of the universe, even as he consciously deconstructs his mystifications of the self and the world, he must affirm and celebrate the process of life by creating new images and ideas. Thus the romantic ironist sustains his participation in a creative process that extends beyond the limits of his own mind.[53]

Romantic irony acknowledges the limits of human perspective and is skeptical of totalizing "structures or myths"—and indeed, as Mellor states, Schlegel's romantic irony emerges from a "post-Enlightenment distrust of the capacity of human reason to ascertain the laws of nature, or, indeed, any absolute truths concerning the ways of the world."[54]

This ironic perspective can historicize the "mind of Europe" and the "order" it dictates but retain the possibility of an order and patterning to the past which resists history becoming merely "mongrel." Thus, on the one hand, as part of the "rational fiction" of his metahistory, Frampton will aspire to make a "grammatically complete synopsis" of "the infinite cinema."[55] On the other hand, Frampton will ironize his own quest as impossible and contingent; in his lecture on early film he says,

> After a century, nevertheless, it is still true that no one knows even how to begin to write the sort of thing that film through its affiliation with

53.   Anne K. Mellor, *English Romantic Irony* (Cambridge, Mass.: Harvard University Press, 1980), p. 5.
54.   Ibid., p. 4.
55.   Simon, "Talking about *Magellan*," p. 15.

the sciences might expect of itself, that is a *Principia Cinematica*, presumably in three fat volumes entitled, in order: I. Preliminary Definitions; II. Principles of Sequence; III. Principles of Simultaneity. The wish for such a thing is somewhat like the wish of a certain aphorist who said—I believe the last of his aphorisms, or at least the last that I have read—that he would like to know the name of the last book that will ever be published.[56]

Frampton does not give up on essential claims, but he places the hypothetical text that would articulate that essence in an absurd and impossible future.

The tone of Frampton's escape from a slavish relation to tradition, and this embrace of an ironic perspective is, I think, best echoed in Frampton's essay on Edward Weston, one of the modernist fathers—like Pound, Eliot's contemporary—whom Frampton had ultimately to encounter and defeat in order to work as an artist: "As an intellectual parent, he amounted, finally, to one of those frowning, humorless fathers who teaches his progeny his trade and then prevents them from practicing it by blackballing them in the union. We are under no obligation to put up with this sort of thing."[57]

Frampton's relation to tradition was always fraught. His artistic biography, as he freely admitted, consisted of a movement through a series of artistic fathers whom he needed, eventually, to outgrow: Ezra Pound when he wanted to be a poet, Edward Weston when he was a still photographer, and, I would speculate, Stan Brakhage in film. One rationale for Frampton stating that the histories of the other arts are perhaps no more than a footnote to the history to film is that it displaces the anxieties of influence that had plagued his earlier "failed" artistic careers. It is in this active spirit—full of humor, confusion, and ambivalence—that Frampton will engage Eliot's tradition, that "mind of Europe," by remaking modernist masterworks from the relics of early cinema.

                                                                          Gloria!

In speculating about the "intellectual parents" he would prefer, Frampton suggests that

since some sort of choice must be made, I would state a personal preference for a chimera . . . a hybrid of Venus Geneatrix, who broods over the mountains and the waters, indifferently donating pleasure and pain to everything that lives, and Tim Finnegan, who enjoyed everything, and most of all his own confusion, and ended with the good humor to preside happily over his own departure.[58]

56.   Frampton, "Invention," p. 17.
57.   Frampton, "Impromptus," p. 159.
58.   Ibid.

Hollis Frampton. Gloria! *1979.*
Courtesy Canadian Filmmakers
Distribution Centre.

In *Gloria!*, Frampton cites two early tableaux comedies to represent the story of *Finnegans Wake*, using early film to prefigure a classic modernist art work.[59]

Appropriately, as the concluding work of *Magellan*, *Gloria!* is less concerned with birth than with death and—given the cyclical nature of the *Magellan* calendar—resurrection. There are two early films in *Gloria!*: a very short one-shot comedy opens the film, while the longer two-shot Finnegan story all but concludes the film. The actual conclusion is a text that dedicates *Gloria!* (and all of *Magellan*) to his maternal grandmother, Fanny Elizabeth Catlett Cross, born November 6, 1896 and died November 24, 1973. She lives from the beginning of cinema to the birth of *Magellan*. She also presides over the passage from the nineteenth to the twentieth centuries, from the height of what Frampton calls in the "Metahistory" essay "the mechanical age" to the dawn of the electronic age.[60] This transition is pointed to in *Gloria!* by the use of both early film and a video computer screen to generate the text that constitutes much of the film. (The screen is green, connoting the Irish roots shared by himself, his grandmother, Finnegan, and Joyce.)

The text that scrolls up the screen begins: "These propositions are offered numerically in the order in which they presented themselves to me and also alphabetically, according to the present state of my belief." The "propositions" about "I," "we," and "she" follow, and serve to describe Frampton's thoughts and feelings in relation to his grandmother. The numerical order of appearance of the propositions is apparently random and chronological, a kind of automatic writing. The alphabetical order of importance (denoted by bracketed letters at the

---

59.   One of the two early films is probably *Murphy's Wake* (Am & B, 1903), although I have not positively identified either.
60.   Frampton, "Metahistory," p. 112.

end of each proposition) attempts to evaluate and structure the propositions, according to the "present state of my belief," i.e., after a period of self-conscious reflection upon the first series of propositions. The metahistorical method of *Magellan* as a whole is encapsulated in this matrix, both contingent and ordered, except now, instead of "footage," video/linguistic transcriptions of Frampton's thoughts (also materially based in electronic signals) are worked through. This matrix is grounded in a most concrete form of tradition: Frampton's genealogical relation to his grandmother. The first proposition, ranked "[A]" alphabetically, reads: "That we belonged to the same kinship group, sharing a tie of blood [A]." This genealogical relationship and the simultaneous continuity and gap it proffers enables Frampton's elastic sense of history and the poetic power of resurrection. In *Gloria!*, narratives of birth and death are linked by the principles of genetic continuity and variation, ontogeny metaphorically recapitulated in phylogeny. The legacy of Frampton's grandmother is formed by the memory of her offspring, "according to the present state of [his] belief." And in the field of cinema, early film is resurrected, and animated with remarkable emotional resonance.

Cadenza I

The prelude of *Cadenza I* offers two creation stories that contain an elaborate set of allusions to origins and beginnings, both physical and metaphysical. The metaphysical origins refer to genesis: "In the beginning was the Word." The film begins with a pan right on a brick wall, which ends on a hand-drawn letter *A*: the first letter of the alphabet (and of the encyclopedia), the beginnings of language. A graphic *A* also refers us to the first image of *Zorns Lemma* (an *A* typewritten into tin foil and magnified), but this letter is found in the world. In the long middle section of *Zorns Lemma*, the "replacement image" for the *A* (which Frampton called a "word image") contains, according to Frampton, a man (Michael Snow) flipping the pages of a book—Antonio Pigafetta's account of Ferdinand Magellan's circumnavigation.[61] *Zorns Lemma*, Frampton's seminal film on language and the encyclopedia, has inscribed within it the genesis of the *Magellan* cycle.

The second creation story in the prelude to *Cadenza I* is scientific and begins after the letter *A* fades to black. The screen soon begins to flicker; flares increase in intensity and frequency, like the effects of light leakage on the beginning (or end) of a film roll. Over this light play is heard the sounds of an orchestra tuning up. Then a thunderclap erupts into the sound track followed by the sound of rain; the colors of the light flares deepen from yellow to red and blue. The tuning of the orchestra just prior to the outburst of natural sound, like the letter *A* preceding

61.   Scott MacDonald, "Interview with Hollis Frampton: *Zorns Lemma*," *Quarterly Review of Film Studies* 4 (Winter 1979), p. 27. Also see Charles E. Nowell's edition of *Magellan's Voyage Around the World: Three Contemporary Accounts* (Evanston, Ill.: Northwestern University Press, 1962), which includes Pigafetta's text.

the light flares, readies the organization of a signifying system (here harmonic music and written English). The physical world is created when lightning animates the dark elements, transforming a black void of matter into life. The sound of rain accompanies the final image of *Cadenza XIV*, a fade-in from black to an extreme long shot of a rain forest at daybreak (or dusk).

Frampton's elaboration of light as a metaphor for creation—moving from abstract components to the depth and substantiality of the three-dimensional photographic image—is embedded most directly in the fifteenth-century text by Robert Grosseteste (as translated and edited by Frampton) that is read in the third section of *Zorns Lemma*. Frampton suggests the resonance of the text:

> The key line in the text is a sentence that says, "In the beginning, light drew out matter along with itself into a mass as great as the fabric of the world." Which I take to be an apt description of film, the total historical function of film, not as an art medium, but as this great kind of time capsule . . . that led me later to posit the universe as a vast film archive.[62]

This metaphor of light drawing itself out to form the world can be seen in terms of Frampton's metahistory of representation: if time expands like the waves created in Eliot's puddle, so the human elaboration and modulation of Light constitutes the human history of (visual) representation. Crucially, Frampton here suggests the need to understand film in relation to the total cultural history of Western representation; film, as the "Metahistory" essay argues, is the ultimate product of the Enlightenment quest for *total* representation. Frampton's metahistory will be the metaphor that points, in Borgesian fashion, to the enormity and absurdity of that quest:

> This is my metaphor because I am a filmmaker. Borges has a wonderful story called "The Library of Babel," in which the entire universe has been transformed into a library of books. While conjecturing as to the actual structure of the library, he manages to reconstruct the entire history of human thought. All through this one metaphor! The cinematic metaphor seems to me more poignant, more meet.[63]

It is this model of a total representational machine that he posits to be devouring, in ways that evoke André Bazin's "total cinema," the substance of the world:[64]

> It is not surprising that something so large could utterly engulf and digest the whole substance of the Age of Machines (machines and all), and finally supplant the entirety with its illusory flesh. Having devoured all else, the film machine is the sole survivor.

62.   Gidal, "Interview with Hollis Frampton," p. 98.
63.   Ibid.
64.   André Bazin, "The Myth of Total Cinema," in *What Is Cinema?* vol. 1, ed and trans. Hugh Gray (Berkeley: University of California Press, 1967), pp. 17–22.

If we are indeed doomed to the comically convergent task of disman-
tling the universe, the fabricating from its stuff an artifact called *The
Universe*, it is reasonable to suppose that such an artifact will resemble
the vaults of an endless film archive built to house, in eternal cold
storage, the infinite film.[65]

A final correlative of Frampton's metaphor of light drawing out the fabric of
the world is his description, via Piaget, of the development of consciousness itself:

To the undifferentiated consciousness all the sensible world must be
continuously, and infinitely, replete. The act of distinguishing an image,
that is, of partitioning a "figure" from its proper "ground" is, if we are to
believe with Jean Piaget, one of the first heroic feats of consciousness. . . .
The infant mind erects a structure that is as intricate as the world,
because, for the purposes of the animal within, it *is* the world.[66]

Film as a "vast metaphor for consciousness" is grounded in a metaphysics of
light—within which Lumière is the prime mover. In what is the first written
reference in Frampton's texts to the Lumières and early film, we discover, in a
handwritten note on one of the *Zorns Lemma* production matrixes, a description
of the word images: "With the exceptions noted, all were carefully framed tripod
shots. I wanted Lumière's static camera—for which all cinematographic images
were numinous and replete."[67]

The prelude of *Cadenza I* (also the prelude to the entire *Magellan*) gives way
to the main section of the film, which consists of nine intercuts of two scenes. The
first scene, shot by Frampton, is in color, a handheld long shot captured by a tele-
photo lens, of a man and a woman dressed in formal clothes, standing on a
bridge, being arranged and shot by a wedding photographer in a lush garden.
The second scene is an early film, *A Little Piece of String* (1902), which features two
men ripping the dress off an unsuspecting woman. These two scenes are punctuated by a piece of animation, a dot zooming in and out of the frame.

The couple in the garden are, of course, Adam and Eve, just after their
union, which sends them out from the garden into the world.[68] From the creation
ex nihilo from God's Word, we fall into sexuality and history. The presence of the
photographer satisfies the complaint of the female historian in Frampton's 1974
essay, "Incisions in History/Segments of Eternity":

The trouble with the Universe, seen from a rigorously historical point of
view, is just this: no one was there to photograph the beginning of it—and

65.   Frampton, "Metahistory," pp. 114–115. Emphasis in original.
66.   Hollis Frampton, "Incisions in History/Segments of Eternity" (1974), *Circles of Confusion*, p. 93.
Emphasis in original.
67.   Frampton, production notes, *Zorns Lemma*, ca. 1970, AFA files. Emphasis in original.
68.   This continuation of the biblical creation story is echoed and interwoven with the scientific
creation story in the rainforest/Eden that concludes *Cadenza XIV.*

presumably, at the end, no one will bother. After all, history, like pornography, couldn't really begin until photography was invented. Before that, every account of events is merely somebody's panting prose fiction.[69]

Magellan as Borgesian metaphor for the history of Western representation begins, in *Cadenza I,* with a creation myth presided over by the photographer, who, within the cosmology of the Genesis story, is either God or the devil. Metahistory will begin intact with its witness, photography.

The first shot of the scene in the garden (which, significantly, contains only the bride) is followed by the first shot of *A Little Piece of String:* a woman exits a store and is engaged in conversation by a man. The two scenes are intercut; in the garden a nonlinear series of events ensues as the photographer gives directions, the couple pose, with all three figures variously exiting and entering the frame. The gag film proceeds in linear fashion. The man to whom the woman is speaking notices a loose thread near her skirt. A second man approaches; as the woman turns to speak to him, the first man begins to pull on the thread with various expressions of surprise and delight. Finally, with a flourish, he pulls the dress off; Frampton cuts, and when we return to the scene, we see the eighth and final shot of the gag film as the dress falls, the woman picks it up and runs back inside the store, and the two men laugh. The ninth and final shot of the garden features the bride alone and then fades to black.

Frampton points to the allusion to Marcel Duchamp's *The Bride Stripped Bare By Her Bachelors, Even (The Large Glass):*

> Among the things you saw, by the way, was another ancient film that is in the *Cadenza,* the film about the bride in which two gentlemen, who we may presume to be bachelors, strip more or less bare a putative bride of some kind. It's a very muddled situation that, given its context, I think someone might get a chuckle out of eventually.[70]

That Duchamp and *The Bride Stripped Bare By Her Bachelors, Even* should have an important place in an ironic meditation on points of origins is appropriate, both within Frampton's own development of *Magellan* from a sculptural project based on Duchampian "hoaxes" from 1964, and more substantially in Duchamp's concern with language understood as a grand contextual framing device constantly threatened by the eruption of sensual and sensuous energy from the phenomenal world. Frampton points to his own affinities with Duchamp's ambivalent place in modernism, and Duchamp's use of aleatory strategies and appropriation, by choosing to begin *Magellan* with this ironic emblem.[71]

69.   Frampton, "Incisions," p. 88.
70.   Simon, "Talking about *Magellan,*" p. 26.
71.   Reno Odlin, "Letters from Framp 1958–1968," *October* 32 (Spring 1985), pp. 43–52. The film project, as outlined in early grant proposals (ca. 1971–73), has two parts with the same titles as the sculpture "hoaxes," "Straits of Magellan" and "Clouds of Magellan."

The conclusion of Frampton's discussion of the Duchamp allusion above is instructive in relation to the importance Frampton attaches to self-conscious appropriation. He continues, "There are films in that collection [Library of Congress] which are interesting now and important now as their posterities have modified them. In itself, the one man engaging the lady's attention while another one unravels her skirt is idiotic."[72] Material from the point of origin of cinema is not valued for its own sake (Frampton does not share certain archivists' fetishization of early film). In fact, in itself, *A Little Piece of String* is "idiotic." The metahistorian searching for the quintessence of early film is faced with its "infantile" rawness. However, by appropriating *A Little Piece of String*, segmenting and intercutting it, and placing it within the larger conceptual framework of *Magellan*, Frampton transforms its slim narrative into a grand metaphor. This metaphor doubles back to ironize the grandeur of its correlative, the already self-ironic Duchampian modernist masterwork it echoes. Frampton, moreover, establishes the metaphor precisely by crosscutting linguistic and visual texts: while the iconography of *The Bride Stripped Bare By Her Bachelors, Even* bears no relation to the title of the early film, the narrative of *A Little Piece of String* alludes only to Duchamp's title.

Frampton here echoes Foucault's ironic relation to historical origins in "Nietzsche, Genealogy, History" (1971):

> History also teaches how to laugh at the solemnities of the origin. The lofty origin is no more than "a metaphysical extension which arises from the belief that things are most precious and essential at the moment of birth." . . . The origin always precedes the Fall. It comes

72.   Simon, "Talking about *Magellan*," p. 26.

Frampton. From the Protective Coloration *series. 1984. Courtesy Albright-Knox Art Gallery.*

before the body, before the world and time; it is associated with the gods, and its story is always sung as a theogony. But historical beginnings are lowly: not in the sense of modest or discreet like the steps of a dove, but derisive and ironic, capable of undoing every infatuation.[73]

Frampton ironizes the Genesis myth and the modernist masterwork with an "idiotic" early film, a concrete instantiation of the cinema's lowly historical beginnings, and thereby grounds the opening of *Magellan* in a productively ironic relation to history and origins.

---

73.   Michel Foucault, "Nietzsche, Genealogy, History," in his *Language, Countermemory, Practice: Selected Essays and Interviews*, ed. Donald F. Bouchard (Ithaca, N.Y.: Cornell University Press, 1977), p. 143.

The Music of His Music: Edward Said, 1936–2003

MICHAEL WOOD

Since the death of Edward Said in September 2003 I have spoken several times, in different places, about his sense of the place of art in life. I confess that I thought of myself on these occasions as correcting or complementing a dominant view, a picture of Edward that was all politics, as if he were nothing other than his admirable set of stances and writings and actions on behalf of the Palestinian people. He would have been a remarkable figure if he were only that; but he was more. Not that politics is necessarily a reduction of the person; but making any single thing out of a complex person is always a form of reduction.

And at no point did I wish to refuse or diminish the political aspect of Edward's work. On the contrary, I want to understand his politics better, and I want to develop a view of their relation to the rest of his work. I even think we might arrive ourselves at a different politics this way. I don't mean change our minds about particular issues, although that would in many cases be no bad thing. I mean change our view, for the better, of what politics is, what a truly open and democratic politics might embrace. So what follows rests on three propositions, each slightly contradictory of the other two, but all three entangled with each other, in conversation with each other. The three propositions are these:

1. That music, like the other arts, is always political, doesn't inhabit a world apart from money, power, prestige; apart from intrigue and all the grubbier aspects of human vanity and weakness. Here's what Edward says on an early page of *Musical Elaborations*, although he is being a little more restrained than we perhaps need to be: "the study of music can be more, and not less, interesting if we situate music as taking place . . . in a social and cultural setting. Think of the affiliation between music and social privilege; or between music and the nation; or between music and religious veneration—and the idea will be clear enough."

2. That music, like the other arts, but perhaps more immediately and more powerfully, creates a space of its own, a form of solitude that doesn't remove us from the world but makes a sort of hole in the world, a secret zone where there really is nothing but music. Edward writes of "the ultimately solitary intimacy by which the special music of an author impresses itself upon a receptive critical intelligence." Edward is commenting on a famous passage in

OCTOBER 109, Summer 2004, pp. 143–49. © 2004 October Magazine, Ltd. and Massachusetts Institute of Technology.

Proust that tells us that books are the work of solitude and the children of silence; and that each author has a particular "tune," which the reader picks up. "I have always thought of Proust's comments as having application of a very rich kind to the musical experience. In speaking about the train of thoughts provoked by the Brahms Sextet variations I found myself coming to a sort of unstatable or inexpressible aspect of his music, the music of his music, which I think anyone who listens to, plays, or thinks about music carries within oneself." Here Edward seems to be speaking about music in general, or about the music we care about, different for each of us no doubt; but he also mentions the idea of variations, and this is important.

3. That some music at least, music that explores the music of its own music, may offer us the image of a future politics, a world where solitude turns into freedom and undiluted respect, a world that is full but not crowded because no invasions—of individuals or of groups—are taking place. We are not alone and we are not silent; but we have given up none of the privileges of solitude and silence. We hear the music, and we hear the music of the music. The music of a possible politics, we might say. Is this utopian? Of course it is, and I shall come back to the idea of utopia.

The first proposition, then, reminds us of the (necessary) politics of music. The second wonders at the moments, in music, where politics can't be absent but seems to have gone completely silent. And the third proposition asks us to reverse the first, and think about the music of politics.

I need to say something about the company Edward keeps when he takes us into these regions of thought. Here's a difficult, but haunting quotation:

> The only philosophy which can be responsibly practiced in the face of despair is the attempt to contemplate all things as they would present themselves from the standpoint of redemption. Knowledge has no light but that shed on the world by redemption: all else is reconstruction, mere technique. Perspectives must be fashioned that displace and estrange the world, reveal it to be, with its rifts and crevices, as indigent and distorted as it will appear one day in the messianic light. . . . It is the simplest of all things. . . . But it is also the impossible thing. . . . The more passionately thought denies its conditionality for the sake of the unconditional, the more unconsciously, and so calamitously, it is delivered up to the world. Even its own impossibility it must at last comprehend for the sake of the possible. But beside the demand thus placed on thought, the question of the reality or unreality of redemption itself hardly matters.

The writer is T. W. Adorno, and these are the last words of his book *Minima Moralia* (1951). Edward didn't talk much, if at all, about redemption—and if he had he would not have said that its reality or unreality hardly matters. But he talked a lot about the impossible, and he talked a lot about Adorno. More precisely,

he thought of the impossible in Adorno's sense: as that which had to be compre-
hended, that is, embraced and understood, and, one day, overcome. Or if not
overcome, registered as the fullest imaginable rebuke to the possible. This, I take
it, is just what Adorno means by redemption.

In a late interview, in 2000, Edward described himself as the "only true
follower of Adorno." We have to imagine his grin, and remember all the ways in
which he was not like Adorno at all. He didn't have his solemnity, for one thing;
and Adorno, by all accounts, had nothing of Edward's warmth. And Edward
couldn't really be a follower of Adorno, because Adorno didn't have followers, and
Edward wasn't a follower of anyone. There certainly couldn't be an Adorno *fils*,
Edward said; the very idea is ridiculous. But then Edward also spoke, in the same
breath, of Adorno as "my model" and "an impossible example to follow": "In this
sort of wonderfully problematic cross-fertilization between the musical and the
immediacies of ordinary experience my model has been Adorno, an impossible
example to follow." And again: "Theory is not really interesting as a subject in and
of itself. . . . I make exceptions. Adorno strikes me as interesting for his own sake. . . .
That's what's great about Adorno . . ."

I don't find Adorno in *Beginnings* (1975), or *The World, the Text and the Critic*
(1983). Or in *Orientalism* (1978). But he is everywhere in Edward's work after that.
Sometimes criticized for his attitude to popular culture, sometimes included
among the unalterably Eurocentric figures who were so much a part of Edward's
own formation. But always admired; and admired above all for his sense of the
impossible. You will have noticed the phrase "wonderfully problematic" above.
Edward also writes of Adorno's "stirringly bleak account of Schoenberg's emergence
and rather repellent triumph." In *Musical Elaborations*, Edward quotes Adorno
himself: "Modern music sees absolute oblivion as its goal. It is the surviving
message of despair from the shipwrecked." Oblivion doesn't sound too good, and
perhaps wouldn't be called a goal by anyone except Adorno. But Edward
responded warmly to the sheer austerity of this vision, and his own vision of literature was often rather similar. Conrad, Hopkins, Swift, Yeats, in his accounts of
them, were writers whose very achievements led them to frustration, whose
immense successes could also be described as forms of failure, and especially by
those writers themselves. I have always found there to be something very moving
about Edward's being so moved by Adorno's relentless aesthetics and by these particular careers. So unlike his own, and yet obviously so close to it in important ways.

A message of despair from the shipwrecked. A philosophy practiced in the
face of despair. Edward didn't believe in despair. But he did believe in and fully
acknowledge the frequent reasons for despair, the sense in which the person who
despairs may be right, and it was for this reason, I think, that he was so drawn to
Adorno's lofty idea of the impossible. Edward would say, as probably Adorno
wouldn't, that a philosophy practiced in the face of despair would have to know
despair, but it wouldn't be despairing. And he would say that a message of despair,
even from a shipwreck, is not only a message of despair. But he would think this a

useful thing to say only when the impossible has been fully folded into the equation—not absorbed, but recognized, like an independent person, or people.

But how do we get from despair to music, or from music to despair? Through politics, I suggest, and through an attempt to understand the relation between Edward's political life and his love of literature and music. This life and this love were not identical, but it is essential to see that they were not opposed. Yet how could this be? There is a genuine puzzle here, and Edward himself saw it as such. In an interview he gave when he was writing *Musical Elaborations* he said that "things that are of particular interest to me . . . again and again . . . converge on the public and the private—the public in an Adornian sense with all of its processes of power and accreditation and authority and orthodoxy; and the private, which is the position of the listener or the amateur or the subjective consumer of music, like myself. I wouldn't call it an autonomous realm, but I certainly think one can talk about it as having a kind of relatively autonomous identity." This is casually put ("kind of relatively"), and not a developed theoretical position. But there is a question of huge significance here.

"I wouldn't call it an autonomous realm." "One can talk about it as having a . . . relatively autonomous identity." These phrases correspond to my propositions one and two, and in almost all of our current discourses, left and right, traditional and progressive, they necessarily contradict each other. The autonomy of music (and the other arts) is either celebrated or deplored; the absence of its autonomy either an article of critical faith or a proof that the world is going to the dogs. Edward would have none of this. Now I don't claim to be able to solve the puzzle he barely sketched, but I do want to insist on its double truth: the worldliness and the unworldliness of music, the striking sense we have that the world is never absent from music, and yet that music produces a curious suspension of the world and its doings, as if time had not stopped but altered its register.

And we can go a little further, and I propose to do so by quoting and commenting on the last pages of *Musical Elaborations*. Edward loved, and wrote lovingly about, Richard Strauss's *Metamorphosen*, but you probably wouldn't (I wouldn't, I didn't) think straight off about the politics of the piece, or its relation to politics. And yet. *Metamorphosen*, a suite for twenty-three strings, was composed in 1944, when the cities of Strauss's musical life, Berlin, Dresden, Vienna, were being totally destroyed by the Allies. Strauss had been a Nazi sympathizer in the early days, but not recently, and he wrote later of that year that it was when "the most terrible period of human history came to an end, the twelve-year reign of bestiality, ignorance, and anticulture under the greatest criminals, during which Germany's 2,000 years of cultural evolution met its doom." We might think that it was not only cultural evolution that met its doom, that many people died too, and I don't think we can really say, as Bryan Gilliam does in a recent book, that Strauss's *Metamorphosen* is "a work that seeks to probe the cause of war itself." I do think the very calm of the piece is haunted by the war, though, and above all haunted by the violence it seeks to keep away. If you listen to this music, you will hear an astonishing series of subtle and brooding variations, or perhaps repetitions rather than variations; a musical journey that really doesn't seem to be going anywhere, that takes its time, as if it had all the time in the world, as if the unavoidable world were not there (but it is there). The opening of the score is pictured on the page at the end of *Musical Elaborations.*

Now an extended quotation, or an extended series of quotations, from Edward's book itself.

> I find myself speculating that two of the main organizational tendencies in Western classical music derive from two different ways of looking at theme, melody, or statement. Looked at horizontally, statement is melody, to be pronounced robustly, carefully developed, definitively ended. This is mastering time according to a linear model, working through the material strictly. Looked at nonnarratively, however, music is not just statement, but statement and infinitely possible variations, not just, for example, the variations written by Brahms . . . but the variations in the use to which I found myself privately putting them. . . .

> Perhaps all I am saying is that in my experience of music the composer's *air de la chanson* I hold onto and whose embellishments over time I enjoy represents a personal obsession of the individual hearer or interpreter . . .

This is the private realm described earlier but seen now as merely private, a turning away from the world, not a suspension of it. Edward doesn't really believe this is what is happening. "Perhaps," he says.

> Perhaps. But I am intellectually impressed by the richness of what I have called the alternative formation in music, in which the nonlinear, nondevelopmental uses of theme or melody dissipate and delay a disciplined organization of musical time that is principally combative as well as dominative . . . .

> Obviously I'm *not* saying that classical forms like the sonata are neurotically un-beautiful. That would be nonsense. But I am proposing that one can think about musical elaboration as something to be returned to for reasons other than its finished perfection, that the essence of the elaboration can be transformative and reflective, that it can occur slowly not only because we affirm and reaffirm its repetition, its meandering course, but also because it too seems to be about the same process . . .

> I do not think it is an accident that the one major twentieth-century composer who intransigently (some would say heedlessly and irresponsibly) followed his own studiously self-devised path despite the innumerable opportunities offered him by serialism, neoclassicism, nationalism, etc.,

is Richard Strauss. In his last years . . . Strauss turned almost exclusively to various quite extraordinary transfigurations of the variation idea. Consider the Oboe Concerto, *Capriccio*, the *Four Last Songs*, and, most remarkably of all, *Metamorphosen*, an essay in almost pure repetition and contemplation. . . .

Glenn Gould calls Strauss's work generally ecstatic, but in the context of what I have been discussing here, it is, I believe, radically, beautifully elaborative, music whose pleasures and discoveries are premised upon letting go, upon not asserting a central authorizing identity, upon enlarging the community of hearers and players beyond the time taken, beyond the extremely concentrated duration provided by the performance occasion. In this perspective afforded by such a work as *Metamorphosen*, music thus becomes an art not primarily or exclusively about authorial power and social authority, but a mode for thinking through or thinking with the integral variety of human cultural practices, generously, noncoercively, and, yes, in a utopian cast, if by utopian we mean worldly, possible, attainable, knowable.

Two things need to be said here. There is no doubt that we are listening to the music of Edward's music, and that the language of these pages reveals this music to be political—in a "generous, noncoercive" sense. But it is important too to see that this music—the music of music and the music of politics—is a dream, the result of a heroic and courtly act of the imagination. Edward is not describing something he finds easy or familiar, something habitual or even likely. He was not himself, to put it mildly, a great expert in letting go, in relinquishing a central authorizing identity, and much of his life was about mastery and discipline and winning. He is not making a world in his own image, therefore, but a world he believes humans need. And second, I think we have to register the pathos of the last words of the quotation, the fact that that Edward, out of sheer, irrepressible hopefulness, is actually bending the meaning of the word utopian. "If by utopian we mean worldly, possible, attainable, knowable." That's not what we mean by utopian. It's just what we don't mean by utopian. When Edward was dying I had a conversation with Jacqueline Rose in which she and I agreed that we were utopians rather than optimists, meaning we no longer believed certain improvements were possible in any world we might live in, only in worlds we could imagine—and ought to go on imagining, of course. Edward, by contrast, was an optimist. His gloss on Adorno's notion that thought has to comprehend even its own impossibility for the sake of the possible would be to stress the future arrival at the possible, however many impossibilities are strewn along the way. The utopian is not what can't happen, it is what will happen, one day: "worldly, possible, attainable, knowable."

Another musical example will take us back to the idea of music as "thinking through." This is one of Strauss's *Four Last Songs*, usually performed as the last of the four, but written first, in May 1948. I'm not going to comment on the song or the poem in detail, but I do want to remind you of the extraordinary pair of last lines, "Wie sind wir wandermüde—ist dies etwa der Tod?" Literally, "How travel-weary we are—can this be death?" The little word *etwa*, usually translated as perchance or perhaps, here really doesn't mean anything so emphatic. *Etwa*'s main meaning is "about," or "around," as in "around two hundred people were there." Otherwise it's used as an expletive or filler, to hint at a sort of approximation rather than a stark fact or number. So the curious semantic effect is of wondering whether this is death or thereabouts, or asking if we are saying this is death, is that what I'm supposed to believe. The tiny word becomes a way of slowing down the line, of faintly underscoring a sense of speculation in the very region where all speculation seems to end. Strauss gets there on a series of rising rather than falling notes, so there really does seem to be some sort of question here. And of course the whole thing is a marvelous musical elaboration in Edward's sense, a refusal of single statement and linear control, a dissipation and delay of musical time. What's more, the song doesn't even end with the word "death" or the human voice; the orchestra resumes what Edward calls its meandering course, and the piece keeps refusing to close. It's a song about letting go; and about not quite knowing how to let go.

CORRECTIONS

In *October* 107 (Winter 2004), the date for Carl Einstein's *African Sculpture* (a different work from his *Negro Sculpture*) was erroneously given as 1915 (p. 146). The correct date for *African Sculpture* is 1921. *October* regrets the error.

M≠C

MODERNITY & CONTEMPORANEITY:
ANTINOMIES OF ART & CULTURE
AFTER THE 20TH CENTURY

University of Pittsburgh
November 4-6, 2004

IN the aftermath of modernity, and the passing of the postmodern, how are we to know and show what it is to live in the conditions of contemporaneity?

SPEAKERS:
Fredric Jameson
Bruno Latour
Antonio Negri
Sadik J. Al-Azm
Susan Buck-Morss
Boris Groys
Wu Hung
Geeta Kapur
Rosalind Krauss
Sarat Maharaj
Mari Carmen Ramirez
and many others

CONVENERS:
Terry Smith
Okwui Enwezor
Nancy Condee

1-412-624-6566
www.mc.pitt.edu
mcsympos@pitt.edu

FUNDERS:
Pittsburgh Foundation
Heinz Endowments
University of Pittsburgh

University of Pittsburgh
in conjunction with the
2004 CARNEGIE INTERNATIONAL

Gloria! The Legacy of Hollis Frampton

A CONFERENCE AT PRINCETON UNIVERSITY

Friday, November 5 and Saturday, November 6, 2004

Events include film screenings, a roundtable discussion, and presentations of papers on Frampton's photographic work, filmmaking, and his relationship to digital media. Participants include Annette Michelson, Mike Zryd, Melissa Ragona, Keith Sanborn, Scott MacDonald, Brian Henderson, Barbara Lattanzi, Malcolm Turvey, Chrissie Iles, Marion Faller, Bill Brand, and Bruce Jenkins.

In conjunction with the conference there will be screenings of Frampton's films at Anthology Film Archives on the two preceeding weekends.

Organized by Keith Sanborn, P. Adams Sitney, and Su Friedrich. Sponsored by the Visual Arts Program at Princeton University. Funded by Princeton University through the Gardner Magic Fund, the Council on the Humanities, and the Amy Knox Fund.

For further details or to register, contact Su Friedrich at sufried@princeton.edu

---

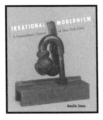